A VILLAGE H

John Davies (1851 - 1942)

Trelewis

**Head of Bontnewydd Board School
which became Trelewis Mixed School
1882 – 1913**

ALUN WATKINS

First published in June 2013

ISBN 978-0-9570426-1-2

Published by Gelligaer Publishing

OldGelligaerFamilies@gmail.com

Printed by www.inkylittlefingers.co.uk

For Caitlin and Euan, my grand-children,
whose interest in and love of History
is growing year on year.

To Alwyn + Anne

Thanking you for your
valued friendship.

Very Best Wishes,

Alan.

A VILLAGE HEADMASTER

John Davies was the longest-serving Headmaster of Trelewis Mixed School. He commenced his duties at what was then called Bontnewydd Board School on April 11th, 1882 and finished at what became Trelewis Mixed School on March 31st, 1913. Most of his professional life was given, therefore, to superlative service in that School and locality. The account which follows is mostly drawn from the chronicle which he wrote in the School Log Book[1] over those thirty-one years.

CONTENTS

5

PROLOGUE: A Personal Statement

In this fast-moving, ever-changing twenty-first century world we inhabit, even nostalgia is not what it was. But when it strikes it becomes a most potent force. It hit me when I attended the Centenary celebrations of Trinity Baptist Church, Trelewis, in July, 2008. Not having been back to the village for many years, this occasion was to prove a sheer delight. I met again fellow pupils of Trelewis Mixed School whom I had last seen over 50 years ago. The lecture on the role of the Church in the life of the village was fascinating as it sketched in many details of which I was unaware. Being there and seeing again places that were formative influences on me as I was growing up stimulated a variety of memories despite the changes which had taken place. The remains of the old Infants' school where I had learned to read, still there. The Junior School now vanished completely and replaced by a row of modern houses. As I looked down on the site of the former school from the elevation of the pedestrian railway bridge, I thought I could hear the syncopated rhythm of our class chanting their tables. I remembered too the solemn, though glad, ending of the school day when, as instructed, with hands together and eyes closed, we sang:

"Now the day is over. Night is drawing nigh
Shadows of the evening steal across the sky."

The smell of the ink as it was poured into the inkwells; the blots on the minimal-sized blotting paper we were assigned; the games, fun and noise of the playground; the serried ranks of small milk bottles arranged, in winter, around the stove to thaw out the contents, (sometimes unsuccessfully); the thrill of discovery as staff broadened our knowledge and increased our skills. These and ever diverse recollections cascaded through my mind.

Much had altered in the village as I surveyed it again. Possibly the only sight which remained exactly as I recalled it was School House, adjacent to the Baptist Chapel, standing proudly, looking down imperiously on all below it. Amongst the larger houses of the village, it was where the Headmaster lived. It was an honour and a privilege if one was asked to deliver a message there. The Headmaster was held to be in a position much above that of ordinary mortals. He was a person to be respected by all for his sagacity, to be obeyed by all his pupils, and to be feared by all who attempted to defy him. His was a crucial role in the development of any community. It was while musing on this that I conceived the idea of finding out more about the Head Teachers who had contributed to the evolution of the village of Trelewis. Initially I had hoped to compile a history of the school set within the context of the growth of the locality. But the more I looked at the primary source, the School Log Book, the more absorbed I became in the work and achievements of John Davies who had the distinction of being the school's longest-serving Head. I ended up instead by making a detailed study of his thirty-one years at the school.

The approach I have taken is to describe briefly the events before he became Headmaster. I proceed to examine every decade (approximately), of his period in office and finish with an account of his years in retirement. This division is obviously purely artificial as each year and decade flows unimpeded into the next. It also results in there being much repetition as the same issues keep recurring. Continuing to record the same factors as they appear in each decade may appear boringly repetitive. But I have done so because their constant appearance in the Log emphasises how important they were to the Head Teacher. From one point of view, then, this study could be regarded as a fairground roundabout. There is plenty of movement but because it is recurrent, it doesn't get anywhere. From my point of view, a better metaphor would be that of a building which requires a number of similar materials but, as they are utilised and fitted together, a complete and useful edifice is built. John Davies was to build a worthy structure and so was to leave a valued legacy behind him in the school to which he devoted most of his life. I found my time well spent, therefore, in making this account of the things which he found important enough to include in the School Log book.

There are other reasons why I did not proceed with my original intention to write the history of the school and with it to include the story of the development of the village. Lack of time is the most pressing of them. My research has proceeded spasmodically, interspersed with the countless activities which crowd into the life of the retired. I was also surprised to find that few, if any, local historians had written anything about Trelewis and that there was a distinct lack of easily-accessible primary and secondary sources to which I could refer. My constant hope was that I would unearth such in some archive or library. Imagine my delight when I made contact with Greg Buick, the Webmaster of Gelligaer Historical Society, and found that he was the great-grandson of John Davies and also of William Lewis, the main benefactor of the village. He was not only able to provide much personal information about them but he most kindly made available to me a chest full of documents relating to Bontnewydd. This was a veritable treasure trove of primary source material throwing light on the expansion of the village. His comments and suggestions as the work was coming to a conclusion have been greatly appreciated. Added to this, he most kindly prepared the typescript for publication. I cannot thank him enough, therefore, for his invaluable help.

I don't know if, by training, Archivists are made to be obliging and supportive. All I can say is that in every Record Office I had dealings with, their assistance and co-operation was superb. My thanks are due to the staff of Glamorgan Archives, Ceredigion Archives, Gwent Archives and Carmarthenshire Archives for their inexhaustible, helpful service. The same grateful thanks are expressed to the staffs of Cardiff Central Library, Merthyr Tydfil Carnegie Library, Bargoed Library, Treharris Library and the National Library of Wales. I am also indebted to oldmerthyrtydfil.com, Alan George and Carolyn Jacob for providing some of the photographs. Friends and family also played an important part in producing this study. Janet Hughes proof-read the manuscript and in so doing corrected many of my infelicities of style and grammar which I have greatly appreciated. (I should add that those that remain are solely my responsibility.) Amongst all these acknowledgements, the most heart-felt is due to my wife. Her unfailing love has accompanied and inspired me in everything I have ever undertaken. I will never be able to re-pay all that she has done for me. Finally, I think that my parents would have been delighted if they had seen, after all these years, that my thoughts and labours have returned to the village where I was born and brought up.

Alun Watkins

Above: John Davies in centre with 41 boys. Below: His wife Rachel with 31 girls. (When and where the photographs were taken is uncertain but probably depicts Ciliau Park Board School.)

Part One

SETTING THE SCENE

Part One SETTING THE SCENE (1851 - 1882)

John Davies was born on October 10th, 1851, at Bettws Leiki in the depths of rural Cardiganshire, the eldest son of Lewis and Jane Davies. His father was a carpenter who moved around the area frequently, possibly bettering himself in the process. Indeed he appears to make progress by being described as "Carpenter and Builder." By the 1871 Census, the family was living at Spring Gardens, Lampeter, having already had at least three changes of address. Being the first born in this family and having four sisters and three brothers, his parents were concerned to do their best for him but also for his siblings. His three brothers trained for the Anglican ministry at Lampeter, (one of them later becoming a Canon), but he was the first of the family to experience Higher Education.[2] On 29th January, 1870, when he was 18, he began his studies at South Wales Training College, Carmarthen, a college founded in 1848 to train men to teach in Church Primary Schools. The course involved a tough, almost monastic regime of training. He survived, completing his course as a Certificated Teacher (Second Class) within 2 years. Then he was off to his first post at the soon-to-be-built new premises of the enlarged Llanover Parochial School in the fertile Vale of Usk with environs very similar to those in which he had grown up.

It was with a certain degree of pride that he made the first entry in the School Log Book on 22nd January, 1872: "I John Davies, late of the South Wales Training College, Carmarthen, take charge of this school today, now for the first time to be conducted by a Certificated Teacher and open to Government inspection."[3] The first Inspectors' Report of 1872 reported the pleasure of HMI's that "so nice a building is approaching completion." That their comments were justified can be seen from the plans and elevations for the School building which had been acknowledged by a letter from the Education Department in Whitehall dated 20th January, 1872. The drawings show what a pleasing school was being built consisting of: a School room (34ft x 20ft); an Infants' Room (18ft x 14 ft); an Entrance Lobby (10ft x 9ft); with playground and Master's House plus garden.[4] The reality, however, may not have been as good as the plans depicted. In

November, 1873, the children had to move back to the old school when on a bitterly cold and wet day, the walls of the new building were found to be rather damp. It was on 24th November, 1874, that he married Rachel Morgan from the parish of Llanfair in Carmarthenshire and they began their married life in the brand-new Master's house.

There had been a school at Llanover previously, built and maintained by Lady Llanover at her own expense, as Slater's Directory of Monmouthshire for 1858/59 records. But despite any shortcomings, what a delight for John Davies to start a completely new chapter, taking charge of a modern school, and even better to have the opportunity of founding its new traditions. For his endeavours, he was to receive the princely sum of £75 per annum from Lady Llanover, paid in arrears. Most interesting are the wages books in which the payments are receipted over a penny stamp. The first entry dated February 12th, 1872, is for £2.17.8 being two weeks salary from January 22nd to February 3rd and the last is dated April 17th, 1876, for £7.4.2 being five weeks salary due on April 8th.[5]

Starting with a school roll of 23 in January, 1872, this had increased to 45 by February. Unusually for a period when the "Welsh Not" or "Welsh Stick" was being used in schools to discourage the use of the Welsh language by pupils, he established an annual Welsh examination which was followed by an ample provision of tea and buns. He was reputed to have been one of the first Head Teachers to start the tradition of recognising St David's Day in the school calendar. No doubt he was delighted when the Managers granted a half holiday for that day and there were evening celebrations in the school. Even better was March 1st, 1876, when Lady Llanover invited his pupils to Llanover House and they marched through the gardens "each adorned with a leek". To him, Welsh language and culture were important, so they were not to be neglected in his school. No wonder that on occasions the Welsh lessons tended to over-run the time allocated on the timetable.

Amongst other innovations which occurred during his headship was the provision of see-saws in the playground, much to the delight of his scholars. As these tended to improve punctuality because pupils loved playing on them before school, they proved to be a worthwhile investment. John Davies had to deploy most of his energy not to play but to schooling and development. The successive reports of Her Majesty's Inspectors (HMIs) show the progress being made. In 1873 they wrote: "This little village school has passed, on the whole, a good examination in the elementary subjects." While the Writing needed more attention and the Singing was very fair, the Discipline was good and the Knitting, excellent. They commented too on the lofty, spacious and well-ventilated new school room and "the private liberality" of Lady Llanover who had financed it. One year later the same HMIs' reported: "The General tone is fair and the order good." The Report for November, 1875, mentioned an unevenness of progress in the different Standards. While Arithmetic was excellent in Standard 2, Spelling was weak elsewhere. The Inspectors accordingly were expecting improvements to be made both in Instruction and Discipline during the next year.

One is left wondering whether this Report was to discourage John Davies as it was the first to contain hints of criticism. Whether it did or not, straight after the Christmas holiday, in January, 1876, he gave notice to the Managers that he intended to leave within three months. Of course, there could be many other compelling reasons for this decision. As he was to return to his native Cardiganshire, that in itself might have been a sufficient incentive. He certainly did not leave Llanover under a cloud. The mutual affection engendered in his first post is revealed in his final Log entry of 7th April, 1876: "This being the last afternoon for the present Master, the children were allowed to play and enjoy themselves in various games around the School. An affecting farewell closed the evening." There is also a description of the children dispersing in a quiet and orderly manner with several of them expressing sorrow and regret at his departure.

Returning to Ciliau Aeron, just a few miles south of his birth place, it must have seemed like a case of "local boy makes good." When he took over the rebuilt Ciliau Park Board School on 22nd May, 1876, there were 21 children present. That was 7 more than his successor at Llanover had found on his first morning. But within two weeks 94 names were included on the Admissions Register. Assisted by Monitors from the older classes and later by his wife Rachel who taught Sewing, he began to make a real impact on the School.[6] The first Inspection report of May 15th, 1877, was encouraging and stated that: "This new school has been brought into a creditable working condition, and the scholars, as presented, passed a creditable examination in the three elementary subjects. The sewing too was very fair."

Needing more assistance, the school eventually gained two trainee Pupil Teachers but these required much help and one of them was dismissed in 1879. John Davies persisted in his labours and the Inspector's report (June 8th, 1880), has real congratulation for him: "The results prove that the school has been very well taught during the past year and it was highly praiseworthy of the Master to present this year, in the Fifth Standard, seven scholars who were last year in the Third Standard." Attendance also kept increasing and in December, 1880, the school recorded its highest ever average attendance of 92.1%.

With everything sounding so promising, why was it that he left the school on April 5th, 1882? He had a young daughter of 4 and his father-in law, William Morgan, had been living with the family in the School House. Certainly he was not averse to moving further away from home and his experience showed that he relished the challenge of developing new schools. But could it be that there were some disagreements with the School Board? There is a possible indication of this in the Log of 1881 when he writes: "Clerk of the Board favoured us today with rather detailed and somewhat stringent regulations to guide and assist in the management of the school." This provoked a reaction from him in which he questioned the practicality of those regulations. However, there is no convincing explanation for his moving away again from his native county.

Whatever the reason, in 1882 he travelled to new, though not necessarily to greener pastures. Leaving Ciliau Aeron in the lush, green valley of the River Aeron, he made the long and by no means easy journey to the Taff Bargoed valley in N E Glamorganshire. Some eighteenth century writers had described neighbouring districts as most agreeable and had paid tribute to the picturesque scenery. In the 19th Century, George Borrow on his journeying through Wales described his walk from Merthyr to Caerphilly via Quakers' Yard in most poetic language. After leaving the industrial grime of Merthyr he speaks of the contrast he found further down the valley: "After I proceeded on my way, the scenery to the south on the farther side of the river became surprisingly beautiful...... On I wandered. After some time, the valley assumed the form of an immense basin, enormous mountains composed its sides. In the middle, rose hills of some altitude, but completely overcrowned by the mountains around. These hills exhibited pleasant inclosures and were beautifully dotted with white farm houses. Down below meandered the Taff, its reaches shining with a silver-like splendour. The whole together formed an exquisite picture in which there was much sublimity, much still quiet life and not a little of fantastic fairy loveliness."[7] Such was the beauty of the area around Bontnewydd before it was scarred by industrialisation. It would be interesting to know what was the impression on John Davies when he first arrived at Bontnewydd School to take over as Master.

He was to find:

1. A CHANGING COMMUNITY

The area called Bontnewydd had been a peaceful rural backwater situated on the eastern side of the clear Taff Bargoed river, a couple of miles before it joined the larger River Taff at Quakers' Yard. It took its name from the new bridge (Bontnewydd) built there, but when that bridge was built is not known. It must have been at least as early as

1601 because in that year the first documentary evidence is found of a mortgage for a 20 acre farm called Bontnewydd by a William Lewis. The site of Bontnewydd farm is close to the bridge over the Taff Barged river where the track meanders up the wooded hillside towards Cwm Cothi. "Bontnewydd" would appear, therefore, to encompass the area adjacent to Bontnewydd farm from the bridge over the Taff Bargoed river to the Pont-y-Squire bridge which crossed the Caiach Brook.[8]

But with the development of coal mining, its simple beauty was going to be transformed by industrial ugliness. In fact almost every valley in the S Wales Coalfield was, in time, to be altered irrevocably by the mineral wealth below and the disfiguring waste above. The 1875 Ordnance Survey map for Gelligaer and Llanfabon Parishes, and the 1879 OS map for Merthyr Tydfil, Llanfabon and Gelligaer Parishes (both surveyed in 1873)[9] clearly show the scattered farms of Bontnewydd, Tir Shag, Tir Bach and, just across the Gelligaer road, the imposing Llancaiach Fawr. Also indicated were the few dwellings around the Inn at Ffald-gaiach, the Smithy at Shinrig, and Pen-y-groes heol together with other habitations at Pandy and at what was known as Glyn Bargoed. In addition, the maps reveal changes which were being made to this rural, sparsely populated community. Most noticeable was the serpentine sweep of the GWR Taff Vale Extension Railway with its three tight curves before it reached Quakers Yard. This line had been opened from Pontypool in 1858 by the Newport, Abergavenny and Hereford Railway Company, later to be taken over by the Great Western Railway. It was a line built in defiance of geography, majestically crossing the Ebbw Valley on its lace-like iron Crumlin Viaduct, and the Rhymney Valley on its sixteen beautiful, curving stone arches at Hengoed. Bontnewydd even had its own much more modest three-arch viaduct of seventy-eight yards enabling the railway to cross the Taff Bargoed river. Photographers captured the rustic charm of this spot until the view through its arches was completely obliterated by the depositing of colliery waste.

The Maps also indicate that the GWR/Rhymney Railway Bargoed Taff Branch was in construction in 1873. The course of the line to Llancaiach is indicated by the building of embankments alongside its junction with the GWR Taff Vale extension. This was to open for goods on January 10th, 1876, running nine and a half miles, with steep gradients, from Llancaiach, (where it connected with the Vale of Neath Line), to Dowlais (Cae Harris). Its raison d'etre was principally to transport iron ore to the Dowlais Works but passenger services commenced on February 1st, 1876.[10] The two railways were already operating when John Davies took up residence in Bontnewydd. Indeed, they were to play no small part in the industrialisation of the locality and in the influx of migrant workers.

Other evidence of previous or existing small-scale industrial activity which can be seen from these maps include the location of Melin Caiach (Corn Mill & Woollen Factory), Pontnewydd Colliery, Air Shafts, some Quarries and slightly further afield Tophill and Llancaiach Collieries. However, overall, the area remained mainly agricultural consisting of fields and scattered woodland.

On the western side of the Taff Bargoed river the maps show that there were further farms but not a great deal of other habitation. Twyn-y-garreg, ("Rock Hillock" - the original name of what became Treharris); Pantanas; Pen-bwlch and Cil-haul are shown together with the Perrott Inn. It wasn't until one came to Quakers Yard, that a growing population was indicated by its chapels and railway station. But the most significant feature of the 1873 survey for the future was the presence of a straight row of small dwellings called "The Huts" leading up to the embankment and viaduct of the Taff Vale Extension. These had been built to house the workers who had been engaged to sink the Harris Navigation Colliery. They had started work in the early 1870's and the signs of their labours can already be seen on the map which shows the location of Engine House and Shafts of the Harris Navigation Colliery on the opposite side of the river from Bontnewydd Farm. Other claims to fame of these pioneers are: that

The Huts, Treharris in 1936   Courtesy Alan George

"The Huts" became the first name applied to the developing settlement; and that their rudimentary dwellings were to last so long.

It was F W Harris, the Managing Director and Chairman of the Harris Navigation Coal Co., who was to give his name to the village, Treharris, which was soon to mushroom around his colliery. After nearly seven years pursuing the sinking operation, the "Merthyr Express" could report on 8th March, 1879,[11] that "last Friday, coal was won at the Harris Navigation Colliery, the No 2 Pit (North), near Quakers Yard. The celebrated four-foot seam of coal has been struck at the enormous depth of 698 yards", adding that this was more than double the depth of local collieries. The No 1 Pit was to be even deeper at 756 yards when it first raised coal in 1881. These accomplishments were to cause the name of the colliery to be changed to Deep Navigation Colliery. The local paper was confident in 1879

The Pithead Baths at Deep Navigation Colliery, Treharris. Trelewis can be seen in the background on the right,   Courtesy Merthyr Library

that at least 2,000 tons of coal would be produced each day. For that to happen there needed to be an expansion of the work force.

While Treharris was to grow significantly, there was also a considerable impact on Bontnewydd. Housing stock was increasing because of the influx of workers seeking employment in the developing colliery and elsewhere. Slowly but surely the village started to grow from a single street of terraced houses, all of it being on land belonging to Bontnewydd Farm. High Street began to emerge, at least from 1875, when Leases were taken out for designated properties in that street. Proof that the population was growing is seen in the Lease taken out in May, 1876, for Capel Ebenezer by Davies & Kinsey, the first chapel to be built in the emergent village. The lease was for 99 years at an annual rental of £2.7.9.[12] In 1879, Ebenezer Welsh Congregational Chapel was opened (a sister chapel to Libanus, Quakers Yard), having accommodation for 300. There had previously been a Protestant cause at Bontnewydd from 1811 associated with the names of Lewis Lewis, William Lewis and George Watson, amongst others. Proof again of an enlarging village community is seen in the erection of St Mary's Church, built as a Chapel of Ease by Gelligaer Parish in 1886.[13] So it was evident that John Davies was coming to an evolving locality with a changing landscape and a growing population. A mainly rural area of fair country was gradually being transformed into a more industrial vista.

This was not the only transformation he was to encounter. Arriving in Bontnewydd he found:

2. A CHANGING SCHOOL

Courtesy Glamorgan Archives

The school at Bontnewydd had opened on January 1st, 1878, and its first Head Teacher (or Mistress), Miss Marian Lewis, had the responsibility of setting it on its course. She starts the School Log with the inscription in beautiful copper-plate script, "Bontnewydd Board School" having a delightful cursive scroll underneath. The high standard of her handwriting was not equalled by her successors although some of them too possessed high standards of calligraphy. The nature of her entries in the Log also set the tone for those who followed her. According to the 1872 Revised Code of Regulations, the Principal Teacher had to complete the School Log Book at least once each week to provide details of the progress of the School or its Teachers. Facts, not opinions, of significant happenings, particularly those which might need to be referred to at a later date, were to be recorded. In addition, the summary of the Inspectors' Report was to be copied verbatim into the Log together with the names and status of each member of staff, then it was to be signed by the Correspondent of Managers. The keeping of the School Log was an important and essential part of a Head Teacher's duty underlined by the fact that, on every visit, Her Majesty's Inspector of Schools would inspect and sign it.

An examination of School Log Books in a Board area will reveal substantial variations. Some Head Teachers crammed them with detail; others included the very minimum. Most of them show that they inevitably became something of a chore by the repetition of stock phrases such as "Ordinary progress". The School Log, while being a valuable source of information for historical research, has some obvious limitations. It does not include everything that happened in the school but only what the Head Teacher has recorded. Because of that, often it raises queries without providing the answers. Nevertheless it supplies essential information about the development of a school.

Miss Lewis was punctilious in recording attendance. There were 50 children present when the school opened on 1st January, 1878. By the end of the month this had grown to 74 with numbers continuing to rise. The highest number which she records as being present was 105 during the Week ending May 31st, 1878.[14] The rapid increase in the numbers on roll and the varying ages and abilities must have presented quite a challenge to Miss Lewis as she only had the assistance of one inexperienced Monitor for the first four months and a second Monitor thereafter. These three were then expected to cope with over 100 children.

The influx of people coming to the village ensured that the school roll would rise, but the flow was not only one way. Evidence of a turnover in population can be found in the Log. In the first week of February, 1879, thirteen pupils were admitted and towards the end of the month a further seventeen. There was a departure of pupils in August, 1880, when several left during the month owing to their parents removing to Tredegar to work. Others were moving on elsewhere in the neighbourhood, for example, to Blackwood. Whether this movement was due to families not finding employment or discovering what they were seeking in the area, remains unclear. Having a fluctuating intake of pupils in its formative years added to the task facing the school. In March, 1881, Standard 1 is spoken of as having children who had moved to "this place whose education has been grossly neglected."

But the constant pressure of numbers on the school's facilities was an ever-present reality with the comment being made in November, 1879, that "the school is rather crowded."[15]

Miss Lewis' two successors were most firmly of the opinion that the school roll should not go beyond what the school could reasonably accommodate. When the Inspectors' Report for 1879 stated that the average attendance was not to exceed 89, J D Thomas, the Master, refused some children admission. Henry Davies, who followed him, tackled the problem differently. As the school became overcrowded, he would not give the names of irregular attenders to the Attendance Officer.[16]

Initially, the physical condition of the School building could have been somewhat problematical. Described by Inspectors as "in very fair temporary premises", the school room was 35ft 6in long and 20ft 3in wide. But in April, 1878, the school had to be closed for two days for "certain repairs." That there were other deficiencies in the building, probably due to overcrowding, is evident from the Log which records visits from the School Board Architect to suggest improvements.[17] To organise the space educationally for teaching purposes must have required real skill. The next Head, J D Thomas, and the third Head Teacher, Henry Davies, were to be vociferous in their complaints about the deficiencies of the temporary building.[18] It was the continual growth of population in the area which caused Her Majesty's Inspectors' of Schools in January, 1879, to ask the Gelligaer School Board and the Merthyr School Board to confer about the site of a permanent school. They pointed out that Bontnewydd was close to the borderline between Gelligaer and Merthyr parishes while the Harris Navigation Colliery was in the latter. Separating them was "a deep ravine" with only the railway viaduct providing a crossing. The dilemma the Boards faced was that the population at the time was divided between both sides of the valley and it was still unclear on which side the greater development would take place. HMI believed that a road bridge would have to be built across the ravine and then one school could serve the population of the two parishes.[19]

The rivalry between the two Boards can be sensed from the comments of Mr W Bell, one of the Members of the Merthyr Board. He recognised that in a matter of months, the Harris Navigation Colliery would be producing coal and that within eighteen months, the population of the district could increase significantly from "the present number of 500 with about 160 children between the ages of three and twelve" to a population of between 2,000 and 3,000. To add strength to his argument, he stated that there were over 62 houses in the course of erection besides those already built. He urged the Merthyr Board to take immediate action and build a Mixed School for at least 600 pupils in their parish rather than allow "the Gelligaer Board to come in."[20]

In the event, both Boards decided to have schools in the respective districts. The existing Bontnewydd School, in temporary premises, continued and it wasn't until November 1st, 1881, that a new building was opened for its pupils. It was to those new premises that John Davies would come, but there were indications that there were imperfections which would have to be amended. One was the absence of gas and lamps which in December, 1881, required the afternoon timetable to be changed because of the lack of light.[21] The Merthyr School Board was also determined to keep up with its neighbouring parish. It formally opened a new school at Treharris on March 27th, 1882, replacing one which had previously been accommodated temporarily in the vestry of a local Baptist Chapel since August, 1881.[22]

The curriculum followed by the pupils at Bontnewydd was typically of the period, confined to the three Elementary Subjects (Reading, Writing & Arithmetic), with extra subjects for the boys being Geography and Grammar, and Geography and Needlework for the Girls. Miss Lewis also liked singing judging by the number of new songs she taught her pupils, sometimes two in a week. By September, 1878, they had mastered the words and music of sixteen different songs. One wonders what some of the older children thought of singing such songs as "Little birdie in the tree" and "The sun is

24

peeping."[23] Attempting to get her pupils to sing by note, she introduced them to the Modulator of the tonic sol-fa notation. This had been adopted and adapted by John Curwen, a nineteenth century English Congregational Minister, from a previous "Sol-fa Ladder." Having personally experienced the problems of reading Staff notation, he had introduced this method for his Sunday School children to derive spiritual benefit through singing hymns.[24] The English Education Department had officially recognised this teaching method in 1860 and by 1891 over two million school children were being taught by this system. Miss Lewis continued to give her charges frequent exercises using the Modulator.

Singing remained a prominent feature of the curriculum under J D Thomas and Henry Davies with many new songs being taught. Indeed an almost permanent feature of the timetable was reported as "Singing and Sewing on Tuesday and Friday afternoons."[25] However, the Log does not mention whether the Modulator was used or not. John Davies, when he had been at Llanover Parochial School had introduced the Modulator there for scale and interval practice in singing lessons. The children had been delighted with the method and showed great interest in it.[26]

Most of the timetable of the school was given to improving performance in the basic subjects. Miss Lewis ensured that: Tables were repeated at the start of the school day; homework was set and followed up. Her successors continued to do everything in their power to raise standards but, judging by their entries, it was a slow process. "Ordinary progress," "backward," "very backward," "still weak," "fair," "improving," "getting on well" are recurring comments on the progress made by the various Standards.[27] In the four years of the existence of Bontnewydd School, the curriculum had not changed very significantly. The daily routine was very similar; but it was differences in the building, and most notably, in the personnel, which probably made most impact on the children. John Davies, starting his tenure there in 1882 would have been very aware too of:

3. A CHANGING LEADERSHIP

For a school to have had no fewer than four Head Teachers in a four-year period would seem to indicate that there was some serious deficiency. Currently, it is not uncommon for football clubs to change their Manager with alacrity when results are not propitious. However, frequent and sudden changes of Head Teacher are not at all common. John Davies must have had much food for thought as he perused the School Log and contemplated the legacy of his predecessors.

Marian Lewis   The TRAIL-BLAZING LEADER
(January 1st 1878 to February 1st 1879)

The school roll grew steadily with average attendance reaching 82.2 by April and 88 by May, 1878. In the second week of the school's existence, a Monitor, Martha Ann Payne, was appointed. She initially looked after the Infants while, at the same time, being prepared herself, for the Standard 5 examination. Martha Ann received one hours instruction each evening on school days from 6.00 - 7.00 p.m. from the Head. Her development as a Monitor was somewhat uneven with the Log recording, on occasions, that she did not seem

Courtesy Glamorgan Archives

to be making any progress in her teaching. It was no surprise to find that she did not make the grade, even under the next Master.[28] In February, 1880, having failed her last examination, the Managers gave her one month's notice.

As the average attendance climbed, the Board decided that the school needed two Monitors. In May, 1878, Elizabeth Lewis was appointed, first of all, to teach Standard 1 with the Head being responsible for

26

Standards 2, 3, 4 and 5. It is interesting to compare her progress with that of Martha Ann Payne as they received instruction from the Head. Elizabeth usually seemed to do better, according to the Log, but it should be remembered that she was also Marian Lewis' sister.[29]

The structure of the school year, which was followed for some time subsequently, was established in the first year. There were two weeks holiday at Christmas, two days at Easter for Good Friday and Easter Monday and a month long Midsummer holiday. The attendance always seemed to go down after any break. There were occasional day or half-day holidays for local events such as Quakers Yard Fair on Whit Tuesday.

Illness and weather, apparently, had the strongest influence on attendance When the Ninnis family suffered from an infectious disease (unspecified), all five children (John, William, Emily Jane, Amelia and Celia) were ordered to stay off school, and the attendance plummeted. These youngsters have the distinction of being the first to be named in the Log book. It was John Jones, the School Board Attendance Officer, who had the endless and important task of chasing up unauthorised absences. This was because the progress of pupils depended on consistent attendance which was essential if the school was to receive its annual grant at inspection.[30]

Amongst the many visitors to the school during its first year were Members of the Board: Rev Aaron Davies (Chairman) and Mr Davies of Merthyr; Managers: Mr John Jenkins, (Secretary), Mr Richards, Mr Evans, Mr Jones and Mr William Lewis. Miss Lewis did not usually state the purpose of the visits but one can surmise that, frequently, they were of an inspectorial nature. The person who made most visits to the school (at least 24), was William Lewis of Bontnewydd Farm. It is most interesting to find that, in November, 1878, just before the Annual Inspection, he supervised the school for one afternoon, with the Monitors, because Miss Lewis was absent ill.[31] This would indicate his real involvement and concern for it.

It is no surprise to find William Lewis playing such a prominent part in the life of the school. He was the most important man in the village owning most of the land on which it stood. It was he who was to give his name to Trelewis just as F W Harris was to give his name to Treharris. From his father he had gained the lease of Tir Shag farm, then in 1866, his uncle, Daniel Lewis, who had no heirs as he had never married, bequeathed Bontnewydd Farm to him with other possessions. The 1891 Kelly's Directory of Monmouthshire and South Wales records him as being Farmer, Landowner and Colliery owner. His standing in the community is further underlined by his being Churchwarden and Guardian of the Poor in Gelligaer Parish for many years. In addition, he became one of the founders of St Mary's Church in the village. A man of such substance was to have a formative influence in the development of all aspects of village life, including the school. His impact there can be traced in the many references made to him in the School Log. It was axiomatic that he would attain positions of authority. Amongst the various posts he held as Manager of the school were those of Chairman and Treasurer. Holding such significant offices probably accounts for the above average number of visits which he made to the school, as did the fact that he lived locally.[32]

The effect of Managers' visits to the school are often revealed in the comments which Miss Lewis made in the Log immediately after they took place. For example, after several Managers had visited in March, 1878, she says that special attention was to be given to order and discipline. Then, after a visit from Mr Lewis in April, 1878, her attention that week was to be directed to "the cleanliness, attire and habits of the children."[33] The Log also reveals that Miss Lewis had some problems in enforcing discipline. She writes in the first week of August, (after the pupils had just returned from the month Midsummer holiday), that she "had some difficulty in getting the children into proper discipline this week." Returning back to school routine after the relative freedom of the long holiday was probably always going to be an effort. To help in doing this, she got the children marching, singing and exercising whilst changing lessons. Evidently the problems continued for, before the end of the month, four pupils, John Ninnis, William Ninnis, Elizabeth Williams and Price Williams were expelled because of their unruly conduct. The Ninnis brothers who had been the first pupils mentioned in the Log for being kept at home due to infectious disease now gained notoriety as being the first pupils to be expelled.[34]

The School year proceeded with Miss Lewis and her two Monitors seeking to prepare the pupils, as adequately as they could, for the very first inspection by Her Majesty's Inspectors of Schools. This was always an important but worrying occasion when performance and attendance would determine the amount of grant the school would receive for the following year. The first Annual inspection occurred on November 21st, 1878, by Mr W Edwards, HMI and Mr Rees, Sub-Inspector. Also present were Rev Aaron Davies, Chairman of the Board, Rev R O Jones and Mr W Lewis, Managers. To conclude this onerous event with a reward, the children, received a treat in the afternoon. Rather ominously, however, Miss Lewis records in the last week of term that although the Inspectors' report had been received that week, she had not seen it as it was still in the hands of one of the Managers. It was not until the first week back after the Christmas holiday, that the Summary of the report was written up.[35]

The Report had faint praise stating that as it was the very first examination for most of the scholars, the results were on the whole creditable. Because, then as now, the inspectorate utilises generalised comments, it is often difficult to gain an exact understanding of the standard being achieved. Reading and Writing were "very fair" and Arithmetic "fair". The Temporary premises were "very fair". Geography was not up to the mark and failed to get the grant. The Needlework needed to improve. But it was the final comment which probably accounted for the delay in Miss Lewis seeing the Report: "The discipline is, as might be expected from the circumstances, as yet imperfect." They did not specify the circumstances but could it be that they were referring to the school being in charge of a School Mistress with two inexperienced female Monitors to assist her?

Although she had not received the Report before Christmas, it would appear that the Inspectors had commented to Miss Lewis about the weakness in discipline. In the week after the inspection special attention was paid to discipline in all classes. To re-assure herself or the Managers, she records just before Christmas that there was "great improvement in discipline this week."[36] Whether or not the Board Members and Managers were convinced that this was happening is not clear. They certainly stepped up their visits to the school in January, 1879, with at least five of them turning up on the last Monday of the month. This did not augur well for Miss Lewis who did not seem to be aware that her remaining time at the school was running out. There is no mention in the Log of her imminent departure. Instead her final entry for the Week ending January 31st, was: "The progress was ordinary in all the various branches of instruction throughout the week." The following Monday she had gone and J D Thomas had taken over as Head.[37]

Within a week of her sudden departure from Bontnewydd, on 3rd February, 1879, Miss Lewis commenced her duties at the small Penybank Mixed and Infants' School, which had an attendance of just 35 pupils. She was to remain there until the Annual Inspection of 21st November, 1879. Mary Snook then took over as Mistress from 24th November, 1879, but the Log is silent about why Miss Lewis left and about where she went. However in the summary of the HMI report on the school it is stated that: "This little school has been well started.......The Discipline is good, considering the circumstances."[38] Miss Lewis at the start of her career as Mistress always seemed to get the tough assignment of initiating things. Whether she eventually made a success of her chosen career is still to be discovered.

John David Thomas   The OFT-COMPLAINING LEADER
(3rd February 1879 - 24th May 1881)

The second Head of the school was to remain there just over twice as long as Miss Lewis. Even so, two and a quarter years' service in post appears very short by modern standards. Also the fact that he was able to take over the school so quickly needs an explanation, which can be found in the pages of the "Merthyr Express." At the monthly meeting of the Gelligaer School Board, in December, 1878, it was agreed to defer a motion that the appointment of Miss Lewis as Mistress of Bontnewydd School be reconsidered. The following month it was decided unanimously that Mr J D Thomas of Blackwood replace her. The Board was aware of his availability because he had been one of four applicants for the post of Master at Pontlottyn. Strong recommendations from the Chairman of Mynyddislwyn School Board and Managers of his school, together with a record of a 95% pass rate there, contributed to this decision. The Board was evidently expecting great things of him.[39]

From his very first entry in the Log he is at pains to remind the Board and the Managers of the difficulties facing him. Stating that he took charge of the school from Miss Lewis, he goes on to use a bleak and blunt phrase that she had been "removed to Brithdir." This, surely, was meant to convey that he had not received a good inheritance from his predecessor and that her shortcomings had resulted in her transfer elsewhere. The impression he seems to give is that it was the three women who were to blame for the school lacking discipline and progress. Now, it was being left to him to rectify their deficiencies. In his first week, therefore, he points out that the staff he had inherited were not up to the mark, being rather "dead & dull over their teaching." It is no surprise that it wasn't long before Elizabeth Lewis resigned with the reason given as "owing to her sister who was my predecessor having left." Martha Ann Payne, however, continued as Monitor for another year until she was given notice by the Managers after failing her examinations.[40]

Mr Thomas also saw fit to record, yet again, the Summary of the HM Inspectors' Report for the year ending October 31st, 1879. This showed the base line from which he started, but also it showed how punctilious he was in keeping the required rubric. Miss Lewis had not listed the staff for the following year at the end of the report when she wrote it up, neither had she ensured that it was signed by the Managers' Correspondent. He did both thus showing that the Managers could expect changes from him. But he doesn't lose an opportunity of painting a dismal picture of the school. Already he had described the staff he had inherited as weak: so too were the pupils according to him. In the first month, he comments on the performance of the various Standards: without exception they are "backward" or "very backward" in the elementary subjects; Dictation and Geography did not seem to have been attempted. Writing in June, 1879, he says: "The intelligence of the children throughout the school is of a very low degree." Even in February, 1881, he says: "Many new children don't even now (sic) their letters and some of them up to 7 and 8 and even 9 years of age." Added to the low ability of the pupils were failings in attendance and punctuality. At the commencement of his Headship, he indicated that some pupils never came into school until after the register was marked and others were very irregular in attendance.[41]

J D Thomas further stressed the defects in the building which militated against progress. On no fewer than 5 occasions, he complains that Geography and Grammar, (the two subjects which failed to get the grant under Miss Lewis), are "most backward" because there is no classroom in which to teach these subjects. The constant repetition of these complaints, especially just before the Annual Inspection, looks very much like him getting his excuse in if the results were not favourable.[42]

It was imperative that the discipline needed to improve in the school and once more he makes plain the difficult task he had. In February, 1879, he writes that order and discipline were bad but better than they had been since he was giving them his full attention.[43] He pointed out that he was in charge now not women. The Log Book does not reveal the exact tactics which he employed since the favourite word that he uses to describe his actions is "cautioned." Among the offences meriting cautions were: being unruly on the highway; throwing stones; breaking down hedges and trespassing, all of which revealed that the school was expected to deal with anti-social behaviour outside its premises. Cautions were also given about lateness, absenteeism, unclean hands and faces, particularly when the Annual Inspection was looming. What he did besides cautioning the pupils when required is not always stated and no Punishment Books recording details of punishments meted out by the school have survived. On some occasions, he speaks of punishment being given, (with details unspecified), as in August, 1879, when the eldest pupils were punished for being "unruly on the road and mocking old people." In addition, in September, 1879, he punished several boys for stealing corn from the harvest field.[44]

Did his issuing of cautions have the desired effect? There are indications of some improvement in April, 1879, even though school discipline wasn't yet as he would have liked. He mentions that the tone of the school was getting better despite several of the older boys still being unruly. In June of the same year he states that behaviour is far better than it had been, particularly on the roads. The problems, however, did not go away and in the first week back after the Midsummer holiday he had to contend with disobedient pupils on their return to school just as Miss Lewis had before him.[45]

Having made sure that the problems facing him were well documented, J D Thomas got down to work with a will and the Log provides a commentary on the progress in the various Standards and subjects. Comments like; "Progressing"; "Good Progress"; "Improving"; "Getting on Well" are now interspersed with "Backward " and "Very Backward." There might have been a low base line for him to start from but he wanted the Managers to know that things were steadily getting better. An intriguing expression is used to indicate the method he was using: he "drilled" the different Standards in Arithmetic, in Spelling and in the Songs to be sung on Inspection Day. The Singing usually occurred on Friday afternoons and included Rounds and what were then new songs like "The Grandfather's Clock."[46]

Assisting him in the teaching was Annie Elizabeth Roberts who had been appointed Assistant Mistress on 1st May, 1879, to take charge of the Infants at a salary of £35 per annum. She had previously been a Pupil Teacher at Pontlottyn Infant School. Her efforts won the praise of the Head on more than one occasion and, what is more important, the approbation of Her Majesty's Inspectors in the 1879 Report. It was that report which was to reveal what J D Thomas had actually achieved in the latter part of the School Year ending October 31st, 1879, after he had taken over the helm.

The Report, as written in the Log, is described as a Summary and is very brief. Progress in attainment and discipline had been made under the new Master with the Elementary work being very satisfactory on the whole. But Geography still failed to get the grant. The Infants had been well taught "under the circumstances" which presumably referred to the deficiencies in the school building. The only improvement which the Inspectors wanted to see in the building was that some of the windows should be made to open. In addition, they cited Article 17c, that because of overcrowding in the school, the average attendance must not in future exceed 89. Evidently, Mr Thomas was encouraged by the Report when he received it in January, 1880, because the results were better than under Miss Lewis and indicated improvement.[47]

In the second year of his Headship, Mr Thomas continued to apply himself assiduously to the task of moving the school on. Miss Elizabeth Jones replaced Miss Roberts as Assistant Mistress in January, 1880. She had previously been a Pupil Teacher at Dukestown Board School. Miss Elizabeth Morgan replaced Martha Ann Payne as Monitress in February, 1880. With the new staff, he was hoping for renewed progress, and was fulsome in praise of Miss Jones who "works regularly and gives every attention." There was some interchange of responsibilities for teaching the Infants and the lower Standards possibly to maximise strengths and minimise weaknesses. In the record of progress made by the Standards, there is a liberal array of comments like: "fairly well up"; "improving"; "greatly improving", amongst the not so favourable ones. One smiles at a comment on the Infants which indicated that Reading was improving but Writing was "backward."[48]

As the Annual Inspection in November, 1880, drew nearer there was a great deal of optimism recorded in the Log about what the outcome might be. Towards the end of September, it was considered that the whole school had made special progress. Increased attention was being given to improving attendance and punctuality. Again he "cautioned" the children. It would be interesting to know what other devices he used in the weeks prior to the Inspection to hide from the Inspectors weaknesses which he knew would be there. Nothing less than concentrated application was required so a sustained effort was made in Arithmetic, Dictation, Geography and other deficient areas. In the week before the Inspection, there had been a recap of all the work of the year, and he exclaims confidently: "Exceedingly well up in the 3R's." Twentieth Century, advertising experts were to use similar words such as "exceedingly good", to seek to convince a sceptical public of the worth of Mr Kipling's cakes![49]

The Summary of the Report for the Year ending October 31st, 1880, is not written up in the Log until the end of February, 1881. The delay might have rung some alarm bells, as it did for Miss Lewis, especially as its content had very faint praise. The Report was even briefer than that for 1879, stating that the pupils had passed a "very fair" examination in the Elementary subjects but that their general level of attainment was still low. More ominous was the comment that the Discipline was "not quite satisfactory." Geography and Grammar were still not awarded the grant. The Inspectors concluded with the observation that the school would probably improve when it entered new premises.[50]

It seems that the Report did have some impact on Mr Thomas because, for the first time, he fails to have the Report signed by the Secretary to the Managers and he fails to record the names and status of the staff. Previously he had been so punctilious in observing the rubric. Continuing to strive to eradicate the weaknesses and failures which the Inspectors had revealed, he recorded some success. In April, 1881, he specially commends Minnie Payne and Mary John, two girls in Standard 5, for the "correctness and neatness of their work." It was rare for him to draw attention to individual pupils but these two were subsequently to become Monitresses and Pupil Teachers in the school and he was proud of their achievements. He states that real progress was being made in Arithmetic with the higher Standards, but Geography and Grammar for the whole school remained backward. As has been noticed, Mr Thomas had re-iterated constantly complaints that there was not a separate classroom to teach these subjects. Almost one of his last entries in the Log about the curriculum pointed out the problem again, that the simultaneous work of the Infants in the same room made it almost impossible to teach Geography and Grammar "to any advantage." The final comment in the Inspectors' report that the new school premises would lead to improvements was perhaps a tacit admission that there was some justification for his oft-repeated complaint.[51]

Their comment about discipline would most certainly have been underlined by Managers and Members of the Board. The "cautions" the Head was giving were obviously not sufficient if order and control within the school were not effective. The administration of School discipline was solely the responsibility of the Head because, in November, 1880, Mr Thomas had received a complaint that Elizabeth Morgan, the Monitress, had been punishing some children which is "contrary to the rules of the school." How then were Monitresses expected to keep discipline with pupils who, in some cases, were only slightly younger than they were? What sanctions did they have? The Head continued to have difficulties himself with discipline. Just before the Christmas break, in December, 1880, he speaks of having trouble with some of the children whose behaviour was "very bad indeed." In February, 1881, Mr Thomas received from the Secretary a copy of Rules and regulations for Managers and Head Teachers of the School from the Board which stated that: "The Managers shall direct that Corporal Punishment shall not be inflicted except by the Principal Teacher and such punishment shall not be inflicted before the expiration of one hour after the commitment of the offence."[52] It is not known whether this instruction was specifically directed to Mr Thomas for breaches in its application, or whether it was sent to all of the Board's schools. Whichever it was, it reveals the importance of correctly applied School discipline to the Board.

Despite his best endeavours, his cautions and his protestations, J D Thomas appears not to have achieved significantly more than Miss Lewis in his two years of Headship. Geography and Grammar had failed to achieve the grant and Discipline was still deficient. So he pays the price and leaves the school. Like his predecessor, there is no warning in the Log that this was going to happen, no explanation and no valedictory comment. His last entry on 20th May, 1881, is: "Usual routine according to timetable." This time, there was no flurry of visits by Managers or Board members to indicate his imminent departure. Just silence. Henry Davies was to succeed him as Head on Monday, 23rd May, 1881. Mr Thomas himself was to remain at the school until Tuesday afternoon, 24th May, thus marking an uncomfortable end to his career at Bontnewydd.[53]

Henry Davies   The SOON-DEPARTING LEADER
(23rd May 1881 to 24th March 1882)

In just over three years since it opened, the school was to receive its third Head Teacher. The question of why the turnover was so rapid is, as has been noted, open to conjecture. Achieving immediate success would have been a difficult task for anyone responsible for a new school in far from ideal conditions. The prevailing and much criticised system of "Payment by results" would have produced added pressures. The Board and the Managers expected and demanded recognisable advancement and were impatient if their expectations were not being realised. The peremptory dismissal of the first two Heads is a powerful indicator of that fact. Now that the third Head, Henry Davies, had been appointed, would he be able to accomplish more than his predecessors?

In his second week, he started an assault on punctuality. After warning, he punished those habitually late. This continued the following week when, again, he punished a large number of children for lateness in the afternoon as well as in the morning. Cautions were not going to be sufficient for him. Punishment was to be the order of the day. When Mr Richards, the Chairman of Managers, visited the school towards the end of June, less than a month after Mr Davies had

37

taken control, he expressed himself "pleased with the order." It seems that Henry Davies was starting as he meant to go on.[54]

In July, Mr Richards had to visit the school again because a Mrs Price had complained that her son had been punished too severely. Mr Davies states that he does remember punishing the boy for "indolence", (the word was underlined in the Log but it could also be read "insolence" as the writing is indistinct). However there is no dated or detailed reference to this incident in the School Log Book. It was either omitted or a separate Punishment Book was being kept. He now puts the record straight after Mr Richards' visit by writing: "He is a remarkably indolent lad, and I believe an occasional thrashing will have a beneficial influence both while he is in school and after he leaves it. He is also very late in coming to school at all times." This incident is indicative of the difficult task of the Head. The Managers wanted him to apply effective discipline but they reacted to parental complaints when it was enforced. After the Chairman's visit, the matter was discussed with Mr Davies at an evening meeting of the Managers. How supportive they were of his action is not known as all that is stated is that he was supplied with the regulations of the Board.[55] Following this meeting, punishments were still meted out for lateness and coming to school with dirty hands and faces. Some improvement ensued as a result. He was not going to be deterred from doing what he felt was necessary to raise standards.[56]

In his first month, he suspended the teaching of sewing on Tuesday and Thursday afternoons because of "the backwardness of the children in their elementary work." It seemed that, from the beginning of his headship, he was putting his foot down to ensure that the pupils performed better under him. But by August and September the usual timetable of sewing was restored.[57] Irregular attendance, the large number of infants, the late arrival of books which he had ordered, the inadequacy of the building, and the shortage of staff for the number of pupils were all pointed out in detail as being factors inhibiting sound progress. Almost his first entry in the Log was to re-iterate Mr Thomas' complaint that Grammar and Geography could not be well taught because of the "inconvenience of simultaneous work in any of the classes." On occasions, he did not give the names of absentees to the Attendance Officer because of the overcrowding. In addition, early in his headship, he applied to the Managers for an extra Pupil Teacher or Monitor stating that it was almost impossible to keep the "whole school fully employed" and receiving good and thorough instruction with the present staff. If he couldn't manage, what chance had Miss Lewis with a larger school roll! When the Pupil Teacher was absent ill, he wrote almost despairingly: "I find it very difficult to work according to the timetable through her absence."[58]

Together with this recital of hindrances to progress, as the annual inspection approached he draws attention in the Log to severe weather and illness affecting attendance. Scarlet fever and ringworm both took their toll in the weeks leading up to the examination. In the very week before the Inspection, there were at least 10 pupils absent because of scarlet fever.[59] On 18th November, 1881, HMI W Edwards, assisted by Mr Rees, inspected the school, with Messrs Lewis & Richards from the Managers and Rev A. Davies, Chairman of the Board, also present. They were doubtless anxious to witness a leap forward or at least a step forward in the pupils' progress. 83 pupils were presented for examination and the average attendance for the year was stated to be 86.4. The usual treat of tea and cake in the afternoon, following the examination, was given which the pupils greatly enjoyed and which they thoroughly deserved. When Mr Davies received the duplicate schedule of the examination results a week later, you can sense the satisfaction he must have felt when he recorded that the children had done "remarkably well considering the state the school had fallen into." The evidence was revealed by the percentage pass which was 98% compared with 63% in the previous year. Probably because of this, he received the Summary Report of the Inspection much sooner than the earlier Reports, recording it in the School Log on 16th December, 1881. The Inspectors found a great improvement in the Elementary subjects with better work all round. Geography had not been presented for the grant; the Infants had performed well except in Arithmetic; Grammar was pretty good except in Standard 4. The

39

Report concluded: "Now that the school has been established in convenient premises with an industrious teacher, it is hoped that a large increase in numbers will soon take place."[60] At last, a Report which would please the Managers and one which reflected well on the Head Teacher. An optimistic view for future development seemed more than justified, particularly as the school was in purpose-built premises at last.

The new school building had opened on the afternoon of Tuesday 1st November, 1881, just over a week before the Inspection. But very little detail of how much it cost, what the premises were like, or of what difference it made, appears in the Log. All we are told is that Rev A Davies, J P Williams and Mr Beddoe, Members of the Board, together with Messrs W Richards, J Jenkins and C John, Managers, were present. (A noticeable absentee was William Lewis.) [61] To have a new school building built specifically for that purpose must have been a tremendous boon. Obviously it would have done much to remedy the shortcomings of the building in which the school had existed since its inception. How illuminating for us if we had details of where the temporary School premises had been sited but there is no record. Where in such a tiny village could there be a room of sufficient dimensions to house a school? There are some intriguing indications which might provide the answer. It could well be that the school's temporary premises were in Ebenezer Chapel, the first non-conformist building in the village, because the Log for 9th September, 1881, records that the school had to be closed on a Monday "owing to anniversary services being held in the schoolroom."[62] This implies that the school was sharing premises with a chapel. Two further facts give added credence to this belief. It was in 1876 that a lease was taken out for Capel Ebenezer, so it is highly likely that the chapel schoolroom had already been constructed.[63] Added to this is the fact that there are other contemporary examples of Board Schools starting their existence in Chapel accommodation. This was to be the case in neighbouring Treharris. So there is a strong possibility from this evidence that Ebenezer chapel was the original location for Bontnewydd Board School.

A renewed and better future was in prospect with the new school building. Hopefully it would end the old complaints about the inability to teach Geography and Grammar in the same room. But Mr Davies soon points out that all was not perfect with it. In December, 1881, he records that the timetable had to be altered because of the absence of gas and lamps. Afternoon school had to begin at 1.30 p.m. and end at 4 p.m.[64] Despite such slight imperfections everything seemed to be improving. More pupils were admitted, with the highest average attendance reaching 103 at the end of January, 1882. The Managers had at last responded to the Head's request for more staff with David Davies, Mary John and Daniel Davies being commended to the Board as Monitors. These were receiving their lessons in the morning before school (not after school as previously) and showed every indication of becoming useful and successful. After the examination, marked improvement was noted in Upper and Lower Standards and in the Infants. All was rosy: punctuality; cleanliness; even the homework was being completed diligently. Then in the midst of all of this encouragement Mr Davies submitted his resignation in February, 1882. No wonder there was a burst of visits from the Managers that week.[65] Here was the first Head of the school leaving of his own accord, and relinquishing his post when apparently everything was going well.

There is no obvious indication of the reason for his decision. At the beginning of February, 1882, however, Mr Davies makes an important entry in the Log about school fees. The only time fees had been mentioned previously was in the Managers' meeting of July, 1881, when the Secretary read a letter from the Clerk to the Board stating that, in future, all bills for school fees were to be delivered to parents by teaching staff, not pupils. Now, Mr Davies writes that he had not entered the paupers' fees received about the middle of last quarter "as I am waiting to enter them together with those due on 29th December, as this will prevent mistakes in reckoning the dates of beginning and ending of quarter - and the fees of the children of Eglwysilan parish have not been received." (Later on in John Davies' Log of June 9th, 1882, we shall find that there were arrears of school fees of £40 since

41

the school opened - not an inconsiderable amount, and to which all the previous Heads must have contributed.) As this information about school fees occurs immediately before Henry Davies' resignation and given the fact that he writes more about them than his predecessors, one is left wondering whether they contributed, in any way, to his decision to leave. After submitting his resignation, he is at pains to say at the annual audit of school books in February, 1882, that the paupers' fees were entered.[66]

Of course, school fees might have had no bearing at all on his decision to leave. Much more likely was that he had been attracted to the prospect of becoming Head in the shortly-to-be-opened new premises of Treharris Board School. Knowing the rivalry between the Merthyr and the Gelligaer School Boards, it is even possible that he had been approached to take over the Treharris School because of his success at Bontnewydd. What is certain is that no time was lost between his submitting his resignation at the beginning of February, 1882, relinquishing his post on March 23rd, 1882 and becoming Head at Treharris on Monday, March 27th, 1882.[67] There was a smooth transition which would appear to indicate that everything had been carefully planned in advance.

Henry Davies becomes the first Head at Bontnewydd to leave a valedictory statement in the Log. (His predecessors had just disappeared without any reference to the fact that they were going.) He writes: "In making this my last entry, I cannot fail to call attention to the very valuable assistance I have received during my stay here from the Teachers, especially Miss Jones, the Assistant Mistress, and Elizabeth Morgan. They have very efficiently discharged all duties which have devolved upon them with the business of the school. I wish my successor a very prosperous and successful year and I believe that with the good class of children that attend the school he cannot fail to secure good results. My duties here have always been a pleasure to me since I entered upon the charge of the school. I hope that they will prove light and pleasant to my successor. He cannot have better results than I wish him."[68] For the first and only time he signed the Log: "Henry Davies".

In the short time during which he had been at the school, Henry Davies had undoubtedly made an impact. Such was his impression upon parents that there were some pupils who were to follow him from Bontnewydd to Treharris Board School when he moved.[69] But whether everything had been completely transformed to sweetness and light remains questionable. His comments about the pupils are so much at variance with those of his predecessor J D Thomas, that one suspects a farewell gloss of self-congratulation. Nothing should be allowed to detract, however, from the best report on the school by Her Majesty's Inspectors since its inception with the highest percentage of passes obtained by its pupils. Henry Davies had propelled the school forward in the right direction.

He was to continue in similar vein at Treharris Board School. Moving from temporary premises in a local Baptist chapel, the new school buildings were formally opened by the Merthyr School Board on the afternoon Henry Davies took over as Head. The pupils celebrated the event with a tea party. The summary of the first Inspectors' Report of his tenure there was to be most encouraging: "The energetic Master who has been a year in charge seems likely to raise the school in due time to a condition of first class efficiency." [70]

So it was to prove during the time that Henry Davies was Head at Treharris from 1882 until 1892.

William Davies   The HIATUS-FILLING LEADER
(27th March 1882 - 10th April 1882)

The gap caused by Henry Davies' departure could not be filled immediately by a permanent appointment so William Davies appears in the Log as a Caretaker Head for just about two weeks. There is no indication of where he came from, why he was able to take over at such short notice, or of where he went afterwards. His comments are understandably brief as he knew he was only there temporarily. His first entry records his pleasure in finding the school "in a very good state as regards education and discipline."[71] Very little else of significance appears afterwards.

So, the scene is set for John Davies' arrival in, Bontnewydd. The small farms and scattered homesteads were slowly but surely being joined by the new dwellings of a developing village. Dominating the landscape across the valley, was the Harris Navigation Colliery with its characteristic twin winding towers and motley buildings. It was to dominate the employment prospects too, of most of those who lived around it, for years to come. The Bontnewydd Board School, after a less than propitious inauguration, was finally sited in a building at the very heart of the village. In December, 1881, it had received the best Inspectors' report since its start and was ripe for further improvement. For this to happen it needed firm, stable and decisive leadership. After four Heads coming and going in four years it was now John Davies' turn to take over the reins.

TRELEWIS FROM GARDEN CITY.

Although the picture says Trelewis from Garden City, very little of Trelewis is to be seen. In the foreground is the top end of Trelewis. At the top of the picture in the background can be seen Deep Navigation Colliery and Treharris which are divided from Trelewis by a small river Nant Bargod-Taf.　　　Courtesy Alan George

Part Two

STARTING THE WORK

Part TwoSTARTING THE WORK (1882 - 1892)

133 /552

April 11. I John Davies formerly of Ciliau Park School under the Llanfihangel Ystrad School Board Cardiganshire this day take charge of Bontnewydd School under the Gelligaer School Board. The Schoolroom seems well built and ventilated and the children are in fair order, but I notice a great tendency to be noisy in their work; whether this be the effect of practice under previous masters or that the children take a little advantage of the frequent change of masters lately. I know not. It is evident that this tendency must be suppressed. The Scholars have gone through a proportional part of the current years work in the three Elementary Subjects but little Grammar and less Geography have been done.

John Davies, in good, firm and clear script, was to make his first entry in the Log on 11th April, 1882. He introduces himself and writes his first impressions of the school in a much fuller way than any of his predecessors: "I, John Davies of Ciliau Park School under the Llanvihangel Ystrad School Board, Cardiganshire, this day take charge of Bontnewydd School under the Gelligaer School Board. The school room seems well-built and ventilated and the children are in fair order, but I notice a great tendency to be noisy in their work. Whether this be the effect of practice under previous Masters or that the children take a little advantage of the frequent change of Masters recently, I know not. It is evident that that this tendency must be suppressed."[72]

Before making that entry, he would most probably have read the account given there of the development of the school. What might have been some of the emotions he experienced as he did so? There could have been a genuine apprehension as he reflected on the fact that in a little over four years the school had seen four Head Teachers. Would he be able to remain longer than any of them? Then he would have considered the huge challenge facing him. While there had been some green shoots of encouraging progress, much still needed to be done to make the school a resounding success. Would he be able to achieve more than the other leaders had done? But in the last sentence of his very first entry quoted above, John Davies revealed the dogged determination which was to characterise his headship. He was going to give his very best endeavours to improve and develop the school which he had inherited. Little did he know that he was to become the longest-serving Head of the school and that he was to spend the remainder of his life in the small village community to which he had come.

John Davies set out with an over-riding objective to construct a sound, secure foundation through a shrewd mixture of academic achievement, productive leadership and discerning improvement. Just as the builders of Rome found, this could not be done in a day or even a year. It was to take time and the progress each year was not necessarily steady and continuous. Set-backs and delays were to abound caused by the manifold problems which he would encounter. Little wonder, therefore, that the onward progression to achieving his objective proved to be somewhat spasmodic.

1. THE PROBLEMS FACED

Consider some of the difficulties he had to deal with:

From his Predecessors - the Absence of Continuity

His first comments about the school already showed up an obstacle which he had to remove, namely the lack of continuous application of common standards. Sound and solid foundations for the development of any new school will best be achieved if pupils and staff have a stable environment without unsettling inconsistencies. Recurrent transitions of leader with the consequent variations in leadership styles and values can be inimical to establishing soundly-based, lasting traditions and customs which are invariably observed. Exposure to diligent, persevering, uniform measures over a period of time stand more chance of success. It must have been unsettling, therefore, for the school to have had so many changes of leader in such a short time. Stability was needed to allow it to develop successfully.

Another consequence of the frequent changes of Head was to present the pupils with an opportunity for them to exploit. Their capacity of finding ways and means of getting one over their teachers, of capitalising on any perceived uncertainty and of seeking to get what they want, is well known. "But Sir, the last Head ALWAYS allowed us to do it," could have been a persistent strategy to employ with each newcomer. Mr Davies at least thought that the noisiness of classes while they were working might have been caused by something akin to this. (Of course he might have been used to rather less boisterous pupils in rural Cardiganshire compared with those of the Taff Bargoed Valley.)

He was determined, therefore, to establish standards of his choosing. There would be no other individuals to lead the school in their own idiosyncratic way for the next thirty years. He would be in continuous charge. The school's progress rested on him and on what he could bring to its development. There were still other difficulties to face but, in all of them, and in the successes he would achieve, he was to leave his own indelible imprint. There were problems also:

From his Pupils - the Challenge of Consistency

Bontnewydd was a growing community from the time that Mr Davies took up residence there. The opening of the Harris Navigation Colliery inevitably led to an influx of people. But the Log reveals that there was still a lot of coming and going throughout his first decade in charge. Writing in June, 1882, he says: "The unsettledness of the inhabitants occasioned by the insecurity of work is a great drawback to the success of the school."[73] What caused that insecurity is not explained. However, the impact on the school was that families were moving into and out of the locality so frequently that the educative work for a number of pupils was interrupted. Mr Davies was to find this most discouraging. After working hard to enable pupils to progress, they left before they or the school could be rewarded for their effort. In March, 1883, he speaks somewhat ruefully of part of the neighbourhood being inhabited "just now by a somewhat nomadic tribe." This state of affairs probably continued for some time with equilibrium sometimes being maintained by the numbers of pupils moving in balancing those who were moving out.[74]

The number of pupils attending the school grew steadily: in 1884, the number reported on roll was 130; by June, 1887, he recorded the highest number of pupils on roll since the school opened - 178, with the number being presented for the annual examination in November that year being 159 (64 Infants and 95 in Standards); by April, 1889, he says that the average attendance was higher than in any corresponding period previously.[75] Despite this enlarging school population there is a great deal of inconsistency in average attendance. Getting the pupils to attend regularly was a perennial problem, particularly in the Upper Standards. Attendance was usually worst on Monday mornings and Friday afternoons and also just before the end and at the beginning of term. The Attendance Officer was one of the most frequent visitors to the school and had an almost never-ending task. He was asked to be particularly active when the date was reached on which all pupils on the Registers had to be presented for examination. It was vital that they attended beforehand so that they would be prepared for it.[76]

The accurate keeping of Registers was of great importance because the annual grant in part depended upon attendance. For this reason, Managers would inspect the registers periodically and sign if they were correct. Usually they were but in October, 1883, Rev R O Jones found that one girl had been marked present by mistake. This had to be corrected before he would sign the Log.[77] Irregular attendance had many causes. Parental collusion often played a part and Mr Davies was concerned that parents evaded the law "wonderfully, by faithful promises and substantial excuses." He urged that parents would encourage regular attendance not through fear of the law but by appreciating the value of education. As the population became more settled, he hoped that this would happen. [78]

It was the Upper Standards which gave most cause for concern particularly amongst those boys who had passed the standard for total exemption and over whom the Attendance Officer had no jurisdiction. They absented themselves with impunity. When the Board's bye-laws ceased to apply to some of the older pupils after they had passed Standard 4, Mr Davies considered asking the Managers to invoke expulsion to deal with the problem. Also parents were not averse to keeping them off school for home duties. By pupils absenting themselves, especially before the annual examination, and not being compelled or persuaded to attend, Mr Davies reflected with feeling that there would be no results to compensate for all the attention they had received earlier in the school. When threats and persuasion did not improve attendance, something further was required. By 1891, the Board raised the standard for total exemption and it was hoped that this would lead to better attendance in the Higher Standards.[79]

Factors such as weather and sickness, quite outside the control of the school had a significant part to play in attendance. Snow, rain and generally inclement weather always had an adverse effect. On one morning in March, 1886, only 28 pupils turned up when there was a heavy fall of snow. As they were wet to the knees, they were dismissed and the school closed except that the teachers remained to clear the snow to improve access. Good weather also brought problems. After a very dry, sultry spell in July, 1886, pupils were kept at home to carry water which was scarce in the village. The following summer the same situation arose although it was hoped that the new pipes which had been laid in the village would not affect absence so much.[80]

Sickness inevitably took its toll, especially when there was an epidemic. A virulent outbreak of measles caused the school to be closed for three weeks in October, 1885, just prior to the Annual Inspection. One of the Infants died and those that did return when the school reopened appeared "sickly and worn." Some, however, were still absent during the vital preparation time for the examination. Again in June, 1889, there was a further Measles epidemic which played havoc with attendance but fortunately this was just prior to the Midsummer holiday. Returning to school after the vacation, many were still suffering the effects which forbade "pressure on them in their work." What Mr Davies described as "Hooping (sic) Cough" seriously affected attendance amongst the Infants in 1889 and forced an early closure of the school before Christmas. Scarlet fever made its appearance in the Log for 1890 with two fatalities amongst the pupils and even one of the teaching staff being absent for five weeks.[81] All of these episodes quite naturally upset progress and added to the difficulties which Mr Davies faced. Inconsistency in attendance was to be particularly difficult to solve as most elementary schools of this period were to find. Added to this was the inconsistency in the abilities to be found in his pupils. Somewhat dolefully he records in April, 1883, that some 7 year old children, all recently admitted, knew "very little beyond the alphabet." They obviously had a lot of catching up to do. Mr Davies' answer to this was to put them in a class with the older infants. In July, 1884, 2 or 3 Infants who had moved up to Standard 1 had to return to the Infants' class because they could not keep up with the work. However, it should also be mentioned that one Infant, on the same occasion, was transferred to Standard 2 showing that it was possible to jump a Standard if the requisite ability was displayed.[82]

51

Even so, it was abundantly clear that, without regular and consistent attendance the performance of his pupils would not improve.

A further impediment he found was:

From his Staff - the Question of Sufficiency

With a growing and developing school, it was imperative that there were sufficient staff to cope with the increasing number of pupils. On occasions, there was a delay between requiring more staff and securing their appointment, which must have been frustrating. When he started his headship in 1882, he had an Assistant Mistress, a Pupil Teacher in her first year and two Monitors to assist him. Monitors were chosen from older and presumably more able pupils. When they were aged 13 they could become Pupil Teachers being apprenticed for 5 years (two of which were probationary), learning the art of teaching practically on the job while continuing their own education with the Head. Each year they were examined at the Annual School Inspection by HMI and in the fourth year they could take the Queen's Scholarship Examination (later King's Scholarship Examination).Those who passed well could then qualify for admission to Training College. However, many chose rather to stay on in schools as Uncertificated Assistant teachers.

With the school roll growing, Mr Davies comments on the sheer amount of work his staff had to do. In 1883, the two Monitors, Mary John and David Davies had signed their Indentures to become Pupil Teachers but he still complains that it was almost impossible to give Standards 5 & 6 "as thorough a training as one would wish with our present staff when there are 3 classes of Infants and 4 other Standards to attend to."[83] Usually it was the Assistant who took charge of the Infants while the Head dealt with the older pupils and the Pupil Teachers and Monitors filled in where they were needed. Slowly, the Staff grew to 7 by the addition of two Pupil Teachers on Probation in 1885. When the school roll reached 178 in 1887, (the highest number since the school opened), there were 8 staff which included the Head, 2 Assistants, 3 Pupil Teachers and 2 Monitors. At the end of his first decade in charge (1892), the number had reached 9 by the addition of a third Monitor who was none other than Lizzie Jane Davies, his daughter. What pleasure that would have given him, even if the total number still wasn't sufficient for the effective running of the school.

Monitors added to the number of staff but they themselves required much assistance to make them fully competent particularly when they had to cope with Standard 6 work as well as preparing for their Candidates' examination to be Pupil Teachers. Even when they became Pupil Teachers, their deficiencies and shortcomings are well documented in the Annual HMI reports.[84]

The sufficiency of the staff, not only in terms of number but also of quality, would determine the progress which pupils could make. Mr Davies was aware of this and did all in his power to improve the standard of teaching. In September, 1882, he commented that the Pupil Teachers and Monitors whom he instructed between 8.00 a.m. and 9.00 a.m. were preparing their lessons more carefully than previously; in May, 1883, he introduced an occasional Criticism lesson for them, to encourage the "intelligent teaching" required by the Revised Code. Earlier in 1883, when they had become somewhat unpunctual in attending lessons at 8.00 a.m., he warned them that they would be reported to the Managers if this continued.[85] To help Pupil Teachers prepare for their annual examinations, he usually allocated them additional time during school hours for revision and also arranged for the Vice Chairman of the Gelligaer School Board to provide them with valuable information about their examination. The whole process must have been very demanding because the examination was usually held in Pontlottyn or Rhymney and this could create additional problems. For instance, in 1883, when there was no convenient train for them to arrive in Pontlottyn before the start of their examination, they had to travel there on the previous evening and then "seek lodgings." Not the ideal way to get ready for what was already an intimidating and important occasion for them. There are also indications of how the task of teaching was made more difficult by new requirements not always being fully explained to teachers. For example, just prior to the annual inspection in

November, 1883, all classes received a test examination. Mr Davies then recorded that the results appeared satisfactory "as far as we are able to understand the new code." Further light was given by HMI's at the annual Pupil Teachers' examination at Pontlottyn and he made sure that their comments were passed on to the rest of the staff.[86]

It must surely have been with a sense of real satisfaction that Mr Davies saw some of his charges metamorphose from Pupil to Monitor to Pupil Teacher and eventually to become Assistants. Mary John, who was a Monitor when he arrived in 1882, had made that transition by 1887. When she left through ill-health at Christmas in 1887, this eloquent testimonial to her appears in the Log recording the fact that she had started at the school as a pupil when it opened in 1878 and then progressed through the ranks: "Her school duties were always done conscientiously and her success in her own studies attest to her industry and perseverance. She is at present unfortunately in indifferent health and unable to accept another appointment." How sad that her death is recorded soon after, with the school paying its tribute by closing on the afternoon of her funeral to allow staff and pupils to attend.[87]

Not all staff were to have such a continuous record of service in Mr Davies' first decade In fact there were no fewer than 23 individuals named on the staff list in this time and, as the highest number on the staff in any one year was 9, there was quite an amount of coming and going. This was not helpful as Mr Davies points out in 1889 when he states that although the staff was numerically strong it had been "unusually changeable." There was also the added difficulty that three of their number were Monitors with little or no experience of teaching. In 1891, when requesting that an Assistant be appointed to replace a Monitor, he again pointed out the need to strengthen what he considered to be, at that time, a weak staff.[88] There were individual staff who were good practitioners as the Log testifies but overall there were deficiencies which Mr Davies steadfastly tried to remedy.

An even greater obstacle arose in these years:

From his Circumstances - the Impact of Tragedy

There were personal difficulties with which Mr Davies had to contend in these years all of which would have had a debilitating effect upon him. In October, 1889, he learned of the death of his youngest brother. Rushing to Lampeter on the same day that he heard the news, he was to remain there until the funeral, leaving the school in the charge of the Assistants. As this was just prior to the Annual Examination in November, this misfortune occurred at a most inopportune moment.[89]

Even worse was to follow in 1890 which proved to be an "Annus Horribilis" for Mr Davies. On October 4th, he had to endure the great tragedy of losing his wife as a result of Typhoid fever. The *Life Change Units Scale*, devised by psychologists, reckons that the death of a spouse is the greatest stress an individual has to bear. The sorrow and pain of this event must have been immense. For its part, the Board responded by closing the school for a fortnight, whether out of concern for the Head or as a Public Health precaution. When the school reopened towards the end of the month, the Log records that all were greatly depressed by the sad event. Attendance too was low because many parents, scared at the continued possibility of catching Typhoid fever, did not wish their children to return.[90]

John Davies and his wife Rachel

Further tragedy was to occur within weeks when Mr Davies' brother-in-law, Rev W Morgan, Calvinistic Methodist

55

Minister at Treharris, also died. In the last week of November, 1890, just before the Annual Inspection, the school was closed for half a day, when the funeral took place. In something of an understatement, Mr Davies writes: "This is certainly a distressing time for me!" Attendance had begun to pick up at the beginning of the month and the revision programme was under way just prior to the Examination, except that the Log states that it was not with "the heartiness and energy that we would wish."[91] These tragic circumstances could not have occurred at a less propitious time as Her Majesty's Inspectors readily acknowledged. All credit to them for doing that because HMI are renowned for describing only what they see at Inspection and not for considering any underlying factors which contributed to their findings.

Already facing a difficult task, the particular four elements described above compounded the situation still further. It is, therefore, real credit to Mr Davies that in his first 10 years at the school, some commendable aspects can be seen in:

2. THE PROGRESS MADE

As Head, it has already been shown that he was determined to lay the components of a strong foundation for the school. His first decade was to reveal distinct progress being made in a number of areas:

By the Pupils - Achievement

Her Majesty's Inspectors of Schools provide the best commentary on this in their annual School Reports and generally show approval of the school's development. In 1882, they comment that passes in the Elementary subjects were very creditable and that Grammar and Geography which had not been taught in the previous year were improving. By 1884, they remark that the number of examinees had increased considerably during the year and the average quality of the work was higher. "It is evident that the school is efficiently conducted and is making its way steadily to a place in the front rank." The work of the Infants' class was also described as "extremely good."[92] John Davies would have been pleased that his efforts were being rewarded.

56

That circumstances could interfere with the school's progress was amply demonstrated in October, 1885. A severe measles epidemic during which one of the Infants died caused the Board to close the school for three weeks, just prior to the Annual examination. In fact, a telegram was sent by HMI asking if the examination could still be held on the following Monday. One of the Managers agreed that it could but it was pointed out that the work had been greatly interfered with by the closure and by half the pupils being ill. The results of the examination reflected this but the Report could conclude "Considering all the circumstances, this is still described as a good school."[93] The school then had to recover the lost ground in the following years and the 1886 Report records this being done, with further improvement in subsequent years. The 1889 report could state that the work of the Lower Standards was very good while that of the Upper Standards was very fair. Admittedly not every aspect of academic life was consistently proceeding forward. In their reports for this decade, HMI drew attention to improvements which were still needed, for example: less prompting in Reading (1884); writing of pupils being cramped and small (1885); more success needed in the Modulator test (1886); greater achievement in mental arithmetic (1891); together with other indications of weakness.

For all these comments, however, the general tenor of the reports is mainly encouraging.[94] Due allowance was made also for factors affecting progress which were beyond the school's control. The personal tragedies of 1890 (which have been outlined above), were acknowledged in the Report when comment was made about the irregular attendance of pupils due to sickness and for what was described as the Head's "very heavy domestic affliction at a very important part of the school year."[95]

That there would be fluctuations in performance and in achievement caused by extraneous factors such as these is readily apparent. The Duplicate Schedule of results in the examination subjects does not appear for every year of this decade. But for the years which are recorded, the highest percentage Pass Rate in the Elementary Subjects was 96.6% in 1883, and the lowest was 87.3% in 1889. John Davies' efforts still had not achieved the 98% registered in 1881. Despite this, it is evident that he was establishing himself in the eyes of parents and the local community as someone who would take the school forward. In his second entry in the Log written in April, 1882, he had said that three boys living in Bontnewydd had followed the previous Head to Treharris Board School, presumably because their families felt that they would do better there. However, within a month they had returned and were re-admitted; also two others from Treharris had been enrolled. Perhaps this was because people were beginning to talk about the good start made by the new Head. He certainly wanted the right books and apparatus for his pupils to progress and made sure that the Managers were alerted when they did not appear.[96]

It is pleasing to note the achievements of girls in Standard 5 or above with a number of them gaining exhibitions offered by the Lewis' School Pengam Charity Trustees at the Higher Grade School for Girls in Pontlottyn. In 1882, at a meeting of the Gelligaer School Board, the need for a Higher Grade Girls' School to serve the parish was raised as Lewis' School had ceased to admit girls from 1876. The Board offered the Lewis' School Governors the use of the West Room in their Infants' School at St Tyfaelog's Church, Pontlottyn. The Governors responded two months later by offering twenty exhibitions per annum of £5 each and £100 for equipment to get the Higher Grade School started. The School opened in 1883 with a roll of 40 pupils, 21 of them having free places.[97] Amongst these first entrants were two pupils from Bontnewydd School, Minnie Payne and Rachel Davies, who had gained success in the competitive examination for exhibitions. They were to begin their education at Pontlottyn in February, 1883. Later that same year, in October, yet another pupil, Emily Jane Ninnis was successful in the examination. However, she did not transfer to Pontlottyn immediately as Mr Davies still required her to be present in school for the annual inspection in November. He didn't want to lose his best pupils before then. It is significant that Minnie Payne, Rachel Davies and Emily Jane Ninnis came back to the school as Probationary Pupil Teachers with Rachel Davies progressing to become an Assistant Mistress in 1889. Minnie Payne left after she had completed her apprenticeship and Emily Jane Ninnis left after her marriage.[98]

There is mention in the Log of other girls sitting the Higher Grade School Scholarship examination: Mary Lewis of Bontnewydd House, (William Lewis' daughter) in October, 1884; Anne Lewis and Anne Jones in October, 1886; but nothing is stated as to whether these three pupils were successful. It was in December, 1888, that five girls are listed as having successfully gained exhibitions: Lizzie Jane Davies (Standard 6), Annie Jane Powell (Standard 6), Annie Jones (Standard 5), Sarah Jones (Standard 5), and Sarah Date (Standard 5). John Davies couldn't resist paying tribute to these because one of them was his daughter. Annie Jane Powell was recommended to be presented at the Government examination for Pupil Teachers and began her service at the school as a Pupil Teacher in 1892. At the same time, Sarah Date and Lizzie Jane Davies started as Monitresses. Three more successes in the Higher Grade School exhibitions were reported in November, 1891: Frances M Clarke; Bessie Davies and Maggie Bevan. The achievements of the girls are seen much more readily than those of the boys. In fact, the only boy recorded as proceeding to Secondary education in this decade was Thomas W Lewis, the son of William Lewis (Bontnewydd House), who gained an exhibition to Pengam Grammar School in June, 1885. Most of the boys, in all probability, left school as soon as they could to gain employment to add to the family income. Certainly, when the Christmas holiday began in December, 1887, the Log says that the Boys from the Upper Standards who had passed the November examination and received their certificates, left school to seek employment at the colliery (the first time there has been a mention of the colliery). It is creditable, nevertheless, to find that there were a number of girls from this small village school gaining success in open competition with their contemporaries in the other Board schools of Gelligaer Parish.[99]

Progress can be seen in these years not only in the achievements of the pupils but also:

For the School - Improvement

There are a number of ways in which John Davies made improvements in the school during this decade. The traditional curriculum of the three R's, of Geography, Grammar, Singing and Sewing which we have seen in operation was broadened further. In 1886, Welsh was introduced as a specific subject to the syllabus approved by HMI. This involved picking out all parts of speech from a simple sentence; translating simple Welsh sentences into English and vice-versa. The Inspectors' Report for that year was complimentary that a satisfactory start had been made, and the following year there was even more success in the subject. There were times, however, when Welsh lessons were abandoned, more especially just prior to the Annual Inspection, in order to give added attention to the elementary and class subjects. Success in these took precedence. It is not surprising that John Davies, with his background and experience, should have encouraged the learning of Welsh. That he did not do more is possibly a reflection on how anglicised the village was.[100]

In addition to the introduction of Welsh, greater prominence was given to Scripture, with the school receiving the syllabus from the Secretary of the Bible Reading Committee and timetable provision being made for its study. Religious Instruction occurred from 9.00 - 9.30 a.m. through the first secular lesson being reduced by 10 minutes each day All pupils took the Annual Scripture examination: Infants and Standards 1-3 being tested orally and Standards 4-7 on paper. In the 1891 Log, we learn that the examination was held under the auspices of the Bible Reading Association in Day Schools and was conducted by Rev J P Jones, Calvinistic Methodist Minister from Treharris and Mr W Powell, Bedlinog. The questions for the Upper Standards were set by Mr Beriah Gwynfe Evans of Cardiff. This amount of detail of the examination is indicative of the status which was accorded it. Success in the Scripture examination was celebrated appropriately. Just before term ended in 1890 for the Christmas holiday, certificates for those successful in the June examination were presented by Dr W W Leigh of Glynbargoed House, with Mr W

Lewis, Chairman of Managers and Mr John Jenkins also present to express congratulations.[101]

Yet another subject appeared on the curriculum with the pioneering of Drawing as a timetabled subject in 1891. This could not commence until the requisite books and materials had been received. An Art Inspector, Mr W Llewellyn, visited the school in the October to conduct the examination which suggests that the Drawing was more artistic than technical. His report recognised a "Fair" achievement. As has been observed previously, the generalised statements of Inspectors do not provide a very exact standard of the proficiency displayed.[102]

Throughout these years, the Log provides particulars of the Object Lessons being given. Object Lessons were a much favoured educational device in the nineteenth century as they promoted Pestalozzi's ideas of teaching through the senses, moving from the known to the unknown and from the concrete to the abstract. Some of the first recorded Object lessons for Infants were: Horse; Cow; Sheep; Dog; Goat. Much depended on how the Teacher presented these lessons. The HMI Report for 1883 praised the quality of the training through using Object lessons but wished that they would be more varied with better means of illustrating them. (School Suppliers subsequently began to advertise "Cabinets of Specimens for Object Lessons.") Bontnewydd School did its best to improve and in 1884, it was stated that every effort was being made to illustrate lessons for all Standards as well as for the Infants. Also that year there were Object lessons additional to those involving animals: Leather; Candles; Silk; the Oak Tree; Slate; Ice; the Sun; the Carpenter; the Mason; House; Summer. In many schools, Object lessons degenerated into boring rote learning and often there was no coherent relationship between the Objects when they were presented. Still, Inspectors in these years mainly continued to praise the use which this school made of Objects.[103]

The list of Songs which were sung during the year, as has been seen, was a common feature in the Log. Now there appears more detail of the Books, Readers, Poetry etc. which were to be used. Some of these lists were signed by Her Majesty's Inspector or Sub-Inspector, which probably indicates that there was greater control being exercised over what was taught. In 1889, Standards 5-7 were to study amongst other things "Kenilworth" and, for Poetry, part of Shakespeare's "Henry V" and, in the following year, selections from "Julius Caesar". The lists for the other Standards also reveal material designed to stretch pupils and to raise ability. How far this actually occurred when these prescribed books were used is not revealed, but the intention becomes markedly obvious.[104]

Everything possible was done to encourage pupils to succeed. In 1882, just prior to the Annual November examination, John Davies brought in Mr J Hughes of the Abercarn Board School to conduct a test examination and to familiarise pupils with the routine they could expect. A Pupil teacher at Ciliau Park School, (where Mr Davies had formerly been Head), David Owen, who was staying with him, also gave added assistance to Standard 3 in October, 1884. To help Pupil Teachers conduct Reading lessons more efficiently, he gave specific instruction to them as to how they were always to question the children on what they had read and to show by their example how to read expressively.[105] Nor did Mr Davies neglect other ways of motivating his pupils. Previously there had been a half holiday after the November examination, but now more information is given of the "Treat" pupils were to receive: buns, apples and sweets were distributed by the Managers afterwards. This type of treat also took place sometimes at the end of the Autumn Term when the school broke up for Christmas. On at least one occasion there is an instance of the Treat being given at the opening of the New School Year in January. This was to give prizes to the "most diligent scholars" and to award Certificates to those successful in the November examination. A Spelling Bee was also incorporated into the proceedings but how much of a treat this was to the pupils is not stated. Perhaps the intention of placing this at the start of term was to encourage attendance which always seemed to be poor then. Concerts were also arranged on a number of occasions to provide money for Certificates and prizes. In 1889, the school gained a half day holiday while staging was put up for an evening presentation of "The Seasons of the Year" and other pieces. The admission proceeds were devoted to the Fund used for Prizes and treats. The intention behind all of this was to encourage regular and diligent work by means of recognition and reward.[106]

There is evidence that the pupils and their parents responded well to this objective of developing a sense of pride and achievement. In 1884, when all who were successful in the November examination were presented with a certificate by John Jenkins (Secretary to the Managers), the Log states that most of them were going to frame the Certificate which they had received. By 1887, when a similar ceremony was held, the comment is made that framed Certificates now adorn the walls of many houses.[107] Pupils were also encouraged to contribute to their learning. A start was made in 1884 to the formation of a School Museum with pupils bringing in suitable articles. Further development to the Museum and, in addition, to the beginning of a School Library came in later years by using money received from the School Concerts. By 1886, it is pleasing to note that objects from the School Museum were often used in lessons by way of illustration. The Library too was increasingly used with pupils eager to read what was on offer. Whether they were allowed to take the Library Books home is not stated. Yet another new venture was the opening of a Savings Bank in School which received an encouraging response from the pupils. There are no details of how the Bank operated or of the amounts saved, but again the School is to be applauded for seeking to develop the good habit of thrift.[108]

The Infants' Class was regularly praised by Inspectors in the Annual Reports with Good Merit Grants being awarded. The consistent record of achievement amongst the Infants is a most gratifying feature of the School's progress. In the 1884 Report where instruction was described as "extremely good", discipline as "very good", a Higher Fixed Grant was awarded with the proviso that separate access be provided from the Infants' classroom to the playground. As a result of this pressure from HMI, the separate entrance was constructed in 1885 which was very beneficial considering the increase in the number of Infants. Later, in 1890, the Board had to consider the enlargement of the Infants' room or the construction of an additional room again as requested by HMI who felt that the Infants' Mistress was working at a disadvantage because of the inadequacy of the room. In the event, a separate classroom for the Infants was started in November, 1890, just prior to the Annual inspection, adding to the problems of adequate preparation of the pupils who were already suffering from the adverse circumstances already noted. The new classroom was completed in May, 1891, but it wasn't adequately furnished until November of that year when a stove and desks were provided. Already the expansion of the Infants' department was promoting change which was to lead ultimately to its complete separation.[109]

Enhancement in the facilities for the Infants were not the only ones which came about in the school building during this period. In Mr Davies' very first term, Dr Dyke, the Sanitary Inspector for the District, inspected the state of the premises with Mr Jenkins (Secretary of the Managers). Gas pipes were fitted in January, 1884, which probably improved the lighting during the winter months. Heating, too, was upgraded with a new stove being installed in 1888. During the Summer holiday of that year decorators were employed, resulting in the premises having a "brighter and more pleasant appearance." Concern for the children's health and well being was also seen. Dr Dyke, now known as the Medical Officer of Health, visited the school in September, 1887, to inspect the building and to advise on precautions for preventing the spread of smallpox, following an outbreak in Treharris. The Secretary to the Managers also wished action to be taken about the water supply to the school when children were found to be drinking water drawn from the school roofs, the only provision available. In April, 1890, the Sanitary Inspector for the District (Mr J Jones) brought leaflets to the School describing precautions to be taken to prevent the spread of scarlet fever. These did not prevent the onset of the disease later that month.[110]

Whether the school improved in its discipline in this period is not readily discernible. There is no available Punishment Book to consult and there are only a few references to Discipline in the Log. From the start, John Davies was determined to give something more than cautions for misbehaviour, stating in August, 1882, that corporal punishment was being used to maintain proper order and that, generally, things had improved. The next month, he records that very severe corporal punishment had been used on George Chapman for insubordination, but although the mother complained of the excessive punishment. she did not justify her son's conduct. The Inspectors, however, could still find fault in the November oral examination where the older pupils displayed a lack of discipline. The following year, another Chapman received corporal punishment for insubordination and was detained after school to catch up on his work. This time the father came in to complain but, after Mr Davies explained the circumstances, it appeared likely that the boy was to receive further punishment at home. Parental complaints on Discipline were also received about Teachers using corporal punishment when only the Head was permitted to use it. Mr Davies looked into the matter but could not find any case proven. One of the Pupil Teachers had to be reproved for punishing and nicknaming pupils. Pupils were punished for being late and loitering on the way to school and older boys living in the village were warned by the Managers about interfering with pupils proceeding to and from school. Apart from these sparse references very little else appears in the Log about Discipline in these years.[111]

One of the improvements in this decade which was to win great approbation, especially from parents, was the abandonment of payment for elementary education. Forster's Education Act of 1870, which had set up the system of Board Schools, did not abolish the payment of school fees in Board Schools but the amount paid was in no case to exceed nine pence per week. There had been no standard rate of fee and previously there had been considerable variation depending on where the school was and who was running it. It was in 1891 that virtually all elementary school fees were abolished when parents were given the right to demand free education. But complete abolition of fees for elementary education was not finally achieved until 1918.[112] As has been seen, children were kept away from school when the school fee could not be afforded or if parents required their offspring to work in order to add to the family income. So the coming of free education was to have the effect of improving general school attendance. The Log sounds forth this development. On 31 August, 1891, the Board gave instructions that there was to be a holiday to commemorate the advent of free education by the Board from that date. The following week the children had no further payments to make. No longer were there to be any worries about the arrears of school fees creeping up with the school having to take steps to devise means of collecting them. From everyone's point of view, free elementary education was a blessing. Some of the improvements which have been outlined in this section were to prove rather transitory. This one, at least, was to stand the test of time.[113]

Progress during this decade was not confined to the school. There was:

In the Village - Development

To trace fully how the village developed between 1882 and 1892 requires more than an examination of the School Log for that only makes incidental and very cursory reference. The growth in the population is mirrored by the expansion of the School Roll. The influence of the church is also indicated in a number of references chiefly to holidays being granted for Anniversary services, walking days, Sunday School treats, tea parties, etc. Ministers of Religion were greatly involved in the life and work of the School as Board Members and Managers and continued to make many visits to the school: Rev Aaron Davies of Pontlottyn (Chairman of the Board for a number of years); Rev J L Meredith (Rector of Gelligaer); and Rev R O Jones (Secretary to the Managers for the majority of these years). There is, too, a reference to the opening of a new Church in the village (St Mary's) which again required a holiday to celebrate. But for any detail about what was occurring in the development of the village, other sources have to be used.[114]

The origins of Ebenezer Welsh Congregational Chapel have already been noted above with the grant of a lease in 1876, and the possibility of its being the site of the School's original temporary premises. In 1879, the main chapel was opened with seating for 300 and Rev John Evans as its first Pastor. Services were held on Sundays at 10.30 a.m. and 6.00 p.m. and on Monday at 7.00 p.m. This remained the only place of worship in the village until St Mary's Chapel of Ease was opened. On a later occasion, John Davies was to give a brief history of its foundation. When he first came to the village in 1882, "from the beautiful hills and dales of Cardiganshire", there was no Anglican Church in Trelewis or Treharris. Services were started in a private house in High Street, conducted by the Rector of Gelligaer (Rev Meredith). John Davies and others then pressed for the construction of a Church building. Plans for it were prepared in 1885, on a site generously given by William Lewis who also made a donation of £50. When the Rector raised anther £50 the work was commenced. In 1887, the Church was opened and consecrated at a cost of £1,200, "for the greatly increased population of that place", as described in Kelly's Directory of 1891. With feeling, John Davies was to state that "it was the oldest Church in the District". It had seats for 250 in a stone building with chancel, nave, south porch and bell turret for one bell. On Sundays, services were at the same times as Ebenezer but its mid-week meeting was on Thursday at 7.30 p.m. An Anglican presence was now to be felt, under the general oversight of the Rector of Gelligaer, with a resident curate, the first of which was Rev J R Jones. For 10 years St Mary's was attached to Gelligaer parish then for a further 10 years to Treharris and subsequently to Bedlinog, finally returning to Treharris. It was in St. Mary's Church that John Davies was to render additional service as one of its Church wardens.[115]

When this village of two Churches is compared with its neighbouring communities, its relative size can be appreciated. Further up the valley at Bedlinog, there were four chapels, (three of them Welsh), together with a Mission Church. Between them they had sittings for over 1,800 people with buildings mainly erected in the late 1870's. But this provision was exceeded by what was occurring across the valley in

Treharris where there were five chapels built between 1880 and 1890 (three of them Welsh), with Anglican services being held in the Board School until St Matthias' Church was built in 1896 at a cost of £3,500. All of this indicates that the greatest influx of population was to Treharris, thus answering the question which the Department of Education had posed when it had commented in 1879 that it was not clear on which side of the valley most people would settle.[116]

The name "Treharris" had soon been applied to the village growing around the Harris Navigation Colliery. It appears in the Log as early as June, 1881, showing that it had originated before then.[117] A natural development was therefore for Bontnewydd to imitate its near neighbour by its expanding community being called Trelewis after its main landowner, William Lewis. The precise time when this occurred cannot be stated with any degree of confidence but the name was clearly evolving in the early 1880's. In the 1884 Kelly's Directory, no fewer than five of the Commercial entries have their addresses listed as "Lewistown, Tre-Harris". (Note the interesting use of the hyphen and capital "H" to denote its derivation.) The 1891 Kelly's Directory lists all the Commercial entries under "Tre-Lewis". The name Lewistown, as used in the 1884 Directory, was presumably given to properties which were built on land belonging to Bontnewydd and William Lewis. Other entries for properties within the area have been recorded differently e.g. Ffald-gaiach properties are designated "Quaker's Yard"; W W Leigh the Medical Officer and Public Vaccinator for Llanfabon District, Pontypridd Union, is listed as "Glyn Bargoed, Tre-Harris". However, even William Lewis' entry appears as "Bontnewydd House, Tre-Harris" and Rev John Evans, Ebenezer's Minister's address, is also given as "Tre-Harris."

It is the increase in businesses within the village which provides an illuminating insight into its growth. The 1884 Kelly's Directory lists five shopkeepers, two grocers, and one boot and shoe maker. But there is only one Public House: the Ffald-gaiach Inn. Of the businesses listed in the 1891 Directory, only three are still listed with the same proprietor as in 1884: Jonah Evans (Grocer, flour and hardware

The Ffaldcaiach Inn which existed before the industrial revolution. It was owned by the Llancaiach estate, as was the land upon which the lower part of Trelewis has been built.

merchant, clothier, draper, boot and shoe dealer and butcher) with premises in Railway Street; Thomas Jones and Co. (Grocers); Mrs Elizabeth Ninnis (Green grocer), in High Street. There were two other shopkeepers recorded (John Burley and Thos. Williams), both in High Street; one Insurance agent (John Jenkin Evans), and an additional pair of Colliery proprietors besides William Lewis (Morgan and Edwards, Gilfach Maen Colliery). Jonah Evans, who had been designated only as a grocer in 1884, certainly seems to have expanded his business interests in this period perhaps by taking over others. Villagers were, therefore, able to get most things which they needed as a result of these developments. Then if there were any deficiencies, it was only a short walk to Treharris where much more was on offer.

The village streets, all of typical valleys ribbon development, can be traced on the Ordnance Survey maps. The older dwellings are still there: the farms Tir Shag and Tir Bach; Efail Shinrig with its smithy; Pandy Cottages; and the Ffald-gaiach Inn with 3 or 4 houses around. The Vale of Neath Railway and the Joint GWR/Rhymney Railway now appear fully. But what a development has occurred on Bontnewydd land! High Street takes its central place through the village with Ebenezer Chapel on the right; Railway Street branches off right; then there is a turning up to the Board school and the School House; but beyond St Mary's Church there is, as yet, no further development on the right hand side of High Street, nor behind the Church up to the Taff Bargoed Railway line; below High Street, Bontnewydd Terrace has been built; beyond High Street on the left is Penygroesheol with the road crossing the Taff Bargoed river on Bont Newydd, up to Cwm Cothi as before. Bontnewydd Farm appears hemmed in by the railway line; crossing the line there are quite large quarries and a coal level. The whole of the village is now prominently named "Trelewis".[118]

There is much useful information about this development of the village in the documents collected by Thomas William Lewis (William Lewis' son and son-in law of John Davies). He and his sister, Mary Edwards, had become the administrators and trustees of the Bontnewydd estate following the death intestate of their elder brother, Daniel, in 1927. In the Second Schedule of the Assent dated 27 October, 1947, there are details of leases affecting the Bontnewydd estate giving name of premises, date, term of lease and rent. Numbers 1 to 4 of these leases relate to 36-43, & 67-79, High Street and are dated 1st November, 1875, so building has taken place by then. On 1st May, 1876, Number 5 lease relates to 50-52, High Street being leased for 99 years at an annual rent of £1.16.1. The schedule continues with 35 leases in all being listed between 1875 and 1890 covering properties in High Street, Penygroesheol, and Railway Street. The lease of Brynffynon granted in 1885 was for 999 years not the more usual 99 years but this was because it was granted to Watkin Lewis who was married to William Lewis' daughter, Elisabeth. Studying these documents, one becomes very conscious of the sizeable annual income William Lewis was receiving from these leases. The village was growing up on Bontnewydd land. Not a bit of wonder that it should fittingly be called Trelewis after its resident landowner.[119]

Amongst these leases is No. 26 for 7, High Street, dated 1 November, 1890, leased by John Davies for 99 years with a rent of 11.8d. This was in all probability John Davies Headmaster, who is found to be the lessee of several other properties in years following 1892. To complicate matters there was another lessee called John Davies, a Blacksmith. (It was this John Davies who was to assign 60, High Street to John Davies, Retired Schoolmaster, on 7 March, 1913.) What is apparent however, is that in addition to developing the school, John Davies was also becoming involved in property development in the village.[120] This becomes patently obvious in a further document retained by Thomas William Lewis. It relates to an agreement made on 2nd November, 1885, between his father, William Lewis, and William Phillips (Shindrig), Jonah Evans (Grocer), and John Davies (Schoolmaster), who were representing the Ffald-gaiach Building Club. By this agreement, William Lewis was to let from his freehold land enough ground for the erection of 13 Cottages with Gardens, to be built by John Lewis, Treharris, with an annual ground rent of one penny per square yard. The land was to be leased to the members of the Ffald-gaiach Building Club for 99 years. How interesting to see that a local organisation had been set up and was actively involved in developing the village. Interesting, too, that, within four years of his arrival in the village, John Davies was participating so energetically in the life of the community.[121]

It is possible to get some idea of the houses being built in Trelewis at this time from more documents kept by Thomas William Lewis. There is an Agreement drawn up in 1886 between William Lewis, described as the owner, and John Lewis, Contractor, Treharris, for the erection of three houses. The drawings and specifications had been made by Aaron Davies (Architect), Pontlottyn. When the Bill for the construction was received, the cost of the contract for three houses was given as £400. Extra work was also necessary in adjoining houses, (all minutely listed), which produced a final total of £514.17.2. In

71

view of all the development taking place on Bontnewydd land, it would not take long for William Lewis to recoup his expenditure.[122]

But it was Trelewis' near and larger neighbour, Treharris, which was expanding rapidly in size and importance. The OS maps again illustrate this perfectly. Going under the railway bridge of the Vale of Neath railway towards Treharris from Ffald-gaiach is Glyn Bargoed Road with about 12 houses , the largest being Glyn Bargoed House. Just before Pont Squire and its weir, the road turns right to proceed to Treharris. There is now a road bridge over the Taff Bargoed river just below the railway viaduct which proceeds up the hill past Twyn y Garreg Huts, all 30 of them. The Huts stand proudly and defiantly just south of the Ocean Deep Navigation Colliery which bestrides the map indicating so obviously its controlling influence over many local residents. Continuing up the hill from the Huts, with Railway Terrace on the left, you reach the Square with its Public Hall. Then there are the ribbons of streets around the colliery many bearing testimony to the Quaker faith of its owner: Fox Street, Penn Street, Fell Street, Webster Street with Cross Street appropriately dividing them and Williams Terrace at its extremity. Just off Forest Road, there are Pritchard Street and Evan Street with the reservoir below. Going South from the Square to the Railway Station are: Thomas Street, Edward Street and Perrott Street with the Board School sandwiched between them. Across the railway bridge by the station are Thornwood Place and a hotel. Proceeding West are Mary Street, Victoria Street and Prosser Street. On the opposite side of the railway are Windsor Place, Susannah Place, the Perrott Inn and Gresham Place. Along the Cardiff Road from the Square are Oakland Terrace and Brynteg Terrace. In such a short time a significant transformation has happened.[123]

The 1891 Kelly's Directory rightly calls Treharris a large modern village rapidly growing into a town. It describes the cottages there as well-built with well-formed streets, lighted by gas and possessing the latest sanitary improvements. There are numerous businesses listed, several non-conformist chapels, a Cemetery (opened in 1888), a

Police Station with a Sergeant and three Constables. Other amenities included: a Library and Reading Room (containing 1,000 volumes, daily and weekly papers, all financed by fortnightly deductions from miners' wages); the Navigation Hotel and a Railway Station, opened in 1880. The population was estimated to be 7,000. Judging by the description, they were very well-provided for in their community. All this had happened because of the expansion of the Navigation Colliery again described as the deepest in South Wales (at 765 Yards Deep) which produced some 35,000 tons of coal per month.[124]

Within 20 years, the locality had changed beyond all recognition from its previous rural aspect of scattered farms and dwellings on wooded hillsides. Rows of neat terraced houses now surrounded the focal point and main source of employment: the Deep Navigation Colliery. Trelewis and Treharris were to be typical of the many mining villages growing up in the South Wales valleys as a result of the rapid expansion of the coal industry in the second half of the nineteenth century. Playing his part in this activity was John Davies, the village Headmaster.

As can be seen, most of the information for this section had been drawn from sources other than the School Log. However, before leaving the record which John Davies made of his first decade as Head there are some intriguing questions to be raised:

From the Log - Predicament

Already the deficiency of relying on a School Log book for a full and detailed account of all that one would like to know has been demonstrated. On many occasions, researchers would wish to get the answers to so many things which are not recorded. When there are obvious gaps in the account, one is left wondering why this occurred. John Davies' Log presents just such a predicament. On February 26th, 1885, at 4.25 p.m., just as the school was getting ready to be dismissed, W Edwards, HMI, made a visit to the school without notice. He states that the children were sent away in an orderly fashion and that the registers were properly completed. Then he adds: "No entry in Log book between January 8th and February 26th." Why did

Mr Edwards make an unannounced visit? Was he checking up on the Head? Why, specifically, did he write about the omission when he could so easily have spoken to the Head about it? Why was it that there had been no entries made in the Log for over a month? These and other questions remain unanswered. After the HMI's visit and the slight slap on the wrist which was given, there is an improvement. In the following week the only entry he makes is: "The attention of the Attendance Officer has lately been regular and efficacious." He may still not be writing much but his words are impressive![125]

It is possible to speculate that amidst all the many duties of being a Head, completing the Log did not figure as a high priority. Certainly as time goes on, John Davies' entries are not so full and explicit as some of the earlier ones. It may well be that sometimes they were written up in retrospect when he had time. Another feature of his Log is that instead of invariably writing up the record for 'the week ending....', which had been the previous practice, there are times when he records the happenings of the actual day that they occurred. This makes it more difficult to spot omissions with a cursory glance. In 1886, there is a gap in the log between March 5th and April 12th and there are two further gaps which appear in 1888, (between October 31st and November 20th and between December 7th and December 20th), but these are not pointed out or commented on by anyone. Similarly when there is further silence between February 3rd and March 3rd, 1890. This is surprising because there were other visits made "without notice", e.g. two by Gomer Jones, Assistant HMI in April, 1889, and in September, 1890, but he does not draw attention to the omissions, merely recording that the registers were completed satisfactorily and that the School was working to timetable.[126] Again we are left with unanswered questions.

The Log does provide evidence that nineteenth century Inspectors of Schools were by no means infallible. When the Summary Report for 1887 was written up, the entry read:

"E J Ninnis has passed fairly, but should attend to History"

"R Davies (Arithmetic, Grammar, Geography and History) - she must improve"

However, a statement has to be included later that, following a communication from the Education Department, it was R Davies who had passed fairly and not E J Ninnis. Was that mistake made by the HMI or by one of the administrators? That was not the only shortcoming to be revealed. When the handwriting of HMI's is compared with that of the Head Teachers in the Log, it is clearly inferior. That of W Edwards, usually written in the ubiquitous blue pencil of officialdom, is distinctly below standard and is frequently difficult to read. The record of his visit without notice in February, 1885, contains two crossings out. Very rarely, if ever, did the Head Teachers have to cross out any of their entries. Perhaps HMI had much in common with doctors as far as their handwriting was concerned.[127]

To point out the intellectual stature and ability of W Edwards is necessary to dispel the disparaging comments made above. William Edwards, (1851-1940), was born in Denbigh and educated at the Liverpool Institute. A brilliant student of Queen's College, Oxford, (1869-1873), he gained a First Class degree in Classics and also in Maths. In 1874, he was elected Fellow of Jesus College, Oxford. Following a brief teaching career, he was appointed in 1877, at a young age, as Her Majesty's Inspector of Elementary Schools in Glamorgan, giving thirty-eight years of dedicated service in that role. Retiring in 1915 he became Chief Inspector for the Central Welsh Board until 1926. For his distinguished service to Education, the University of Wales conferred the Honorary degree of Ll.D. on him in1925. With his wife, he resided in Merthyr Tydfil and together they entered fully into the social and cultural life of the town. He died at Merthyr on February 12th, 1940. William Edwards was to have a major role in the development of elementary education in South Wales and his comments on the Inspections he made provide a rich commentary for researchers. He was able to see, at first hand, the character and value of John Davies' Headship.[128]

It was William Edwards who conducted most of the Annual Inspections of the school. When he was not personally responsible, his Sub-Inspectors and Assistants reported to him. Amongst these were:

D Isaac Davies, Gomer Jones and a Mr Rees. They all witnessed the sound start which John Davies had made to his headship between 1882 and 1891 and saw how he was leading the school forward in a positive manner. Yes, there were still weaknesses and problems to address. The circumstances which he had encountered during these years made this inevitable. Between 1882 and 1891, John Davies had many vicissitudes with which to contend: difficulties to surmount; personal tragedies to overcome and changes to master. Despite all these obstacles, he had made a sound start as Head at Trelewis. He had already been in post longer than any of his predecessors and had met the first real test of his mettle with some success. A brighter future beckoned. This small, village school was developing and keeping pace with the expansion of the locality. His strong will and determination to succeed is evident in all that he sought to do. The indifferent start and deficiencies which had been bequeathed him were being systematically removed and forgotten. But there was still much to do and achieve before he could be completely satisfied with his incumbency.

Part Three

SUSTAINING THE EFFORT

Part Three   SUSTAINING THE EFFORT
(1892 - 1902)

During this decade there were further challenges and opportunities to be encountered, some of local, some of national origin. Perhaps most significant nationally was the gradual breakdown in these years of the unloved "Payment by Results" system. Introduced by the Revised Code of 1862, teachers and pupils had been subjected, amongst other things, to a narrowing of educational experience and the devising of ways to outwit the Inspectors in the annual examination. It was an encumbrance which many had wished to end. Fortunately the rigidity of the Code had been revised on a number of occasions. Gradually other "specific subjects" such as Grammar, Geography & History had been added to the elementary subjects to attract grants and the curriculum was slowly broadened by the inclusion of further subjects. But attendance remained throughout as the basic element to gain the award. It wasn't until 1897 that the revised Code finally came to an end, although its effects were to continue for much longer than that.[129] John Davies was to face up to these developments and other even more pressing matters with his characteristic determination. As the Log unfolds, there is a palpable sense of "deja vu" as the problems of the first ten years continue to occur. The same concerns, the same difficulties pour out from the record. Reading the account can be repetitive, even tedious. However it is essential to an understanding of the issues which pre-occupied John Davies in these years.Writing about them, therefore, is done not to weary the reader by reiteration but to emphasise their significance and importance in the development of the school.

John Davies still had to contend with:

1. OBSTRUCTION FOR ADVANCEMENT

There were a number of obstacles to successful teaching during these years, a few of major and some of minor significance. Hindrances to regular and continuous attendance were especially harmful and attendance could be adversely affected by circumstances over which the school had no control. No teaching can occur if pupils are not present and Mr Davies was powerless to alter some of the factors which caused pupils to be absent. Of these perhaps the most harmful were:

Epidemics

It is not altogether easy to discern the vagaries of school attendance in this period. The School Log for these years does not contain such full detail about numbers on roll and average attendance as was previously recorded. Presumably this was because such information was available elsewhere with the advent of School Admission Registers, and other documentation required by School Boards. In January, 1892, the number on registers was stated to be 211 and the average attendance 172.8. By September, the average attendance had reached 178.4 but a year later it had decreased to 111.9. The reason for this was that from May 1st, 1893, the Infants Department had been detached to become its own School. The next mention of average attendance is in October, 1898, when it was 128 and the school was described as "uncomfortably full." With such sparse information it is difficult therefore, to judge exactly how many pupils were in regular attendance.[130]

However, it is far easier to see the reasons for enforced absence. Epidemics arose so easily in Valley communities and spread virulently among its children. Childhood diseases are still with us today and any close-knit community such as a school will be subject to epidemics from time to time. In the 19th Century, these were far more serious and when outbreaks of illness occurred, as they did with frightening regularity, the effect on attendance was severe. Scarlet Fever was the first to appear in March, 1892, and quickly spread throughout the District. Dr Dyke, the Medical Officer of Health, immediately issued instructions that no child was to attend school from any of the infected houses and no child was to be re-admitted until 6 weeks after the onset of the illness. It wasn't until the middle of May that the outbreak of scarlet fever appeared to be abating. Even so, it returned again at the beginning of November, just before the annual inspection. One is left wondering how religiously the instructions of the Medical Officer were observed. The next mention of Scarlet Fever affecting pupils came in May, 1901, when several had to be excluded "because of the prevalence of scarlet fever." Throughout June and July of that year the disease spread in the village with more pupils having to absent themselves as a result.[131]

Measles was also a regular visitor and was the next on the scene in these years. Starting slowly, it accelerated in intensity among the Infants causing much absence in the first two months of 1893. Presumably, the same precautions as were introduced for Scarlet Fever became operative. In September of 1897, a further measles epidemic of such severity occurred that the Medical Officer of Health ordered the school to be closed for 21 days. The school reopened in October but in November measles re-appeared again just before the HMI Inspection. While it was Infants who suffered the worst, their siblings were also forbidden to attend. It is with some despair that Mr Davies writes at the end of November: "New work begun for each Standard will either have to be done again or absentees re-classified." The situation was taken out of his hands when at the beginning of December the MoH ordered a further closure of the school for 21 days and the school did not open again until after the Christmas holidays. Attendance began to improve slowly in the New Year. There was then a gap until several more cases of measles occurred in June, 1900. This got so serious that once again the school was closed by order of the Medical Officer and did not reopen until late August after the Summer holiday. The incidence of measles refused to go away and in February and March, 1901, more cases developed with the usual consequences.[132]

It was uncommon for any year to pass without a record of childhood illnesses reaching epidemic proportions. However, there does appear to be a disease free interlude in 1894 when no impact on attendance from illness is recorded. But in September, 1895, a more threatening illness is chronicled. Typhoid reared its ugly head requiring exclusions from school as before, from those whose houses were infected. How severe this was and how long it lasted is not made clear but in February, 1896, much sickness (unspecified) is still being noted with medical certificates being required from those affected. Thankfully, no deaths of pupils from any of these infectious diseases are mentioned in the Log. In fact there are only two records of pupils dying recorded in the Log in this decade: a Standard 1 pupil, Beatrice Taverner who died "very suddenly" in April, 1895 and Sarah J Jones, a girl in Standard 2, who was accidentally burned in a house fire in December, 1898. While it is encouraging to see that the infectious diseases had not, at this time, proved fatal, as they could be, that did not mean that their impact was minimal on the school and on the community.[133]

Absence caused by these periodic epidemics and the resultant school closures was inimical to academic progress and Her Majesty's Inspectors recognised this in their Annual Reports on the school. For example, in the 1898 Report the comment is made: "This year also the school has suffered from epidemics. It is to the credit of the Headmaster and teachers that a very fair standard of efficiency has been maintained." (Incidentally this is the first time in the Log that the term "Headmaster" has been used.) But the Report was adamant that any leniency given, in awarding the Higher Grant because of the special circumstances of 1898, could not be expected the following year. The quality of their mercy was obviously strained.[134]

The impact of epidemics on individuals, families and the locality in general, is not so easily discovered but can be imagined. When the school had to close, it was unlikely that the children would remain cooped up in their homes for the whole period of closure. Families were often large and the children would probably devise some means of getting out to play with others. To contain the spread of disease in the family would have taxed the ingenuity of even the most cautious parent. What is really discernible though, is that, for generations of children in the village, there grew up a general fear of "the Fever" (as it was called) and of what it could do. This was increased with the advent of Isolation Hospitals, (often known as Fever Hospitals) located remotely on hillsides above the Valley floor. Many fearful stories were told about children who had to be taken there. Indeed, as late as the 1930's and 1940's, whenever an Ambulance appeared in the village, children would engage in the ritual of touching their collar repeating the saying: "Touch your collar - Never swallow - Never catch the Fever."[135]

Other issues which caused concern to Mr Davies were:

The Weather and Occasional Holidays

These were minor irritants rather than major issues in causing sustained absence. The impact of the weather, not always as benign as one would wish, in South Wales, was to decimate attendance on occasions. The amount of rain which falls in the valleys is proverbial but it is not constant, as some would have us believe. In fact the climatic conditions throughout a year can be remarkable, ranging from hot, sultry summers to cold, snowy winters with every conceivable variation in between, mostly punctuated by outbreaks of rain. The Log book for this decade gives ample evidence of this. It was the weather which was to bring intermittent interruptions in education although not nearly so long lasting or so serious as those caused by epidemics. Between 1892 and 1901 over 11 days of schooling were lost due to half-day or full day closures because of weather conditions. The causes were: "heavy falls of snow"; "stormy weather"; "heavy rain"; "rough weather"; "thick snow"; "severe weather"; "storm of unusual severity"; "rain falling incessantly all day"; "exceptionally wet weather" etc. Also frosty conditions could affect the water supply in the village and pupils were kept home in order to carry water from wells. While most of the closures were in the winter months of December, January and February, some occurred in March, June, and October. There were instances of the school being kept open despite appalling weather as in March, 1897, when Mr Davies writes: "As I could not notify the closure of the school to HMI and because it would be cruel to turn out those who have come as the storm continues, the school remained open with work as near as possible to timetable." But sometimes, the weather frustrated his best intentions.[136]

Another feature of these years which caused interludes in the teaching programme was a seeming expansion in the number of occasional holidays. The set allocation of vacations was as indicated previously: two weeks at Christmas; two days at Easter (Good Friday and Easter Monday) later expanded to a week; one day at Whitsun (Monday) later to become one week; and five weeks for Midsummer. Attendance tended to be poor immediately following any of these breaks. At intervals, as has been seen, pupils managed to increase their entitlement by just not turning up. So few used to appear on Whit Tuesday because of Quaker's Yard Fair that the school had long since granted either a full day or half day holiday to deal with this situation. The reasons for giving more occasional breaks were many and various and included: Church functions (Sunday School outings, Anniversary services, Rechabites meetings, Singing Festivals, Band of Hope activities, etc.); Local events (Nelson Fair Day, Quaker's Yard Fair, Ploughing matches, Weddings, Funerals, Prize Days at the Endowed School, Sheepdog Trials, Eisteddfods, etc.) National occasions (the Queen's Birthday, Mabon's Day etc.) Elections (for Board, for District, for Parish Council and Parliamentary elections, etc.) Not all of these happened every year but there were sufficient annually to cause further interruptions to teaching. John Davies expressed his exasperation in April, 1894, when he wrote after one such holiday: "It would be well if tea parties and outings of the locality could be arranged for the same day so that the attendance of children at school might be less interfered with." His pupils would not have agreed with him. Many of them were astute enough to benefit from the tea parties and outings of both Ebenezer Congregational Chapel and St Mary's Church.[137]

Much more worrying than the periodic disruptions to attendance due to weather and holidays was to be found in:

Staffing Difficulties

When the children were present it was essential that the teaching should be of the highest standard possible given by teachers who knew, understood and regularly taught their classes. However,

83

frequent changes in staff composition were to be a major cause of worry to John Davies. Starting in April, 1892, when Mrs M Watkins (nee Meredith) relinquished her post as Senior Assistant, after her marriage, and after 8 years of service at the school, there was to follow an unsettling period of staff changes. Mary Davies, the Assistant in charge of Standards 1 and 2, also resigned in August of that year, leaving no one to teach Sewing. Mr Davies reported that "as the staff was weak" he hoped that a replacement would soon be appointed. But at the end of September, Mr Davies rather plaintively records that: "School is now rather full and no appointments have been made." Work was becoming difficult to maintain and the annual examination was on the horizon. He complained to the Rector of Gelligaer and another Board member who promised to do something as soon as possible. But another month went by until Miss E A Morgan of Deri School was appointed as Assistant. As soon as she took up her duties, at the end of October, 1892, James L Jones, the Senior Pupil Teacher and Lizzie J Davies, Monitress, "broke down with illness" the very use of those words being indicative of the stress and strain they were under because of the pressures on the staff. Indeed Lizzie Davies had been absent for a week at the end of September (with no reason stated) and James L Jones had not restarted school immediately after the Summer holiday because he had met with an accident in Cardiff while attending the Queen's Scholarship examination. When he did return at the end of August he seemed "incapable of much exertion." Illness and absence of staff continued into November with Mr Davies stating that "their absence seriously hinders the revision of the year's work for the Examination." The term was to end with the two Assistants leaving, Miss E A Morgan returning to Deri and Miss E Lewis seeking to be employed elsewhere. The obvious consequence was more unsettling staff changes for the school and for the pupils.[138]

It would appear that the Managers were well aware of the problems staffing was causing as they made a statement to HMI prior to the examination in November, 1892, doubtless outlining the situation and also the impact of the outbreak of scarlet fever and illness during the year. The 1892 Report did make allowance for "the exceptional difficulties of the year" as a result and concluded: "But for the drawbacks the school would probably have made more progress." In their Report on the Infants' Class, HMI mentioned the difficulties of the year. But, in addition, they delivered a rebuke to the Managers and the Board by depriving the school of a grant for the Infants because six months had elapsed before a Certificated Teacher had been appointed to teach them. It was evident that HMI did not condone delays in appointing staff qualified to meet the needs of pupils. Whether this was to speed up the action of the Board in making future staff appointments remained to be seen. However it may well have precipitated the decision to create a separate Infants' School.[139]

The changes to staffing continued the following year. Two new Assistants started in January, 1893, and another staff appointment of an ex-Pupil Teacher from Bargoed School was made in April much to Mr Davies' relief, who noted that: "The Staff may now be said to be complete and it is to be hoped without further changes at least for the current year." His hopes were to be dashed when at the beginning of November, Martha J Davies left, to be followed by one of the Assistants at the end of the month and the other at the end of term. To add to his woes, Mr Davies himself was off sick for 2 days in mid-November and was only able to pay occasional visits to the school. The Board did react by sending a Supply Teacher to cover Martha Davies' class. Yet again one can imagine the problems caused by these upsets. Just before the end of term, two new Candidates as Pupil Teachers began teaching at the school (Bessie Davies and Frances Mary Clark.)[140]

Surely, the Board and the Managers should have been convinced by now that the instability in staffing the school could not be allowed to continue. But continue it did in 1894. Two new Assistants commenced in January to join the two new recently appointed Pupil Teachers. At the start of term, John Davies notes that "as nearly all the teachers are strange to the children and some are inexperienced, some difficulty has been encountered in organising classes." Just as he was recording that things were settling down with the teachers getting used to the

85

children and to routine, one of the new Assistants resigned at the beginning of April. She was replaced at the end of the month by an ex-Pupil Teacher from Deri School. (At least the Board had acted promptly this time.) The other Assistant was to follow by giving her resignation to the Board in September. This time the Board was not so prompt in replacing her leading Mr Davies to moan: "It is unfortunate that the staff should be weakened at the most important part of the school year." But the Assistant who had been appointed in April left the school abruptly at the end of October, leaving word that she was going home and that another could be appointed in her place. A temporary Supply Teacher came to help with work before the examination but left immediately afterwards producing a further deficiency in staff until the Christmas holidays. The only way that Mr Davies could deal with this was by asking the Infants' school to retain the new Standard 1 until matters were resolved.[141]

As a general principle, lightning does not strike in the same place twice but resignations of Assistants at Trelewis School in these years are recurring themes. The Log Book does not help us to account for this. All that one can see is that, in both 1893 and 1894, the Assistants had time off owing to illness, (not always specified). In fact, the incidence of sickness amongst Assistants in these years appears to be greater than that recorded in previous years. Whether they found the stress and strain too much for them or whether they had been directed to the School by the Board and were displeased with their appointment there is not revealed. Another possibility could be that they were hoping to gain more congenial positions elsewhere. The fact that there was so much disruption to the teaching staff is proclaimed loudly and clearly but the reasons for it remain unknown. The pupils and the school were to bear the brunt of this uncomfortable situation.[142]

The downward spiral caused by the instability in staffing was to recur yet again in 1895. In fact, throughout the years 1892-95, the Assistants who started at the beginning of the year had left before the next year began, except for Margaret H Williams who starting in January, 1895, was to continue in post until April, 1898. Her colleague, Miss

Elizabeth Jasper, who had started with her in January, was transferred to Tirphil Board School in June, 1895. She also had some weeks off sick. In one of his entries in February, 1895, Mr Davies writes "Jasper absent all week." Could it be that exasperation had caused him to use her surname only when on all previous entries he had used Titles, and usually Christian as well as Surnames? Again there was a long interval before her successor was appointed by the Board. At the end of August, Miss M C Phillips had begun as Assistant but she was to leave within a month. This time an explanation is given. Miss Phillips had just completed her course at Cardiff Day Training College. Before coming to Trelewis, she had applied for Headships and soon after she started, one of these was successful. The Board allowed her to leave without giving the usual notice. They did not move so swiftly to appoint her replacement. It wasn't until mid-November that Miss Isabella G Williams, an ex Pupil Teacher from Deri School, started at the school as Assistant.[143] It was from her appointment that staffing became more settled and the greater stability resulted in greater progress for the pupils. Why the Board allowed this unsatisfactory state of affairs to continue for so long is inexplicable especially as HMI had indicated explicitly in their Reports the consequences for the school.

In the Report for 1893, attention was drawn to deficiencies in discipline with pupils answering out of turn and not always being silent when required. There was a further rebuke in the 1894 Report when discipline was stated to be "not firm enough." The many changes and the inexperience of the staff were undoubtedly being felt and was again acknowledged by HMI. who commented on the many changes to staff during the year. But, in 1895, there was more praise as the school had done better and the pupils were more disciplined. For the remainder of the decade there was to be continued improvement. This was probably due to the more welcome stability in staff after the unsettling situation caused by frequent comings and goings. During the consecutive years, 1896-1898, the same Assistants remained in post (Isabella Williams and Margaret H Williams.) In addition, the same Pupil Teachers had been in post since 1894 (Frances M Clark and Bessie Davies); both became Assistants under Article 50 in 1899 and continued as such until 1902 alongside Isabella Williams.[144] What a pity therefore, that the obstructions which have been chronicled had continued for so long without being rectified.

John Davies was well aware of the obstruction which the elements recorded above were causing the school. But, as has been seen, he tried his best to minimise their effect. It is pleasing that there is plentiful evidence in these years of:

2. CONSOLIDATION FOR PROGRESS

in Teaching Quality

Mr Davies, as he had always done, ensured that his Pupil Teachers and Candidates to be Pupil Teachers were well-prepared for their examinations. In 1892, Annie J Powell (First Year Pupil Teacher), Sarah Date and L J Davies (Candidates), had a week's revision before taking the Annual Examination in June, under the auspices of the Governors of Lewis' Endowed School. Annie Powell and Lizzie Davies were successful. This system of revision was to produce dividends: in the May examination of 1894, Annie J Powell, Lizzie J Davies and Frances M Clark were to gain First Prizes; this resulted in a half holiday being given the school in June for them to receive their awards at the Prize Giving of the Endowed School. As his own daughter was one of the recipients, doubtless John Davies attended, swelling with parental delight.

But before the October Pupil Teacher Examination in the same year, little or no revision could be assigned in school time because of the absence of the Assistant. Mr Davies would not have been best pleased at this because his daughter was again involved. In the years 1895-1901, the usual practice of revision time was resumed and there was a pleasing accumulation of First Prizes once again. It is interesting to note that the Log records some of the quarterly examinations for Probationers being held under the auspices of the NUT as well as the Governors of the Endowed School. Places where the examinations occurred included: Pontlottyn; Pengam; Abermorlais; Rhymney;

Merthyr as well as Trelewis. This suggests that neighbouring School Boards cooperated in the process.[145]

Greater proficiency would have been secured if the Teachers were able to concentrate on the work of the same Standard from year to year. This would have enabled them to master the relevant curriculum. The constant changes in staff noted above tended to militate against this. However, when it was possible, the Log indicates instances when this was done. For example, Lizzie Davies had responsibility for Standard 4 in at least two consecutive years. Almost invariably, Mr Davies himself took charge of Standards 6 and 7. Possibly that is where most trouble would come from. He did his best to foster the professional development of his teachers so that they would perform well. In 1895, the school received a number of textbooks not for pupils but for Teachers; in 1900 he closed the school in the afternoon so that the teachers could go to Pontlottyn to hear HMI give instruction on the New Code. As has been indicated, there were a number of amendments to the Code throughout these years and it must have been difficult to keep up-to-date.[146]

The impact of all this, particularly on the work of the Pupil Teachers, can be readily appreciated in the HMI Reports for these years. After the downbeat Report of 1894 improvement rapidly follows. "The school has done better this year... ... ... Some of the scholars show good proficiency... ... The children behaved well on the day of inspection... ..." - all from the 1895 Report. The good progress continued and there was high praise in the 1897 Report: "This school is in an efficient condition... ... there can be no doubt as to the industry of the teaching." There were still weaknesses to be addressed but at the end of the decade when the reports are much briefer it is obvious that significant progress had been made. "The teaching is well-directed and the discipline very satisfactory" and "The instruction is very carefully given." Such criticisms as were made then referred to the premises rather than to the teaching, all of which pointed to the fact that much had been accomplished thanks to a committed and settled staff. Contributing to this satisfactory state of affairs was Lizzie Jane

Davies. Her pleasing input and that of her fellows is well-documented in the Reports: not only did she pass her examinations but the Reports state she "Passed well." In the 1896 Report comes the statement: "E J Davies has obtained a First Class in the Queen's Scholarship Examination." Her father would have been delighted to have written that and also the comments about her in previous years. But his pride would have known no bounds when he penned the following words in September, 1896: "Elizabeth J Davies, my daughter", (the first time that the Log had mentioned that), pupil and teacher at the school for upwards of 12 years, has left to attend the Day Training Department at University College, Cardiff." She has the distinction of being the first pupil of the school to be recorded in the Log as entering Higher Education. That would have given John Davies added pleasure. Lizzie had undoubtedly benefited from her schooldays at Trelewis and had proved her worth as a teacher. A bright future beckoned her.[147]

The Day Training College at University College, Cardiff, was one of those original establishments, opening in 1891 for both men and women. It accompanied the men's colleges at King's College, London, and Owen's College, Manchester, together with the women's college at Mason's College, Birmingham and the mixed colleges at Durham and University College Nottingham. They had a vitally important role to perform in the development of education as they were the predecessors of modern University Departments of Education. Students like Lizzie who attended such institutions had an altogether richer and fuller experience than those who attended the residential Teacher Training Colleges. They mixed with students who were going on to professions other than teaching and the course they followed attempted to widen their intellectual background as well as making them competent, practical teachers. Again, it would be most illuminating if we had a record of Lizzie's progress there.[148]

It is not until January 3rd, 1899, that documentary evidence has been found relating to Elizabeth Jane Davies' subsequent career. On that date the Log Book of Merthyr Vale Mixed School records that she started there as an Assistant Teacher.[149] This was a large elementary school whose roll was to increase to over 450 by 1903. To provide for such numbers was to require a staff of: Head Teacher (Edwin Thomas); 12 Certificated Assistants; 1 Assistant, Article 49 and 2 Pupil Teachers. As one would expect, specific references to Lizzie Jane in the Log are few & far between. Those that do appear provide some interesting features. The HMI Report for the year ended January 31st, 1900, states: "The Certificate for Miss E J Davies will be issued after 3rd July, 1900, upon application to the Board, if she continues in this school until that date." It would appear from this that final certification depended upon demonstrating practical teaching skill after completing the College course. This was to present no problem for Lizzie Jane. Most of the other references to her in the Log were to record her absence through sickness: once, for 3 weeks in 1899 suffering from pleurisy; once in 1900 suffering from quinsy and once again in 1901 for the same reason, together with 3 other absences through ill health (unspecified). It is to be hoped that this recurrence of illness did not disadvantage her in her early days as an Assistant. Judging by the HMI Reports on Merthyr Vale School, she had much to gain from her experience there. The 1902 Report concluded: "The efficiency of instruction has been maintained in a most creditable manner owing to the conscientious steadiness with which the school is always conducted." The major problem of the school was that it was "seriously overcrowded." Temporary premises were provided to ease the situation and in 1903, a new school was opened in Aberfan to which presumably some pupils and some staff were transferred. When Edwin Thomas left in June, 1903, to be succeeded as Head by Edward Williams, the number of pupils present had been reduced to 272. Also the list of staff had decreased to 3 Assistants, 3 Ex Pupil Teachers, 1 Pupil Teacher and 2 Candidates. As Elizabeth J Davies is not included in the list, the assumption is that she transferred to the new school at Aberfan. Throughout this time that Lizzie Jane was beginning her career as an Assistant, her father was readily available for help and advice. As he had always done, John Davies would have encouraged her in all that she encountered and assisted her to flourish as a Teacher.[150]

91

Meanwhile, the other Pupil Teachers who remained at Trelewis school after Lizzie Jane had left to go to College, (Frances M Clark and Bessie Williams), were also fine products of the school and likewise made their contributions to its advance. Their development as Teachers can also be traced in the HMI reports. Eventually, in 1898, they both gained a Second Class in the Queen's Examination and the following year were made Assistants at Trelewis under Article 50 continuing their good work at the School until 1901/02. They did not proceed to Teacher Training as Lizzie had done but chose to stay on at school as Uncertificated Assistants. This was not uncommon. Pupil Teachers at the end of their apprenticeship took the Queen's Scholarship examination and those who passed gained a grant to allow them to enter a Training College for a 3 year period. However, many chose either not to proceed there, or to leave at the end of one year and become Uncertificated teachers instead. Financial and other practical considerations were often the reason for this. So frequently did this occur that eventually the Training College Course was reduced to 2 years.[151] That Frances Clark and Bessie Williams opted to stay on at the school was to allow their accumulated expertise to be deployed to the obvious advantage of their pupils. A settled, contented, committed staff was what John Davies had been seeking for some time and in the last years of this decade it had finally been achieved.

There was to be further consolidation for progress:

in Refining Curriculum

It would appear that the curriculum of previous years was to continue with the concentration on the elementary subjects and with the pervasive presence of Object lessons. But there seemed to be more direction from HMI. In November, 1892, Edward H Short, the Sub-Inspector, wrote out neatly and carefully in the Log a detailed list of Books, Object lessons, Recitations and Songs. This was done the day after the Inspection and the lengthy list gives some idea of the kind of education expected. His writing, in ink, was far easier to decipher than the blue pencil comments of W Edwards, HMI. After the Infants separated from the Mixed School in 1893, HMI omitted

Object Lessons (although these still continued in the Lower Standards) but included more Welsh components in their Songs and Poetry lists. The extra subjects such as Geography, Needlework, etc., were still inspected for purposes of grant. Scripture continued to be examined by local clergy appointed by the Bible Reading Association, with Drawing being examined by Colonel Clancy. Nevertheless, the curricular diet for pupils had been extended through the various revisions to the Code even if these are not always apparent in the Log. Some additions did not always seem to be well thought out, as in January, 1896, when new books and apparatus had been received for the year which included provision for a new Code in "Varied Occupations." But by March, 1896, when there was some doubt about "Varied Occupations" being included as a compulsory subject, instruction in this was discontinued and the time given to Object Lessons.[152]

Increasing use of educational technology can be traced in these years. In October, 1893, "Views of the British Empire" were projected by Magic Lantern much to the pleasure of boys in the Upper Standards. Other diversions from normal routine included Pottery Demonstrations by a Travelling Practitioner in May, 1897, with pupils being allowed to make vases and other objects. Talk and Chalk might still be the staple of instruction but these practical hands-on opportunities would have been welcomed. Cookery lessons for girls were also occurring in these years despite there being occasional problems in the instruction. An intriguing entry records that some of the girls had to go to Bedlinog, in October, 1898, for their cookery lesson. One wonders how they got there. More formal learning was to remain the norm. In 1898, a new syllabus for Religious Instruction was received from the Board and a new syllabus for Welsh was being prepared. Before the latter was introduced in February, 1900, the school had already been implementing some of its features. Mr Davies, as one would expect from his background, probably wanted to expedite their inclusion in the curriculum.[153]

Although it is not possible to discern completely the exact changes in the content of the curriculum during this period, far clearer and far more important are the changes in the way the curriculum was structured. It was the Day School Code of 1895 which was to herald the end of the annual examination by HMI and of the consequential Payment by Results. The chief innovation was that the Inspector's Annual Visit could, in future, be substituted by occasional visits (as a rule two), to be made without notice. But schools which were adjudged by HMI to need a closer test of their efficiency could still be examined annually. The impact of this was that Payment by Results was finally abolished in 1897.[154] But it was also to have repercussions on the way that schools organised themselves. In January, 1896, Mr Davies drew up a syllabus of work to be covered by each Standard within that month and seemingly repeated the process monthly. This is the very first time that this useful device has been seen which gave teachers short term goals to achieve and a regular means of discovering if they had been successful. To check that the scheme of work had been covered efficiently there now followed Periodical Examinations throughout the year (usually four in total), instead of one crucially important one. There were to be occasions when the intended Periodical Examination had to be deferred usually because of disruption in schooling due to epidemics. After the Periodical Examination, the results were to be entered into Progress and Record Books, yet another valuable innovation. Action was taken on pupils who did not keep up with the work expected to be covered in the Periodical Examination: they were re-classified. E H Short, HMI Sub-Inspector, made two visits to the school in 1896 under Article 84, one in March and the other in October. Presumably these were the visits without notice to assess the progress the school was making. Things were being tightened up for the benefit of the school, its pupils and its teachers. This appeared to be far more productive than the system which it replaced. After the October visit, the Head notified the staff that until the end of the school year, full attention was to be given to the weak points indicated by Mr Short. These were not listed in the Log but one hopes that they were addressed.[155]

The benefits of having a more stable staff have already been seen in the HMI reports from 1896 onwards. Also it is likely that improvements in performance owed much to the new system of Periodical Examination and the better records of progress. The comments Mr Davies made on what was necessary for staff to concentrate on become more frequent and fuller than previously. Here are a few examples: - 1896 "Mental Arithmetic and class subjects require most attention in Upper Standards and Object Lessons in Lower"; - 1898 "points of revision marked out for Teachers"; - 1899 "Standard 2 seems to be the weakest class"; - 1900 Arithmetic in all classes is to receive "special attention" especially Mental, Theory and Simple problems. His remarks about the results of the Periodical Examinations are mainly encouraging and include: "decidedly promising on the whole in every Standard and subject"; "more even progress in class subjects"; "Syllabus will be well covered in the appointed time." If further evidence is required about the improvements subsequently achieved it can be found in the success of pupils in examinations for Lewis' School, Pengam and for the Higher Grade Girls' School. There have not been many references in the Log to these annual tests in the first part of this decade and nothing about successes gained, but in 1899 we read that 4 pupils, three girls and one boy, (Richard Morgan, Mary Jane Kinsey, Kate Jones and Kate Brace) had gained scholarships. In 1901, four boys and three girls sat the examinations but only three boys were listed as being successful (William Lewis, Henry Lewis and Bertie Bevan). Another independent view of what was happening in the school is provided by an entry in the Log by the Rector of Gelligaer (Rev T I Jones), in July, 1899: "Examined the school in Religious Knowledge and found the work uniformly and excellently done. The recitations were correctly rendered, the hymns well sung and the children, especially Group IV, showed unmistakable signs of careful and thorough preparation. It was a pleasure to hear the intelligent answers." The enhancement of achievement was becoming obvious to all who cared to look.[156]

One further and important change in structure came about in 1898. This was the first time that the School Year began after the Summer holiday, on August 29th. The previous practice had been for pupils to move up to their new Standards when they returned after the Christmas holiday and after the results of the November examination were known. The ending of Payment by Results no longer made this necessary and the modern practice of the Academic Year starting in September, not January, was to evolve in elementary schools. Pupils proceeded to Standard 1 from the Infants' School and all classes commenced work of a higher standard. In its first year of operation, (1898), there were problems to overcome, for as Mr Davies observed: "As the work proceeds, the unpreparedness of some scholars to be advanced a Standard after a shortened School Year becomes more obvious." They had lost a term's work. But by the end of December most had made encouraging progress. After the first year the position regularised itself and the start of the school year after the long summer holiday was to become a permanent feature. However, as far as attendance was concerned, we still read in 1898 of the School Year ending on 31st October even though pupils had started their new Standards in September.[157]

The Government had introduced compulsory attendance in School for children up to the age of 11 in 1893 and up to age 12 in 1899. Legislation was the easy part: it was altogether harder to achieve consistent, regular attendance in practice. It is thanks to Mr Davies' tenacity that fresh attempts were made by the School in handling this difficult problem, to secure progress:

in Improving Attendance

The value of using both Carrot and Stick has not always been appreciated in securing modifications in behaviour. Often attention has been focused exclusively on one or the other which has produced inferior results. When both carrot and stick are utilised, in appropriate, not excessive amounts, there have often been more lasting benefits. The Board in 1896 decided to provide incentives for improving attendance by introducing a prize scheme for attendance. "Prizes, Medals and Certificates" were to be awarded for regular attendance and the introduction of this new venture was to be widely publicised.

What the distinction was between these three categories of award is not described in the Log but were probably dependent on levels of attendance. A sense of occasion was stimulated by either the Chairman of Managers, the Chairman of the Board or the Rector presenting the awards, at the end of school, with parents encouraged to be present to hear "kind and encouraging" words.[158]

As the curriculum had benefited from a more structured approach so too did the school's method of dealing with attendance. In August, 1894, Inquiry forms issued by the Board were distributed. This may have been precipitated by the well-known and oft-repeated decline in attendance immediately after a School holiday. Later, in 1897, we read of the school having to complete monthly forms for attendance which prompted the observation: "Attendance has decidedly improved since the introduction of these forms." The forms were given to the pupils as a personal reminder of their attendance record. Teachers, no doubt, seized this monthly opportunity to remind them of what was still needed to gain attendance prizes. It would appear that refinements occurred in the process as, in October, 1901, we read that a new attendance scheme had been in operation since the summer holidays. This time the monthly attendance forms were to be sent to the Parents/Guardians presumably to get their co-operation as well. How effective all of these measures were in improving attendance is not readily detectable. (As has been pointed out, the Average Attendance figures are rarely recorded in the Log for these years especially after monthly returns of attendance were made to the Board.) All that there is to go on are scattered and disparate comments which Mr Davies included, for example: Number of absentees "comparatively small" (May 1897); "fairly good" attendance (September 1898); "quite up to average" (after Christmas holidays in January, 1899); attendance "uniformly good" (November 1901). Nevertheless, the more businesslike way in which the problem was being tackled and the greater emphasis on reward would surely be repaid.[159]

The use of the carrot did not mean that the stick was cast aside. Throughout the Log the Attendance Officer constantly appears and his

97

ministrations were relied upon by School Boards to see that children attended regularly. Often the Attendance Officer was a feared and fearsome figure - the "Board Man", the "Whipper In", the "Kid Catcher" or other more uncomplimentary titles given him by parents and pupils. Mr Davies would have wished on occasions for added activity from John Jones, the Attendance Officer, as he writes somewhat sarcastically in 1894 that the school was "honoured with two visits of the Attendance Officer this week- a unique experience." Later in 1900, John Davies was to write: "It would be well if he could call during the first week and early in the week after a vacation." That was a continuing problem for attendance no matter what methods for reducing it were employed. When, in 1901, John Jones was succeeded as Attendance Officer by R Saunders, there seemed to be more regular visits made that year possibly as a result of the new broom. The Attendance Officer had one final sanction if all else failed: resort to a Magisterial order for removal of the Offender to the Truant School. In October, 1899, Richard Bray, a Standard 4 Pupil, who had been absent from school since the summer holidays and was developing into an "incorrigible truant", was to be the first pupil named in the Log as receiving this deterrent. The following year, in June, when the Attendance Officer visited twice in one week, he threatened to resort to prosecution in the worst cases. The threat was probably enough because the unknown horrors of the Truant School at Quaker's Yard were to trouble the minds of pupils at Trelewis for many years to come. Parents were not averse to trading on those fears when they wished to bring recalcitrant children into line.[160]

The South Wales and Monmouthshire Truant and Industrial School at Quaker's Yard had been certified on 8th November, 1893, to accommodate 90 boys in purpose-built premises, set in grounds allowing 2 acres for cultivation. Even a brief examination of the Rules of the School (signed by the Chairman and Secretary on 5th December, 1895), is sufficient to confirm the worst fears of children who knew of its existence. The object of the School was to apply a short, sharp shock, (as a later age would express it), to deter persistent truants from continuing in their delinquency. A harsh regime is indicated by the punishments meted out. For a minor offence: up to four strokes of the Tawse on the hand; for more serious offences: not more than six strokes of the birch on the buttocks. Other punishments included: solitary confinement (but in a lighted room); loss of privileges; reduction in quantity and/or quality of food, etc. In any case, the food provided was almost reminiscent of Victorian workhouses. Breakfast at 8.00 a.m. was invariably Oatmeal porridge (not quite Oliver Twist's gruel!); dinner at 1.00 p.m. did provide some slight variation e.g. 4 ounces of meat on Sundays, Tuesdays and Thursdays; supper at 6.00 p.m. was uniformly Bread and Dripping. The best that can be said is that there were three regular, if plain, meals per day. Those admitted were to be between the ages of 8 and 14. For a first offence they were to be detained for 3 months; for a second offence 4 months and for a third offence 6 months. Their day began at 6.00 a.m. and they were to receive instruction in the three R's, Spelling, a little Geography, History, Religious Instruction and Singing. There was also an attempt to provide a small amount of vocational training mainly in Gardening or Housework with some Handicraft, if possible. The inmates' day concluded with bed at 8.00 p.m. Parents/relatives were only permitted to visit once per month and sometimes even this limited visiting could be suspended.[161]

Proof that the tales of the harsh treatment of Truants at Quakers Yard were to continue unabated well into the 20th Century, comes from a contributor called Emrys, to the web site of Tredegar Forum, in May, 2008. He recalled an incident from his schooldays. Having been absent from school because of illness, he was visited by the School Attendance Officer who was not pleased to see him at home. Emrys continues: "He berated me in front of my mother as though I was the worst offender…repeatedly telling me that if I didn't mend my ways I would end up in Quaker's Yard, a boys' correction centre. He then proceeded to tell me how hard the discipline was there."[162] One would have hoped that, together, the harshness of the stick or the increasing attraction of the carrot would have been sufficient to gain more consistent attendance with very few defaulters. But despite all of the effort which was made, the Log states in March, 1900, that pupils were

John Davies seated on left. The board held by the two girls at the front says "Trelewis Group 4". The date of the picture is not known, but comparison with other similar pictures suggests it might be as early as the late 1890s.

still indifferent regardless of the fact that "no effort is spared without undue harshness to induce them to attend regularly and to persevere in their work." In September of that year, attendance is recorded as being low because children have been sent into the fields to collect blackberries. [163] Truancy continues to be a problem in the 21st Century. It was far more difficult to correct in the 19th and early 20th Century when parents, for their own purposes, actively promoted absence for domestic or other reasons. Mr Davies valiantly continued to consolidate the activities of the school in teaching quality, in curriculum and in attendance whenever possible. Progress was assuredly made but full success was still some way off.

A major change which happened in 1893 was:

3. SEPARATION FOR INFANTS

The Board had decided that the Infants' Department be separated from the Mixed School and that it should have its own Head Teacher and individual organisation. This was to begin on 1st May, 1893, with both schools continuing in the same building for some years. Structural alterations had been made previously to aid this progression, for example, in April, 1885, a separate entrance to the Infants' Department had been constructed. The 1886 HMI Report had remarked on the fact that the number of Infants had been increasing with the added observation of the unusual proportion of boys exceeding that of girls by two to one. Numbers had continued to grow and the 1889 Report had drawn attention to the overcrowding in the room requiring either an extension or an additional classroom. Work on a new classroom was to begin in November, 1890 and a year later a stove and new desks were installed there. The 1892 Report was insistent that as the average attendance of the Infants was more than 50, under Article 100, the Board should "at once" appoint a certificated teacher to take charge. As has been shown, the Reports on the Infants' Department prior to this had invariably been good, often with real praise. For example: "the Infants are vigorously and intelligently taught and the results are highly creditable to the teacher" (1888); "the order is very good" (1889). It seemed a logical development, therefore, with the appointment of a certificated teacher, with the increased numbers and the good progress, for a separate school to be established, and this took place in 1893.[164]

Very little now appears in the Log about the relationship with the Infants' School in the years from 1893-1901. The fact that they shared the same building could possibly have led to some friction but this is not documented. The building itself was to cause problems which needed attention, in particular the drainage. As early as January, 1893, the Board's Architect had met the Managers to discuss ways of improving drainage. The 1893 HMI Report had also required action to be taken in respect of the lavatories. Managers again met with the District Sanitary Inspector about this but concluded that it was impracticable at that time to connect them with the drains. A very heavy storm of rain in October, 1894, alarmingly revealed the deficiencies in drainage: the drains on the East side of the building just couldn't cope, the main teaching room was flooded and the children had to be sent home. This produced a rap across the knuckles in the next HMI Report, displeased that the recommendations of the previous year had not been followed: "The improvements required last year in the offices should be carried out without further delay or the grant will be endangered (Article 85a)." This time the Architect for the Board reacted promptly. The power of the Inspectorate and the necessity to gain every penny of grant were persuasive stimulants. In the 1895 Report, HMI complained about the lighting which cast shadows upon the pupils' work. The Architect again responded quickly deciding that the Boys' Lobby should be removed for a window to be put into the pine end of the building. The disruption caused by the building work resulted in a school closure for two days as the Boys' entrance was blocked. Meanwhile the School Roll was growing. In October, 1898, the building was described as "uncomfortably full" and some classes, particularly when there were oral lessons, had to be held in the porches. That would have put additional pressures on the teachers. The pupils would not have been too pleased either for this to continue as winter was approaching.[165]

Presumably the need for additional accommodation persuaded the Board to commission a new building at a separate location for the Infants' School. An adjacent site of half an acre, 193 feet long and 113 feet wide, on Bontnewydd land, behind St Mary's Church, was designated in an Agreement drawn up between William Lewis and the Gelligaer School Board on 17th April, 1900. The cost of £302.17.6 was to be paid to William Lewis on 1st June, 1900 and the Board was to erect a stone and mortar wall not less than six foot high, replacing the existing wall and gate to the field. and constructing appropriate drains, etc. William Lewis or his solicitor, John W Lewis, drove a hard bargain with the Board. It is fascinating to see the alterations made, in red ink by Frank James & Sons, Merthyr Tydfil, in the Agreement for the Board, seeking to moderate some of what were considered to be excessive demands of William Lewis. In November of 1890, the Log states that work had started on the erection of the new buildings. The following year, the construction was completed.[166]

On Monday, 26th August, 1901, the new Infants' School was officially opened, by W Coslett Beddoe, Vice Chairman of the Board. This freed up space for the Mixed School to utilise and not before time. It meant that Cookery lessons could recommence in a "new and commodious room attached to the Infants." But there was to be further disturbance. In September, 1901, W Edwards, HMI, during his Inspection visit had written that the opening of the Infants' School now allowed the Mixed School building to be rearranged. He directed that: the galleries should be removed and all desks replaced by dual ones; the playground should be of asphalt or other firm material, not rough ashes, as previously; the Infants' playground should also have a similar surface. The Board complied with these instructions and the resulting structural alterations caused upset in school organisation affecting, amongst other things, the Periodical Examination. In the long run, however, there were to be significant advantages for the school.[167]

It wasn't only the school which grew in this decade. There was manifestly:

4. EXPANSION FOR THE VILLAGE

By the end of this decade, there were two schools on adjacent sites in the village, indicating an expanding population which would have required further property development. As previously, information about this has to be derived from sources other than the Log. The information derived from OS maps showing additions of new streets, etc., does not provide the exact dates for their construction. This is because the maps for this area, available in Glamorgan Archives, which have been consulted, provide only the date of the original survey (usually 1873) and the dates of subsequent revisions. For example the Second edition of the 1900 OS Map states it was surveyed in 1873 and revised in 1898. It is not clear therefore as to when the building of any new developments occurred. The information derived from the leases held by T W Lewis are a better indication.

In the Second Schedule of Assent for leases on the Bontnewydd Estate there are records in 1893, 1894, 1895 and 1898 for more properties in High Street. Also in 1895 and 1896, leases were granted for additional

A photograph of Trelewis taken some time in the 1890s. The only parts of Trelewis then built were the lower part of Bontnewydd Terrace, that part of High Street behind it, and Railway Street (not visible in this photo). The big house on the middle right is Glyn Bargoed House, and above it can be seen the farm Ty Bach. Towards the left can be seen St Marys Church which was built in 1887. It would not be possible to see it if the Bontnewydd Hotel and that part of High Street to the north had been built. The 1900 OS map does show this part of High Street indicating the photograph must have been taken some time in the 1890s.

houses in Bontnewydd Terrace. Most significantly, a Lease for Bontnewydd Hotel, (with coalhouses, stables, building yard and garden), is assigned on November 1st, 1899, to M Roberts, (William Lewis' eldest child) and her siblings for 99 years at a rent of £5 per annum. There are a number of draft documents in the T W Lewis' collection relating to this together with requests for Counsel's Advice and a final date of 1st January, 1900 This would appear to cast doubt on the plaque on the outside of the hotel which proclaims:

"This hotel, built in the 1880's retains the original district name (Bontnewydd means New Bridge). After the arrival of the miners and

their families the name changed to Trelewis, named after a local farmer, William Lewis." Merthyr Tydfil Heritage Trust

The Trust was obviously only able to give an approximate date for the opening of the hotel. But with the evidence from the lease quoted above, OS maps for the period and contemporary photographs, it is more likely that the Bontnewydd Hotel opened in 1900. Trelewis at last had a Public House on Bontnewydd land in addition to the older Ffald-gaiach Inn. The miners would have welcomed this acquisition which provided an extra amenity.[168]

The Bontnewydd Hotel

Attention has been drawn above to the business acumen of William Lewis and his Solicitor, J W Lewis. This is revealed again in the long process taken in drawing up the lease for the Bontnewydd Hotel. The Lessees were to be his nine children in equal shares described in the Lease as : Margaret Roberts, wife of John Roberts, farmer of

Llanishen; Elizabeth Lewis, wife of Captain Lewis of Brynffynon; Joan Lewis, widow of Llwyngolau Farm; Hannah Matthews, wife of John William Matthews, New Tredegar, Furnace manager; Daniel Lewis of Abercynon, Colliery Manager; Lewis Lewis of Bontnewydd Hotel; Mary Lewis, Spinster of Bontnewydd House; Thomas William Lewis, Bontnewydd House, Quarry Proprietor; Edward Lewis, Bontnewydd House, Quarry Proprietor. All nine of them were to share in the costs of the erection of the hotel but not in equal parts. In drafting the lease, their father was determined that the Hotel was to remain in the family in perpetuity and that is why there are a number of requests by J W Lewis, his Solicitor, for Counsel's advice on this and other matters. The advice was given by G E Cruickshank of Bell, Broderick & Gray, Queen Victoria Street, London, showing that William Lewis would spare no expense to ensure that his wishes were fulfilled. There were no family concessions made in the lease either: his children were expected to fulfil their obligations as any of his other lessees. After much discussion, it was ultimately agreed that Captain Watkin Lewis, the husband of Elizabeth Lewis, Brynffynon, was to be appointed as the lessees' representative or agent with full powers for life, but with no right to sell the premises. William Lewis, the shrewd business man, is shown again as being meticulous in securing his self-interest in the expansion of Trelewis.[169]

In the Kelly's Directory of Monmouthshire and South Wales, 1901, Lewis Lewis, (William's second oldest son), is listed as the Landlord of the Bontnewydd Hotel. There is a growing list of businesses too included in the Commercial Section for Trelewis in that year. At least nine businesses are listed in High Street: Grocer; Butcher; Tailor; Insurance Agent; Post Office; Boot Dealer and three unspecified shopkeepers. In Railway Street there was a Grocer, Draper, Boot Repairer and a Furniture Dealer while, in Bontnewydd Terrace, a Sewing machine Agent and unspecified shopkeeper could be found. The growing array of establishments in such a small village (compared with those which appeared in the Kelly Directories of 1884 and 1891), is testament enough to an enlarged clientele. It is also pleasing to see the Ffald-gaiach Inn now listed under Trelewis in the same Section.[170]

While we have to look elsewhere than the Log to get details of these developments, there are occasions when the Log speaks of events which were shared with village as a whole. In August, 1895, practically the entire village turned out to welcome a visit of the 41st Regiment of Foot to Treharris. In 1881 this had been amalgamated into the Welch Regiment which had a strong following in the County of Glamorgan and an impressive battle record. As a consequence the school was closed. Village-wide celebrations also occurred during Jubilee Week in 1897 (21 June - 26 June). When the Board's notice was received by the school, the pupils reacted "with joy" which increased all the more as the M.P., Alfred Thomas, gave them a treat on Jubilee Day (22 June). Another village celebration occurred on May 25th, 1900, to mark the Queen's birthday and the relief of Mafeking. The children marched through the village in the afternoon singing nationalistic songs. The Log has been noticeably silent about the children's singing for some time compared to the abundance of entries in earlier years. But national occasions roused their singing abilities which were shared with the village. Indeed, prior to the Jubilee celebrations in 1897, they had practised singing patriotic songs. To develop further their appreciation of the occasion, they had read articles from various periodicals which illustrated the achievements made by the country during Queen Victoria's reign. Patriotism flourished in the school. So no doubt there was a real sense of loss, when on February 1st, 1901, the school was dismissed, without afternoon registration, following a short address on the life and death of the beloved Queen.[171]

There are some other entries in the Log which are indicative of all being not well in the village during these years but the information given is too sketchy to comment on in a meaningful way. In May, 1898, the following appears: "There is reason to fear that some of the children attending the school are insufficiently fed owing to the prevalent distress. An effort is made to supply a mid-day meal to the most needy from a fund collected locally for that purpose." There is no indication of what the distress was. Most probably it was due to a lock-out at the colliery. Neither is it stated who decided on those "most needy." Could this have been Mr Davies' role? It would also be informative if the nature of the meal and details of who had provided it were given. One would need to look elsewhere for further enlightenment. Later that year, the Log appears to suggest that employment in the colliery was at the heart of the problem. At the beginning of September, 1898, it was recorded that only a few of the senior pupils who had passed the required Standard had left school. But there was this addition: "when the colliery is in full working order," they will probably be withdrawn then. Once more the deficiencies of the Log in providing a full and accurate picture have been demonstrated.

The colliery which had resulted in the evolution of Trelewis and in the growth of its school had a fundamental part to play in its life. No one could forget that, not least John Davies. His task, however, was to ensure that, whatever happened, his pupils were brought up, vigorous in mind and body, to be loyal, useful and enriched members of the local community. That he was achieving some success in this is testified by the experiences which have been documented in the decade 1892-1901.[172]

Part Four

SECURING THE OBJECTIVE

Part Four SECURING THE OBJECTIVE (1902 - 1913)

It was during these years of the Twentieth Century that John Davies became the longest-serving Head Teacher of Trelewis Mixed School. Most of his professional life had been given to the school and many of the fears which may have beset him in 1882 had long since subsided as tangible and evident progress was seen from his labours. At all times he strove to enhance the performance and development of the school and his imprint upon it has already been seen in the Log. Reading through the account given for 1902 - 1913, one is conscious of the fact that the entries tend to be briefer and less detailed than those of earlier years. Also the number of gaps seem to occur more frequently. While there are new experiences for the school in these early years of the new century, old difficulties continue unabated. Inevitably, recurring features of its many facets of life and activity feature prominently and repetitively in the record. Because of this, it is possibly helpful to consider first, in these last years of his Headship:

1. NEW FEATURES

There were indeed aspects which were completely novel and some which were given a new twist to deal differently with longstanding situations. Perhaps the most important and certainly the longest-lasting of these was the change that occurred in:

Organisation

John Davies had taken over the leadership of a Board School when he arrived. School Boards were established as a result of Forster's Education Act of 1870 and were authorised to set up schools where there were deficiencies in the voluntary provision. In the Counties, School Boards were: to be elected by ratepayers; to charge fees of a few pennies a week and to receive financial support from government grants and local rates. The Gelligaer School Board remained responsible for Trelewis School until the Balfour Education Act of 1902 which abolished School Boards, some 2,559 of them. In their place, Local Education Authorities (LEA's), 330 in total, were to be

110

established by County and County Borough Councils. These were charged with developing the existing system of elementary schools and also with establishing new secondary and technical schools. Board Schools as a result became Council Schools.[173] The 1902 Education Act was to set up the idea of the local administration of education which was to last, with some modifications, up to the present day. By the Act, education became one of the local services for which Councils were responsible. No longer was it the responsibility of a body which was separated from the main system of local government. LEA's were to appoint Education Committees to carry out their duties. Members were to be chosen by the Council but others who had a special knowledge of education and of the District could also be appointed. The Glamorgan Education Committee was to take over the responsibility for Trelewis School. This was a major change as is indicated by one writer who describes the far reaching effects of the 1902 Act in these words: it "brought administrative order where there had been chaos, and set up an organised system of elementary, secondary and technical education."[174]

Slowly the changes in organisation brought about by the creation of the Glamorgan Education Committee began to manifest themselves in the Log of Trelewis School. Differences in bureaucratic procedures were inevitable. One of the first recorded mentions of the Committee was in May, 1904, when the Whit holiday is stated to be May 20th - May 30th "by order of the Education Committee." How perceptive that the long standing problem of attendance during the period of Quakers Yard Fair had at last been recognised with a week's holiday being granted instead of two days. Paper work and other procedures altered and probably increased. New forms had to be completed weekly to record each child's attendance. A new Attendance Officer was appointed to work exclusively in part of the District instead of in the whole Board area. Permission had to be given for the granting of occasional holidays, and this sometimes came at very short notice. There were other delays noted too, as when, at the start of the term, in September, 1905, all classes were working on a new syllabus, previously submitted, but which had not received approval from the

111

Education Committee. At the end of the financial school year, annual returns, together with registers, had to be sent to the Chief Education Official, (the high sounding title given to the Executive in charge of Education within the County). Regulations were received to submit Forms of Entry, Certificates of Birth and other documentation for candidates seeking Scholarships and Probationerships at County Schools. More form-filling seemed to be the concomitant of administration by the County Council. New systems and new people were now to grace the pages of the Log. An example of this increasing bureaucracy is found when Mr Davies writes that: "in compliance with regulations" he had submitted the Book and Stationery order to the Education Authority. No doubt further regulations and instructions were to follow.[175]

It would appear that, in theory, there was to be closer and more professional supervision of schools by the Education Committee. Whereas the School Board had utilised its own strategies for administration, it had tended to rely on the visits of Her Majesty's Inspectors to discover a school's strengths and weaknesses. Members of the Board did themselves visit schools frequently, as has been seen, but they were mostly interested and concerned members of the local community, (often clerics), rather than educationalists. The new Education Committees were to appoint County Inspectors of Schools to monitor and supervise their schools. W Bryn Davies, County Inspector of Schools was assigned to Trelewis School and paid his first visit there in February, 1905. Following that, the Log records that he was to visit, on average, twice a year, (although no visits appear for him in 1910 or 1913). As far as can be seen, he concerned himself mainly with staffing and attendance. Educational achievement still seemed to be the preserve of His Majesty's Inspectors.[176] What contribution W Bryn Davies made to the running of the schools for which he was responsible is not easily discerned. At least one of His Majesty's Chief Inspectors for Elementary Education was very disparaging about County Inspectors. In a report to the Board of Education he opined that: "there are special reasons why the bulk of the local inspectors in this country should be unequal to the discharge of their responsible duties." This was based on his observation that most inspectors for LEA's had been appointed from the ranks of elementary school teachers who had grown up during the period when the Revised Code was in operation. This experience, he argued, had given them a cramped and narrow view of school education.[177] Obviously there would have been many exceptions to such a generalised statement and it is to be hoped that some of them were to be found in the ranks of Glamorgan's County Inspectors.

There were to be new features in these years other than those emanating from the changes noted in school organisation. As one would expect, there would have been alterations in:

Curriculum

Evidence of a greater degree of central control is found when we are first introduced in the Log to Dr John James, the Chief Education Official. Glamorgan County Council had established its first education post in 1891 when it appointed an Organiser of Technical Instruction. His responsibility was to report on and organise technical education in the County. After the Education Act of 1902, nearly all education in the County became the responsibility of the Council and in 1903 the Organiser of Technical Instruction's post was subsumed into the new post of Chief Education Official. (Eventually, in 1929, when Dr James retired after 26 years in the post, the title was changed to Director of Education.) By 1909, the Chief Education Official had a staff of 9 and from this developed the County's Education Department. With such a large County to administer, bureaucratic delays might be expected. This can be seen when Dr James is first mentioned in the Trelewis Log. In May of 1905, Dr James had issued instructions that the Scheme of Work for the ensuing year, together with a projected timetable, was to be submitted. While that was duly done, when the school started back in September to begin work on the new schemes, approval had not been received from the County. (This requirement was to continue in future years with the instruction that the Scheme of Work and Draft Timetable be sent to the County

Inspector.) It is to be hoped that the administration of the new LEA improved to keep pace with these developments.[178]

New subjects began to appear in the timetable though there is no evidence as to whether this was due to local or external initiative. In 1902, lessons were introduced which included readings from relevant extracts to stimulate the pupils' interest in "facilities for Nature Study which the locality affords." The following year, in May, sunny weather allowed various classes to go on Nature Study rambles. How excited the children would have been to find that they could learn outside the classroom as well as inside it. This also won the approval of HMI who commented in their Report: "The school excursions in pursuit of Nature Study appear very interesting and instructive." Full marks, therefore, for making creative use of the local environment as an educative tool.[179] The lower Standards were also given some change to their usual lessons when brush-work was introduced for them in 1904 and appropriate apparatus was ordered then and in subsequent years. Practical work of this nature would have had an enriching effect. So it was to prove. Possibly the younger pupils having enjoyed the experience wished it to continue. In 1908, there were to be changes in timetable with the express purpose of gradually introducing brush drawing throughout the school. Standards 1 and 2 had some of the time allocated to Arithmetic reduced in order to give them experience of elementary exercises with the brush. That would have made the experience even more enjoyable.[180]

There were other new aspects which appear in these years. Saint David's Day had more attention paid to it. In 1910, on March 1st, special lessons on the life of St. David were given with emphasis being placed on "patriotism and conduct." Welsh songs were another feature of the celebrations. But probably it was the half holiday which was given on that day which made it such a memorable occasion for the children. Generations of Welsh pupils have had their feelings of nationalism strengthened by the way in which schools have celebrated St David's Day in Wales. When this is contrasted with how schools in England seem virtually to ignore St. George's Day, Welsh children are culturally privileged. A half holiday to celebrate their Patron Saint's Day is a small price to pay for such a rich reward. (It is to be regretted therefore, that the practice of giving a half holiday on St David's Day appears to be disappearing from schools.) John Davies had long been a keen advocate of all things Welsh stimulated by his origins and also by his early experiences at Llanover where Lord & Lady Llanover were powerful influences. In his last years of headship at Trelewis there appeared to be more regulation of what the school was expected to do on St David's Day. In 1911, the special programme for the morning of March 1st had to be approved by HMI and the same approved programme was to continue in 1912 and 1913. This gives additional evidence of more centralised control.[181]

Some minor innovations are revealed by examining the requisitions for teaching materials. As early as 1902, amongst the order for books and apparatus are included, for the first time in the Log, pictures which could suitably adorn the "bare walls". There is no indication of the subject matter or of the purpose of these pictures but their inclusion in the list of teaching materials marks a move forward from earlier practice. Previously the only apparent decoration for the walls had been the application of paint at infrequent intervals. This use of illustrative materials might well have been the start of an improved educative experience within the classroom environment. Nowadays the practice is universal of Junior Schools making the fullest use possible of classroom walls to provide a lively, pictorial backdrop designed to assist learning Another interesting inclusion in the requisites for 1911 was an order for Contour maps of the British Isles and the Continent. This was in direct response to a request made in the HMI Report for that year.[182]

Of all the changes which can be observed occurring in these years, those that enhanced the welfare, health and general interest of pupils were to produce tangible dividends for the future. The State had begun to realise its responsibility for their:

Well-being.

Ever since the 1870 Education Act had increased the numbers of children in schools, it had grown more and more obvious that many of them were under-nourished and in poor health. This became increasingly apparent when thousands of those who had presented themselves for military service in the Boer War were declared to be unfit.

This had led to a Government Committee being appointed in 1904, to examine Physical Deterioration[183] and in 1907 to the Education (Administrative Provisions) Act, which called upon LEA's "to make such arrangements as may be sanctioned by the Board of Education for attending to the health and physical condition of children in Public Elementary Schools." This Act was to see the establishment of a School Medical Service and the advent of compulsory medical inspections for pupils in elementary schools. A limited start had been made to improve the health of pupils but it was only a start. Initially parents were not even obliged to carry out the recommendations of medical officers. Much more remained to be done and much more was to follow including ultimately the provision of treatment.[184]

The first record we have of medical inspections at Trelewis School is in June, 1908. The legislation had soon resulted in action when Dr T Evans attended to examine medically all the school leavers. A year later, Dr S Fosdick spent two days at the school engaged in medical inspections. Thereafter, there were to be annual medical examinations, mainly, it would appear, of the upper standards and these were carried out either by Dr Thomas Evans or Dr Arnold Davies. In due course the benefits of systematically monitoring the health and well-being of pupils were to result in their being stronger, fitter and better-nourished.[185] John Davies was also to call upon the services of the local nurse, Nurse Vaughan, mainly to give the benefit of her expertise to the older girls. In 1909, she gave them a lecture on the nursing and feeding of infants. School was being used profitably to equip them for a future role as wives and mothers. The next year, in addition to speaking to the older girls, she was asked to visit the parents of pupils "reported as in unsound health in course of the last few days." This was also to happen in future years. Medical advice and help, albeit of this very restricted nature, was to be an invaluable, additional feature for the community.[186]

There is evidence, in this period, of the school fostering social, along with physical well-being. Most significant was what seems to have been the first School trip, (at least it would appear to be the first recorded), which involved 60 scholars and some teachers. They travelled to Cardiff, on Wednesday, July 21st, 1909, to witness the re-enactment of the National Welsh Pageant, described by the "Western Mail" as: "an absolutely unique event in the long, stirring and glorious history of Wales." Over 60,000 school children had booked seats at the dress rehearsals, held in the week before the Pageant opened. The South Wales Railway companies had offered special Cheap Tickets to attract attendance from all over Wales and beyond. With a cast of thousands, (including over 1,000 children), elaborate costumes and staging of 5 episodes of Welsh History with 5 interludes, it must have been a sight to behold. The consent of the Education Committee had to be obtained and presumably of parents who also had to afford payment for their children to attend. What an occasion it must have been! Visiting the big metropolis was always a memorable day for valleys' children and, for some, going to this spectacular event might have been their first time. It would have been interesting to know just how many teachers accompanied them since modern Health and Safety rules require a high Pupil-teacher ratio for school visits. The Log does not mention any more school trips taking place (up to 1913) which were unconnected with the curriculum. There would have been numbers of pupils inevitably excluded from any such visits simply on grounds of cost. That was probably the main reason why children had to wait until times of greater affluence before the school trip became a common and exciting feature of the school year.[187]

There were other more local treats for pupils to enjoy. David Davies of Llandinam, owner of the Ocean Coal Company and so of Deep

Navigation Colliery, Treharris, decided to give a tea for the children, as a mark of his beneficence. The Managers of Trelewis School responded by granting a half-holiday for preparations to be made. National events were also celebrated appropriately. On Coronation Day, 1911 (June 26th), after a week's holiday to mark the event, a tea for pupils and parents was arranged in school. To add to the occasion, sports were held in an adjacent field. There may not have been street parties in the village but the school was at the heart of the festivities. All the expenses in connection with this event were raised entirely by public subscription so everyone was able to participate. Another treat which pupils were able to enjoy was when the Education Committee designated a Half-Term holiday of two days, in October 1911, to break up the long Autumn Term. This new departure was assuredly welcomed.[188]

It was inevitable during this period that there should be alterations in the:

Buildings

The structural work on the flooring and other aspects, which had commenced in December of 1901, had not been completed for the start of the Spring Term, 1902, so an extra week's holiday was sanctioned. But the Contractors did not finally complete the work until well into February. By this time, the school had also taken delivery of new locker desks and John Davies was able to say with some satisfaction: "Teaching is greatly facilitated." There were still problems with water in the school and one of the Board members, later in the year, pointed out the wastage of water in the latrines. His intervention resulted in the Architect and Builder installing "more accessible and workable stop-taps to regulate the flow."[189] There is nothing more recorded about the Buildings until May, 1907, when Pugh Jones, the Council Architect, made a general inspection of the school premises. His report has not survived but subsequent events indicate that he had suggested various additions and alterations for which a number of Contractors submitted tenders. That work was badly needed was seen shortly after the Architect's visit when the main room was flooded by a heavy down-pour of rain in June, 1907, which caused the pupils to be sent home for the afternoon. Just over a year later, there was a repeat performance with pupils having to be sent home again because of flooding. The work required by the Architect was still progressing in February, 1909, and was creating some difficulties for the school, one of which was the necessity for Boys and Girls to use the same entrance. It wasn't until November, 1909, that the full extent of the work was completed after almost a year's disruption. But the end result was the provision of: a new classroom; a Head Teacher's room; a store room and a new lavatory for boys. These improved facilities were much appreciated.[190]

It is revealing to find different attempts being made in the early 20th Century to deal with the age-old problem of:

Attendance

In effect they really amounted to variations on the practice of using carrot more than stick to gain improvement. One of the last prize-givings for attendance carried out in accordance with the Gelligaer School Board's instructions was held in October, 1902. The Rector of Gelligaer presented books to 9 pupils who had 100% attendance and to 53 pupils who had 90% attendance. His address was said to be "interesting and encouraging." But by the end of term, as Christmas was approaching, it was noted that the attendance had been "dwindling for some days." What might the new LEA do differently to increase attendance?[191]

One of its new weapons was to offer a school a half-day's holiday if attendance reached over 92.5%. Instead of rewarding individuals for their compliance, the whole school was to benefit if, collectively, the target was reached. One can imagine how this would have promoted peer pressure on those who might have let the side down by their absence. In November, 1905, however, Mr Davies regrettably writes that the school is "continuously falling short" of the average attendance qualifying for the half holiday and blames the prevalence of infectious diseases. However, in March of the following year, the percentage climbed to 92.6, just over the target figure and the school was entitled to a half holiday in April. Further half holidays for attendance were recorded: in October and November 1906, (with attendance reaching 93.4% on the latter occasion; in October, 1907, (92.7%) and in October, 1908. All of these were approved by the Chief Education Official who might have felt pleased that this new venture was having a beneficial effect.[192]

John Davies once again gives more details about attendance, recording averages for the week, for the year and giving percentage figures , but not consistently so. In December, 1902, the average attendance for the previous 5 weeks was 140.9; in March of 1905, the weekly average was 141.8, (91.5%) with current yearly average 137.1; in February, 1906, the number on roll was said to be 170 with a monthly percentage of 90; in October, 1908, at the end of the financial school year, the average attendance was 173.2 (88.1%) and the average number on registers 196.5. In November, 1909, the average attendance was 174. Registers, as has been seen, had to be meticulously kept and were rigorously inspected and checked. But more bureaucracy accrued. From April, 1904, the LEA required sheets recording the attendance of each child to be sent to the Attendance Officer every Friday afternoon; monthly attendance returns had to be sent to the Clerk; from November, 1905, annual returns had to be completed with registers sent to the Chief Education Official at the end of the financial year. With all the form filling involved, a half holiday would have been well and truly earned.[193]

The Attendance Officer (R Saunders) who had succeeded J Jones was also prepared to try fresh rewards for attendance. Having previously stated what was required, (but not reported for us), 24 pupils who had met his conditions were rewarded with either a photographic trip or a photograph. The Log does not specify which it was. Anyway this reveals that he was happy to experiment with different ways of promoting attendance. The LEA was also to re-structure its handling of attendance. In October 1904 it appointed a new Attendance Officer (D. Roberts) whose role was to be confined solely to part of the District only, which included Trelewis. In future, the intention was that he was to call at the school and also chase up absentees weekly. This increased activity was probably one of the reasons why the school was able, for the first time, to reach the target for attendance and gain a half holiday under the new scheme. The LEA was also to appoint a Superintendent Attendance Officer, (W R Thomas), to supervise the working of the whole system. His visits were described as thorough and detailed, for he "enquired about the attendance of particular individuals". In 1911, a new Attendance Officer, W Yemm, began to make weekly visits checking the attendances on the sheets.[194] A more systematic approach and a greater supervision, which has been seen in other aspects of the Education Committee, was obviously being applied with the object of raising attendance levels.

While in these years there is evidence of new features appearing in the life of the school the majority of entries in the Log are concerned with:

2. OLD FACTORS

Having tried to isolate, above, the newer trends in dealing with attendance it is still very much the old, old story that we discern about:

Absence

The entrenched triumvirate of inhibitors to regular attendance: illness; weather; and occasional holidays are recorded in full and recurrent detail. Infectious diseases appear and re-appear with monotonous regularity. Thankfully, however, there are no prolonged or, indeed, any closures of the school recorded as a consequence which had happened in the previous decade. Starting in February, 1902, there were several cases of Scarlet Fever which resulted in those affected being excluded on medical advice. In March, 1903, there was an outbreak at the home of Henry Taverner, the Pupil Teacher, and he was kept off school for a time. Again in March, 1907, the incidence of the disease began to grow before subsiding later that year until it returned in February, 1909, when two families had to be excluded. There seemed to be nothing to prevent it re-appearing with the Medical Officer of Health repeatedly notifying fresh out-breaks. The pupils affected were hit twice over: they suffered in their illness and they were deprived of their schooling. From the record available, it seemed that Scarlet Fever was the most prevalent of the Infectious diseases which afflicted pupils at the school.[195] Measles outbreaks were comparatively fewer in number only being recorded in January, 1903, and in April, 1910.[196] Diphtheria could have had a more serious impact with pupils being excluded in May, 1903, in October, 1904 under the Infectious Diseases Act and once again in February, 1905. Thankfully, there were no deaths recorded due to infectious diseases so the precautions being taken and the treatment given were apparently successful. Schools were places where such illness could spread and it was imperative that the County Council did everything it could to mitigate its ramifications. In June, 1910, the School Medical Officer issued revised regulations relating to infectious and contagious diseases.[197] How successful these were is not known but at least there were no further outbreaks of disease recorded by Mr Davies in the remaining years of his Log.

As one reads these pages, there is much to support a commonly held view about weather in the Valleys, that it is more often than not inclement. Rain repeatedly stopped pupils attending and even those who braved the storm sometimes had to be sent home as in April, 1902, March, October and December, 1903, February, 1904, June, 1907, and September, 1908. Mr Davies comments frequently about: "exceptionally wet weather"; "continuous wet weather;" "heavy downpours;" "continuous torrent of rain;" "exceptional downpour of rain;" "very stormy;" "very rainy for several days" etc. He also notes: severe winter weather; sleet; ground covered with snow for most of week; slippery roads all of which adversely affected attendance. Nevertheless, there were still pupils who braved the elements and these were duly commended. Weather forecasters wishing to discover historical trends in weather patterns in South Wales would find the Log a most productive source.[198]

The litany of days and half-days when the school was closed for occasional holidays continued unabated. Church events (Band of Hope/Sunday School Treats, Singing Festivals); Local Events

122

(Sheepdog Trials, Nelson Fair, arrival of Circus, Coronation celebrations, Funerals of local dignitaries and of people associated with the school); School used as a polling station for elections: the sheer multiplicity is all recorded in the Log, as had been done previously. The LEA had also contributed to this catalogue by awarding holidays for good attendance.[199] Interestingly, many of the entries have the addition of the phrases: "with consent of the Chief Education Official"; "granted by Managers"; "with consent of Managers"; "by order of the Managers"; "by order of the Education Committee." This would indicate that a closer eye was being kept on such occurrences. In these years there are a number of holidays given to attend the opening of new schools: at Pontlottyn; Deri; Bargoed and at Bedlinog. The re-opening of Hengoed School and of Pengam County School for Boys warranted half day holidays as did the inauguration of the Higher Elementary School at Bargoed.[200]

The well-rehearsed phrase "Attendance below average" continues to be seen in the week before and/or after a school holiday period. Nothing positive had occurred to alter this commonplace pattern since the school started. Pupils seemed to take a delight in anticipating the break from school or prolonging it, by absenting themselves. It was almost as if they considered that it was their right to do so.[201] The Managers' visits to check the registers were not carried out regularly and systematically if the Log for these years recorded every occasion they came. None are mentioned for 1902, only one for 1903 by Thomas Thomas, one in 1904 by David Prosser, and two further visits by Thomas Thomas in 1907 and 1908. However, when Jonah Evans took over the responsibility in 1909, there was a more consistent and more frequent sequence He would visit every two or three months between October, 1909 and January, 1913 writing in the Log that the registers had been checked and found correct. The entry and his signature were sometimes in blue pencil or purple ink, almost as if he wished to copy the way HMI sometimes made their entries. It has already been noted that Jonah Evans had expanded his business interests in the village. These activities show that he was also prepared to expand his role as a Manager.[202]

Staffing

The hardy perennial of staffing difficulties constantly appears in the record. Illness and personal circumstances regularly interrupt the attendance of teachers. Henry Taverner, who had started at the school as a Probationer in 1899, was particularly badly hit in these years. At the start of 1902, after remaining at home to help look after his father who was seriously ill, he had the trauma of attending his father's funeral shortly after. In March, 1903, due to an outbreak of scarlet fever at his home, he had to be excluded for almost a month. At the start of the year, in 1904, he had not been attending regularly as he was unwell. Mr Davies was to add that even when he was present "he seems dispirited." Henry Taverner's spirits would have drooped still further, when, in March, he learned that he had failed the King's Scholarship examination which his fellow pupil teachers, (Lettice Davies and Margaret Ann Morgan), had passed. Worse was to follow when almost immediately afterwards, his mother was to die as a result of an accident. While there are no more reports of his absence or of adverse circumstances, it comes as no surprise to find John Davies writing in February, 1905, that Henry Taverner had left the profession on 31st January "for something else at which I trust he will succeed." Mr Davies included the comment: "He has always been willing and obliging in his conduct but not so persevering in his studies as I would have wished." Focusing on this individual, who probably had more upsets in his teaching career, compared with his contemporaries on the staff, contributes to our understanding of the problems faced by Head Teachers in running their schools.[203]

It would take far too long to give a complete account of the absences of all the staff in these years and, in any case, most were only of minor duration and significance. However, the leaving and sometimes the absence of Assistant Teachers could have a more serious impact. Annie Pugh Assistant (Article 50) since 1902, resigned at the end of November, 1903, having gained an appointment nearer her home. She was prevailed upon to continue until the Christmas holiday but when school resumed in January, 1904, her Standard 4 class had to be taken by Lettice Davies, the Pupil Teacher. At the end of January, the Senior

Assistant Teacher, Isabella Williams married, but the Managers persuaded her to remain in her post until the end of the Spring Term. Losing such gifted and experienced staff was always going to be a blow to the consistent development of the school. As vacancies were now advertised by the Education Committee, it was inevitable too, that there would be some delay in appointing a successor.[204]

More staffing disruption occurred when Lettice Davies, who had become an Uncertificated teacher on passing the King's Scholarship examination, was appointed to a post at Bargoed School in June, 1904. By July, Mr Davies writes with some impatience: "The staff has been so weakened lately by the removal of Assistants that the present state of efficiency cannot be maintained unless it is strengthened forthwith." Instead, the situation worsened. Before the end of the Summer Term, Miss M A Morgan, who had also become an Uncertificated Teacher through passing the King's Scholarship Examination, had gained a post elsewhere and would not be returning in September. When the school reopened, the 28 pupils who had been drafted in from the Infants had no teacher. The Clerk to the Group seeing the emergency wrote to say that Lettice Davies would be re-appointed to the school, subject to the approval of the Education Committee. Within a week, Lettice Davies was back. John Davies' worries continued when, towards the end of September, the Chief Education Official sent the school the resolution of the Education Committee that pupil teachers who attended Pupil Teacher Centres must only be employed half-time in teaching. Fortunately, no pupil teachers from Trelewis School attended such a Centre but as Mr Davies pointed out he could not have complied with the resolution anyway as there were only two Article 50 Assistants on the staff. When Bryn Davies, the LEA's Education Inspector, paid his first visit to the school in February 1905 he was met with the continuing problem of vacancies on the staff.[205]

The staffing situation deteriorated further in April. John Davies reported then, that two Standards had to be taught together by one teacher if any member of staff was absent. A month later his Senior Assistant, Bessie Davies, was absent from school with "Debility" given as the reason on the medical certificate. That could have been a twentieth century pseudonym for stress. It wasn't until July that Bessie Davies was able to resume her duties. In the meantime John Davies repeated his calls for assistance as a matter of urgency. His calls were heeded and a teacher from Pontlottyn Infants was drafted in temporarily and an Uncertificated Assistant, (Miss Jennie Edwards), was appointed before Bessie Davies returned. It was Miss Edwards who took charge of Standard 1 when 24 children arrived from the Infants in September. More staff changes and absences caused ever lengthening cries of anguish. When a new pupil teacher, (Mary Packer), started in October, although she had passed some Central Welsh Board exams, it was reported, somewhat regretfully, that she had no previous experience of teaching and it was not apparent what were to be the terms and extent of her employment. This resulted in Mr Davies noting that the staff was too weak to do good work "in the various classes and syllabuses." The individual attention which some of his pupils required just could not be afforded. He was almost beside himself in December, when Jennie Edwards and Mary Packer had been absent for over a week, writing in the Log: "It really is most difficult to work the school properly in their absence as not one of the classrooms is large enough to hold two classes even if one teacher could keep them employed." One can sense his desperation and his unspoken message: "When is someone going to listen to me and do something?" Supply Teachers were obviously not part of the set-up in the early years of the century.[206]

At the start of the year in 1906, a new Certificated Assistant, (Miss Amelia Morris), was appointed and there is a complete list of the deployment of the staff for the term:

Standard 6	Head Teacher	
Standard 5	Jacob Morgan	Uncertificated Assistant
Standard 4	Bessie Davies	" "
Standard 3	Jennie Edwards	" "
Standard 2	Kate Jones	Pupil Teacher
Standard 1	Amelia Morris	Certificated Assistant
	Mary Packer	Pupil Teacher - To assist as directed

It is almost as if Mr Davies is rejoicing that at last he has a full complement of staff. Rarely had he recorded how the staff were to be deployed and more rarely did he have a member of staff to fill the gaps. All of this was not to last: Kate Jones and Jennie Edwards were to leave although Kate Jones was to return later that year as an Uncertificated Assistant on the permanent staff. After the Summer holiday, Mary Packer was required to attend Pupil Teacher classes at Hengoed for half of the week and so was only available to teach her class part-time. At last, the requirement of the LEA was being met but at the expense of Trelewis pupils. Early in 1907, Miss Amelia M Morris was to gain promotion being appointed Head Teacher of Bedlinog Infants School. She was replaced by Miss Maud Mary Phillips. Mary Packer was to leave at the end of August and a new pupil teacher (Minnie Morgan) started in her place. Mr Davies renewed his well-worn complaint when 40 Infants entered his school in September: "It is difficult to arrange the classes for working successfully with the Pupil Teacher attending school part-time." The County Inspector, Bryn Davies, had to deal with this and he recommended the appointment of an additional teacher. But it wasn't until November that Joshua Christmas Williams, a trained Certificated Teacher, started as Assistant.[207]

From 1908 to 1913, there are no more pleas for assistance with staffing despite absences through illness and occasional temporary re-location of individual teachers. For example: in 1908 Jacob Morgan, Uncertificated Assistant, was required by the LEA to take up temporary duties at Nelson School on at least two occasions of a fortnight each. There were some changes too in staff during these years. Winifred Davies was to start as Pupil Teacher in September, 1908, and she too was required to attend classes at the Pupil Teachers' Centre. She was joined by William Percy Thomas in September, 1909, after he had passed the Junior Central Welsh Board examination. He worked as a Pupil Teacher on Mondays and Thursdays and attended classes at the County School for the rest of the week. Within a year, his employment at the school was ended with the terse statement: "his services are discontinued." Winifred Davies completed her time as a

127

Pupil teacher in September, 1911, when she was appointed as an Uncertificated Assistant at Bedlinog. Miss Ceridwen Evans replaced Kate Jones as Certificated Assistant at the start of the Autumn Term in 1912 when Miss Jones left to be married. At the same time Jacob Morgan left to enter Training College and after a temporary appointment, he was replaced as an Uncertificated Teacher in December of that year by Herbert Powell who had a CWB qualification. It is difficult to trace the changes in staff for this period 1908 - 1913 because there are only two HMI Reports written up and no lists of staff for any of the years. But judging by the entries that appear, the inference can be made that the staff was more settled and did not cause Mr Davies too many problems. One of his final statements about staff made in February, 1913, pays tribute to them as being "earnest and industrious." A small addendum indicates, however, that he still had to help with Standard 4 as Herbert Powell was young and inexperienced.[208]

The steady rhythm of school life, interspersed with its crescendos of concern and cadences of calm, unfolds year on year. The necessary recapitulations all designed to enhance the harmony are occasionally disturbed by discordant notes as has been seen.

Many of the old factors continue to appear in school:

Routine

Learning activity was inevitably followed by Periodic Examinations as before but by July, 1903, the phrase "Terminal Examinations" begins to appear. This probably meant that the Periodical examination was now being held, logically, at the end of each term. There is also an indication that the Terminal Examination could sometimes be taken in parts and not confined to one day of testing.[209] Pupils continued to be examined in Religious Education by members of the clergy and detailed reports on the performance of the various Standards are recorded. A most fulsome report is given in September, 1902, by Rev Ambrose Lewis of Maesycwmmer and Rev. R E Peregrine of Rhymney. Scholars in Standards 1 and 2 had a thorough and intelligent grasp of the work; Standards 3 and 4 acquitted themselves excellently and some of the scholars in Standards 5, 6 and 7 were described as exceptionally bright. The only other detailed report we have is for the following year when the content of the examination is more fully described. Standards 1 and 2 were well versed in the history of the childhood of Jesus Christ; Standards 3 and 4 had mastered the selected Parables and Miracles; some children in Standards 5 and 6 showed a wonderful knowledge of Gospel history but others seemed to have forgotten what they had learned in previous Standards. No other Reports appear on examinations in Religious Instruction for the remaining years. Could it be that the LEA incorporated this into their own examinations rather than have external testing by clergymen?[210] The pupils, most of whom regularly attended Sunday Schools, did not go short of biblical knowledge at this particular time.

Terminal Examinations were for all but other examinations that were sat had a more limited clientele. Most select of these were the examinations for entrance to the Gelligaer County Schools at Hengoed for the girls and Pengam for the boys. The selection of candidates for these not only depended on ability but also on finance, for, despite scholarships being awarded, those wishing to go to secondary school were still involved in additional expense. The Log for 1902 - 1913 does not always record the number of pupils who were entered for the Scholarship examination, usually giving only the number who were successful. However in 1903 there were 7 who attempted it of whom 3 were successful. Amongst the other examinations described in the Log were those for the Labour Certificate or the Certificate of Proficiency. The Employment of Children Act, 1903, had stipulated that no child could enter employment until they had earned a certificate of proficiency demonstrating that their school work was of a reasonable standard. The Labour Certificate was usually taken by pupils in Standard 6 and once achieved could lead to their leaving school to start work. As a result, those from the poorest families would often leave as soon as they could to begin earning a living. Bright pupils, therefore, felt this pressure to forego their education to add to the family income. Those who did not achieve the requisite standard of proficiency had to continue at school until they reached school-leaving age. These examinations were held usually more than once in a year and pupils sat them elsewhere, for example-in Treharris, Merthyr Vale, and Llancaiach. It must have been an unsettling experience for them to be examined out of their normal school environment and could have affected the outcome. The largest number participating at any one time of which we have knowledge was 22.[211] The chronicle of routine examinations also included those taken by the Pupil Teachers. They had to pass in order to be Candidates and then would proceed to take the King's Scholarship examination which was required for entrance to training colleges (until it was abolished in 1907). Amongst the places where the examinations were held were Merthyr, Hengoed and Porth. The former practice of allowing the pupil teachers time for revision, if possible before the examination, was continued. Mr Davies always wanted them to do well and get the best possible results.[212]

No longer do we have long lists of songs learned during the course of the year. That did not mean that music and singing lessons were discontinued. In 1902, the two clergy who examined the Religious Instruction reported that Standards 1 and 2 "sang very nicely." There is also mention of one of the school Managers, Thomas Thomas, in 1904, enjoying and appreciating the pupils singing.[213] Silence in the Log about such activities probably meant that the routine was proceeding without comment. Cookery still managed to find its way into the record, as it caused difficulties from time to time. In 1906, it was reported that Cookery lessons had become somewhat irregular as the teacher was having difficulties meeting the new regulations within the normal timetable structure. The following year, the teacher had the practical and demonstration cookery lessons changed to Thursday afternoons while in 1908, the Cookery lessons had to be suspended for a term with no reason stated. When the same thing happened again, towards the end of the Summer Term in 1910, it was attributed to the course being completed. Further change was made in 1911, when Cookery was transferred to Wednesdays after a new syllabus and timetable was approved. As can be seen from this, it was Cookery which was mentioned more than other subjects in the curriculum and mainly because of variations which it made in routine.[214] Other problems in the normal running of the school occurred as a result of delays in receiving orders for books and apparatus. In 1908, only part of the order was received as the remainder had been sent to Trebanos, in error. As late as 1912, there were still unaccountable delays resulting in all classes being short of exercise books. These irritants were all part and parcel of school life but generally it would appear that the routine of the learning process carried on undisturbed.[215]

While there are no giant or remarkable leaps forward in the years 1902-1913 there is plenty of evidence of:

3. CONTINUING ADVANCE

for the School

Reports from Her Majesty's Inspectors of Schools for the years 1902 - 1905 are brief but most complimentary. The 1902 Report speaks of the lessons being conducted in "an assiduous and successful manner." High commendation is seen the following year: "Great praise continues to be due for the manner in which this school is conducted. Signs of honest steady work are seen year after year." What a testimonial to John Davies and his staff for the effort which they had made and were making. But the staffing problems which have been noted caused HMI, in the 1904 Report, to call for an additional Assistant to be appointed as all of the 3 lower classes had to be taught by Pupil Teachers without qualified assistance. Mr Davies' worries had been taken on board by the Inspectors as the whole report is taken up with the staffing issue. In 1905, the Report is confined to a single sentence: "As usual, the Headmaster and his staff work very conscientiously and the scholars are making sound progress in each of the branches of instruction."[216]

In March, 1907, A Taylor, the Drawing Inspector, visited the school when he was impressed with the work which he found. He was able to provide very practical suggestions for further development. No more HMI Reports are included in the Log until April, 1908, when there is a copy of the Report made by W Edwards, HMI following his visit in

March, 1908. Then there is more silence and only one other Report appears, namely of W Edwards' visit in October, 1911. Previously the importance of including a copy of the HMI's Report in the Log and having it signed by one of the Managers had been emphasised. So it is a bit of a mystery why regular annual Reports do not appear. Also after Frank T James, the Clerk, signed the 1902 Report, no one else signed any of the remaining Reports. Possibly the Reports given to the school were verbal with the written Reports being recorded elsewhere. Certainly there were more visits of Inspectors during the course of the school year mentioned in the Log but often without a note being made of the outcome. In 1902, there were 2 visits by G Jones, Sub-Inspector, in January and June; in March, 1903, W Edwards made his inspection and in October and November, 1903, John Evans, Sub-inspector, visited. John Evans also visited in June, 1904, and G Jones made the Inspection in December. The following year, the only HMI visit was by G Jones in October then there were 2 visits, in 1906, by J Evans, in January and July. The only recorded visit in 1908 was that of W Edwards noted above. G Jones, Sub Inspector, inspected the school in May, 1909, and again in March, 1910. J Evans made 2 visits in 1911, one for inspection in February and one concerning Registration in September. He visited in July, 1912 and also in March, 1913, just prior to Mr Davies' departure. HMI continued the practice of writing in the Log to indicate their visit, sometimes in purple ink or pencil, in red ink, in blue pencil and sometimes in ordinary ink. The earlier comments about the legibility of their writing also continue to apply. Regrettably, in these last years of John Davies' headship, the lack of copies of annual reports and the increasing brevity of the Log leave us in the dark about the official view of the school.[217]

W Edwards HMI had known the school ever since John Davies became Head and he would have first-hand knowledge of the ups and downs of its fortunes. Perhaps it is significant that in his final two Reports which are recorded for us, most attention is given to the state of the premises rather than to educational matters. In his 1908 Report, after noting that the growing number of pupils would soon lead to extensions being necessary for the school, he makes 4 requests for improvement: to the heating (stoves were inefficient and smoky); for adaptation to the Dado (assisting free arm drawing); for playsheds in both playgrounds (beneficial in wet play times); for a glass sliding partition in the main room (increasing classroom space). His 1911 Report comments on the improved premises which now had sufficient classroom accommodation. He also mentioned faults in the planning of 2 classrooms as they had no independent exits and could only be cleared through other rooms. There is: praise for the excellent state of the playgrounds which provided plenty of space for physical education; requests for: Contour Maps of GB and the Continent; more varied Readers for all classes; and for better arrangements for the teaching of Welsh. He comments that the Headmaster assisted by a strong staff (at last!) maintains "a creditable state of efficiency" although there were traces of some old-fashioned methods, particularly in Arithmetic. (This is understandable considering the number of changes that had occurred in the revised codes over the years.) But he concludes that the "earnest and capable" staff would soon be able to up-date their practice by studying what was now required. He describes the pupils as being "well-behaved" but draws attention to some of the boys needing to improve their "personal cleanliness." Overall these final Reports bear testimony to the hard work and determination of the Head and staff which had progressively led the school forward over the years.[218]

for the Pupils

Commendation for the progress made by pupils is found in this period but sometimes their names are omitted. Recording success in the Scholarship examinations for the County Schools had always been a matter of pride. But, in September, 1902, Mr Davies merely records that two pupils had been successful and had started their studies there without naming them. The next year he specifically states that Winifred Davies and William Asaph Jones had passed the Scholarship examination out of the seven candidates who had attempted it and Esther Frowen had been awarded a half- scholarship. Between 1904 and 1907, there is silence in the Log about any pupils sitting, let alone passing, the examination. In 1908, some scholars in Standard 6 wished to be entered and of these, two (un-named), were required to attend Part Two of the examination held at Hengoed. Whether that meant that they were to be ultimately successful is not clarified. The 1909 examination required Forms of Entry, Certificates of Birth or Declaration to be submitted on behalf of candidates but no indication is given of the number who were presented. Interestingly, the Log describes the examination, for the first time, as being for Scholarships and Probationerships. Presumably the Probationerships applied to those who wished to become Pupil Teachers. One boy and 4 girls were later named as qualifying for Part Two of the examination (Owen Hamlet Lewis, Kate O M Watts, Catherine Williams, Edith Salmon, and Mary Gwen Davies). In 1910, Edith Lambert, Annie Powell, and Gwyneth Davies attended Part Two of the Scholarship and Probationership examination at Hengoed and of these Edith Lambert and Gwyneth Davies were later to accept Entrance Scholarships. There were 5 pupils who sat the examination in 1911 and of these Rachel E Storey, John Williams and Roderick Mcdonald Finlayson qualified for Part Two. The last entry about these examinations is in 1912 when all that is recorded is that 2 candidates sat for Probationer Scholarships at the County School.[219] It has already been commented on that some pupils, who might have entered and been successful in proceeding to secondary education, were not able to do so because of the need to earn a living and contribute to the family income. Those that did succeed undoubtedly had their future prospects advanced and tribute should be paid to them with commiserations at the same time to their less fortunate peers. From this small village school, there were to be those who would carve out for themselves successful careers.

Again, the record we have shows a rich heritage for those who had been pupils, pupil teachers and teachers at the school. There was indeed a continuing advance:

for the Teachers

It was as far back as 1846 that the pupil-teacher system had been introduced to improve the quality and supply of teachers. Schools which had received a favourable Inspector's Report could be recognised for the training of pupil-teachers with Head Teachers providing them with one and a half hours instruction each day. After a 5 year apprenticeship from the age of 13 they could present themselves for the Queen's Scholarship Examination and gain exhibitions to study at a Training College. In practice many did not enter college but either left the profession or became uncertificated teachers. It was the Cross Commission which pressed for the improvement in the training of pupil-teachers. Pupil Teacher Centres had gradually emerged to improve the instruction of pupil teachers whom the Cross Commission had criticised for teaching badly because they had been badly taught. In the late 1890's, apprenticeships for pupil teachers were to begin at age 15 and Matriculation or Senior Local examinations could be substituted for the Queen's Scholarship. In 1900, the period of apprenticeship was reduced to 3 years; after 1902, it was reduced to 2 years with the minimum age for entry raised to 16. Pupil Teachers were required to spend half their time at a Pupil teacher Centre and half their time teaching or observing in a school. (John Davies, as has been seen, had some reservations about this because of the shortage of staff in his school.) The Board of Education went on to make further changes: after two (later 3) years instruction at secondary school, pupils who wanted to become teachers could gain a bursary enabling them to train for a year as a pupil teacher or go to Training College; in 1907, the King's Scholarship examination was abolished being replaced by Preliminary examination for the elementary school teachers' certificate. These developments led to a decline in the number of pupil teachers. But, in the period 1902-1913, pupil teachers at Trelewis School received from Mr Davies the commendation which he had given his own daughter when they followed her route from pupil to pupil teacher and on to better things.[220]

In July, 1902, Mrs Frances M Lewis (nee Clarke) was praised for her 10 years or more at the school as pupil, pupil teacher and Assistant. Even longer was the time spent at the school by Lettice Davies. She had been in almost continuous attendance there for 17 years starting as a pupil and finishing as Assistant before leaving to train at Swansea Training College. Because of the need for more teachers to staff the growing number of pupils in schools, LEA's had been encouraged to establish their own Training Colleges and the Swansea Municipal College was amongst the forerunners of these new institutions. Lettice Davies, who had received a good grounding in her years at Trelewis, now entered higher education to equip her further. In June, 1906, Jennie Edwards, who had been an Uncertificated Assistant for a year left to train at University College, Cardiff. The progress on to Higher Education seemed to be becoming more customary in these years. It was in September, 1912, that we have the last recorded entrant. Jacob Morgan who had been Pupil, Pupil Teacher and Assistant at the school over a period of 16 years left for Training College. John Davies would have been delighted to see such progress from students whom he had personally nurtured.[221]

It must have been a source of rich satisfaction too when he recorded the successes gained by his staff. In the Log, he records assiduously their successes in the Pupil Teachers' examinations, the King's Scholarship examinations and the Preliminary Certificate examinations. It is pleasing to trace their individual progress and the level of achievement, whether First, Second, or Third Class, and for Part One or Part Two. The success of Kate Jones is most praiseworthy. She had started as a Monitress in 1902, having won a County School Scholarship 3 years earlier and passed the Junior examination of the Central Welsh Board. This exempted her from the first year Pupil Teacher examination in 1903. But, in the HMI Report for 1903, this statement appears: "The Board of Education cannot advise Kate Jones to take up the profession of teaching as the cataract of her right eye will almost certainly debar her from recognition as a Certificated Teacher." Despite this, the Log goes on to record her success in the King's Scholarship Examination of 1905. She is transferred temporarily to Graig Infants' School in May, 1906, but returned as an Uncertificated Assistant on the permanent staff in July of that year following Miss Jennie Edwards leaving for Cardiff University College. In November, 1907, we read that she was granted leave of absence to sit the Certificate Examination. It is almost with a note of triumph that John Davies writes in April, 1908: "Miss Kate Jones has been notified by the Board of Education that…she will be recognised as a certificated teacher from August 1st, 1908." With further pride he wrote in August, 1912, that "Kate Jones, Certificated Teacher, leaves today to be married after over 18 years here as Pupil, Pupil Teacher and Assistant." HMI had been proved wrong and the Head would have rejoiced in his part in Kate's accomplishment.[222]

Miss Amelia M Morris was the only Certificated Assistant on the staff, apart from Mr Davies, when she was appointed to the school in January, 1906. Having spent 14 months at Trelewis, she left in March, 1907. The next time her name appears is in January, 1908, when John Davies records that the school had been given an extra day's holiday to mark the opening of Bedlinog Infants' School. The reason stated is that Miss Amelia M Morris, previously Assistant at Trelewis, was to be the Head Mistress. Congratulations and celebrations would have been the order of the day for the promotion of a former member of staff. Warm tributes were paid too when valued staff severed their links with the school following their marriage. In January, 1904, Isabella Williams, the Senior Assistant, was married and became Mrs Isabella Watkins. However, the Managers prevailed upon her to remain in post until March 30th, when John Davies writes that Mrs Isabella Watkins, who had been "a diligent and successful Assistant here since November 14th 1895 leaves today with the best wishes of teachers and scholars for her future welfare." From a 21st Century viewpoint, it seems such a shame that promising teaching careers could come to an abrupt end because of the prevailing view that the place for married women was in the home not in the schoolroom.[223] It was not until the 1944 Education Act that women teachers were no longer forced to leave their jobs on marriage. Even then it took until 1953 for equal pay to be accepted in the teaching profession.

for the Village

The village which had been expanding over the years to provide workers for the colliery, continued to grow and the leases granted for

137

Courtesy Alan George

properties on Bontnewydd land provide useful information on where and when development was occurring. In Leases Nos. 68-75 dated November 1st, 1905, there appears the first mention of Richards Terrace. The lease rental required for each of the 9 houses is stated as 12 shillings. New developments also appear to have taken place in St. Mary Street with Leases 110-123 dated November 1st, 1909, (stating a rental of 13 shillings each) and development of Field Street, (Leases 124-152). Neither street had been mentioned before. The next leases on the Schedule are dated November 1st, 1912, (Nos. 153-159) and refer for the first time to Edwards Terrace. This time the lease rents are given as £1. The money received from these leases by the Lewis family was obviously steadily increasing. Other leases are for properties in High Street (Nos.77-96 dated November 1st, 1906) and for Bontnewydd Terrace (Nos.99-109 dated November 1st, 1909). Slowly additional ribbons of terraced housing were joining the main high street through the village.

In the Schedule of Leases, it is revealing to note Thomas W Lewis, (William Lewis' son), expanding his portfolio. In addition to

138

Courtesy Alan George

properties in High Street, Richards Terrace, Field Street and Edwards Terrace, he leased his home "Coed ceirios" for 99 years on November 1st, 1907, for a rental of Four Pounds and One shilling (Lease no. 97). John Davies is also listed amongst the lessees in these years with 5 further properties, in High Street, Bontnewydd Terrace, St Mary Street and Field Street, assigned to him (Leases 78, 96, 117, 145, 161). The last of these was dated November 1st, 1912, and was for "Tawelfan" on a 99 year lease for a rental of One Pound Fifteen shillings and six pence. This was to be the home where he lived after his retirement. The business acumen which he had showed earlier had not deserted him. Prominent among the other lessees are members of the Lewis family: Mary Edwards, Joan Lewis, Lewis Lewis, Edward Lewis, Mary Lewis, Jane Lewis and Hannah Matthews. Elizabeth Jane Lewis, (John Davies' daughter), the wife of Thomas W Lewis, was, from 1st November, 1911, the lessee of 35 Bontnewydd Terrace at a rental of eleven shillings and one penny (No. 107). She was no doubt following the lead given by her father and her husband.[224]

But there was also to be expansion of the village which took place on land other than that owned by the Bontnewydd estate. From OS maps,

139

Warren Street, (just below the Shinrig), Caiach Terrace and Mackintosh Terrace (running to the bridge over the Taff Bargoed Branch Railway) and Park Terrace which was situated opposite the Ffald-gaiach Inn, can all be traced. The problem remains of finding the exact dates when these habitations were constructed as the maps only provide an approximate timescale.[225] What is abundantly clear is that the continued influx of inhabitants over these years made the village more and more anglicised. W Edwards, HMI, in his Report on Trelewis School in 1911, had commented: "This was once a very Welsh District but, with the influx of newcomers, has, of late, become very much anglicised." Accordingly, he had recommended a change in the organisation for teaching Welsh in the school. Instead of class teachers teaching Welsh to their own class irrespective of their proficiency in the language, he suggested that the timetable should be altered so that only fluent Welsh speakers should give Welsh lessons to pupils. Within a week, John Davies had taken appropriate action: Standards 5 & 6 were to be taken together for Welsh by J C Williams; Standards 3 & 4 were to be taken separately by the Head and Jacob Morgan. The order of the first 2 lessons on Mondays, Wednesdays and Fridays was altered so that Miss B Davies could change classes with Miss M Morgan for the Welsh lesson.[226]

A more sympathetic attitude to the teaching and learning of Welsh had manifested itself towards the end of the 19th Century. As has been seen, the old Gelligaer School Board had sought to promote the teaching of Welsh in its area. Mr Davies himself, throughout his career, has been observed seeking to encourage the teaching of the language and in this period continued to do so. Earlier, in 1902, among books and apparatus he ordered, there were sheets for teaching Welsh by the Direct Method. These were added to in 1906 but he made the comment that, although Welsh was now taught regularly throughout the school, there were some teachers who did not feel competent to teach the subject. He then publicised details of Welsh classes for teachers, in the Summer holidays, to be held at Rhyl and expressed the hope that some teachers would attend. However, the expense and the distance probably inhibited the take-up of many from South Wales.[227]

Despite all these actions, designed to encourage and build up the use of Welsh, the school was powerless to halt the rising tide of anglicisation. With the waves of immigration from England to the mining areas of South Wales, even the Sunday Schools in the chapels were forced to resort to the use of English to communicate with their new scholars. Also, as children played in the streets, it became increasingly common for them to converse in English.

More evidence of this trend in Trelewis can be found in the opening of Trinity English Baptist Chapel in 1908. The first non-conformist chapel to be built in the village had been Welsh (Ebenezer Congregational). This had been followed by the building of St Mary's Anglican Chapel of Ease. If villagers wished to attend a free church service to worship in English, they would have had to walk to Treharris where there were a variety of denominations available. But in 1907, W D Nicholas and others took out a lease of Bontnewydd land for Trinity Baptist Chapel to be built (Lease No. 98 dated 1 November, 1907). This was for 99 years at a rental of three pounds and eight pence. The chapel was erected on land immediately adjacent to School House where John Davies lived. The village now had an English chapel of its own and its Sunday services were at 11.00 a.m. and 6.00 p.m.[228]

There continued to be commercial advance in the village alongside this additional provision for spiritual needs. Kelly's Directories for 1906, 1910 and 1914 list a number of new businesses or change in owner of established ones. Jonah Evans, who has been observed expanding his role as a Manager of the school, again appears in a multi-faceted capacity as grocer, clothier, draper, boot and shoe dealer, florist, and hardware dealer. In 1906, he took out a lease for an abattoir at a rental of £2 p.a. for 99 years.[229] He would appear to be one of the most prominent business men in the village. Amongst the other businesses are included: some grocers (joined towards the end of the period by a branch of the Co-operative Society); butcher; fruiterers; furniture dealer; confectioners; boot dealers; greengrocers; insurance agent; fried fish dealer; sewing machine agent; china and glassware and other unspecified shopkeepers. There was also a sub-Post Office in the village and we are informed that letters were delivered at 8.00 a.m., 11.00 a.m., and 6.30 p.m. Collections were dispatched at 8.10 a.m., 11.55 a.m., 4.00 p.m. and 7.30 p.m. Compared with the present lack of businesses in Trelewis and the truncated service provided by the modern Post Office, the village in the early years of the 20th Century was a much more vibrant place in which to live.[230]

On 10th July, 1911, Trelewis could boast of the opening of its first railway station, (later called Trelewis Platform), on the Taff Bargoed Joint Railway (GWR/Rhymney Railway). The station was very basic as the platforms had been constructed from old sleepers and ballast. Prior to this, to make a railway journey one had to walk either to Treharris or Nelson and Llancaiach stations. In July, 1904, there is recorded a Band of Hope outing to Barry Island , the first time in the Log there has been mention of a trip to that seaside Mecca for countless numbers of South Wales children. Did that outing begin with a walk to the nearest station? Also the pupils who had attended the National Pageant in Cardiff in 1909 would have had to do this if they had travelled to Cardiff by rail.[231] Now the village had the benefit of better transport connections. Indeed there were 4 trains a day on weekdays either to Ystrad Mynach or Hengoed High Level and two of these were through trains to Cardiff. There were even two trains on Sundays. A second station, Trelewis Halt, opened on 9th July, 1934, as a consequence of increased competition from buses. The station, on the Vale of Neath GWR line, was again most unpretentious with two small wooden shelters on both platforms and no connecting bridge between. It was strategically situated adjacent to the main road to Nelson immediately after the rail bridge across Glyn Bargoed Road. By this date, the village was said to have about 3,000 inhabitants. Trelewis now had a claim to fame greater than that of its two neighbours, Treharris and Bedlinog, as it was served by two railway stations not one. But it was only to be for about 30 years as Trelewis Platform closed on 15th June, 1964, when passenger services between

Nelson and Dowlais ceased. Trelewis Halt closed to passenger traffic in the same year.[232]

It was the Taff Bargoed Branch of the Joint GWR/Rhymney Railway which caused a great stir in the village when it carried King George V and Queen Mary during their Royal visit to South Wales on 27th June, 1912. Imagine the excitement when it was known that, as part of the Royal Visit, their Majesties were actually to pass through Trelewis on the Royal Train en route for Dowlais, Merthyr and Aberdare. The visit had started in Cardiff on June 25th and was to continue until June 28th. After an extensive programme in the capital which included laying the Foundation Stone of the National Museum of Wales in Cathays Park, the King had expressed the wish to see something of the Welsh coal Valleys. On June 27th, an exhaustive (if not exhausting) tour was arranged. King and Queen travelled to Pontypridd by train then up the Rhondda valley to Treherbert by car. On returning to Pontypridd they boarded the Royal Train for the journey to Dowlais Cae Harris via Trelewis. An imaginative administrator must have arranged this itinerary allowing the King and Queen to see contrasts between the valleys: the Rhondda with its closely packed communities running into each other almost without pause; then the Taff Bargoed Valley more sparsely populated with much hillside and moorland undisturbed by habitation. But when they returned to the Royal yacht in Cardiff Docks that night how much had King George V and Queen Mary really seen of the deprivation, poverty and industrial ugliness which existed there? These could all have been hidden by the cheering crowds, the red carpets and abundant decorations. At Dowlais, even the works locomotives gleamed with unaccustomed brightness and cleanliness. There too, the impressive Coal and Steel Arches, which had been erected for the occasion, stood magnificently but gave no indication of the human cost involved in producing their raw materials.[233]

Nothing could, however, lessen the patriotism and pride which was seen in the valleys during the visit and which was mirrored in Trelewis. The pupils of the school had been given a holiday and they, with the villagers, thronged to every possible vantage point to witness the royal journey in the luxurious Taff Vale Railway Directors' carriage. The platforms of the tiny station would have been crammed; bridges over and embankments alongside the line were likewise crowded. One wonders just how much of the royal couple they were able to see and for how long. The likelihood was that the time taken to find a suitable viewing position far exceeded that of the actual view. Nevertheless it would have been a memorable event for all who were there.[234]

During this particular decade the pupils and villagers had also been part of two other royal celebrations. In June, 1902, there had been a week's holiday when preparations were made to mark the coronation of Edward VII. Suitable songs had been learned by the pupils beforehand showing that their singing had not been neglected. However, the actual Coronation Day (June 26th) had to be postponed until August 9th because of the King's appendicitis. The activities for the pupils were not postponed and they enjoyed their planned tea and sports on the 26th. Mr Davies writes that "a pleasant afternoon was spent in the field adjoining the school." It is not recorded whether they had to wait to receive their Coronation Mugs until the coronation had actually taken place. What is certain is that Coronation Mugs were to be prominently displayed on many Welsh dressers. Another was to be added to the collection on June 22nd, 1911, when King George V had been crowned. This time, both pupils and public enjoyed the festivities which included tea, then sports on a neighbouring field. The expenses incurred had been defrayed by public subscription. This was surely a happy time when the whole village came together to rejoice.[235]

A sadder occasion which involved everyone in Trelewis was the death and funeral of William Lewis, its founder and benefactor. The school was closed on 30th April, 1903, the day of the funeral, as a mark of respect to one who had played such an important part in its development. He had served the school in a number of capacities most importantly as Chairman of Managers for a number of years. Mr Davies could, with feeling, express thanks for the "active interest"

William Lewis had always shown in the school since its inception. Many staff, pupils and former pupils would have joined village people in expressions of gratitude and genuine grief for one who had done so much in his lifetime to establish the local community. The importance of William Lewis to the parish of Gelligaer can still be seen today by a visit to St Catwg's Church. His is the most prominent of all the memorials in the Church, situated in the nave, on the wall, just above the lectern. It reads:

'In
Loving Memory of
William Lewis
Bontnewydd
Who died April 26th 1903
Aged 75 years
And of Mary his devoted wife
Who died July 28th 1906
Aged 74 years

William Lewis of Bontnewydd farm, the Lewis who gave his name to Trelewis

The former was Churchwarden and Guardian of this parish for many years, and was one of the Founders of St Mary's Church in the village called after his name - Trelewis

"All things work together for good to them that love God"

This tablet was erected by their 9 sorrowing children'

Such a fitting memorial is not the only one to remain. As long as there is a community bearing the name "Trelewis" there will be a perpetual commemoration of William Lewis.[236]

145

The final section of this survey of John Davies' Headship includes some personal matters mentioned in the Log:

4. CONCLUDING OBSERVATIONS

Mr Davies' attendance record throughout this period was exemplary as there are practically no absences recorded for him except when personal circumstances or professional duties required it. As a stalwart of St Mary's Church he would have been expected to be closely involved in the work and ministry of the Anglican Church in Wales. It is no surprise therefore to see the Managers granting him two days leave of absence in October, 1909, to attend some of the Church Congress meetings held in Swansea. As was usual during a Head's absence, the school was left in charge of the Assistants. Another occasion when this happened was on 13th April, 1911, when, with the permission of the Chief Education Official, he had the afternoon off. He gave no reason or any indication of where he was going or for what purpose.[237]

There were some sadder occasions which required him to leave the school. In early September, 1904, on receiving news of the death of his mother, Jane (aged 76), he was absent for over a week. Further tragedy followed within seven weeks, in October, 1904, when his father, Lewis (aged 78), died suddenly. To have the trauma of sadness and grief in such a short period of time was difficult to bear. Mr Davies' wrote: "This has temporarily quite incapacitated me for work." It was with a heavy heart that he travelled to Lampeter on both occasions. One might have expected a longer absence the second time with the school left in charge of the Assistants. In fact he was to have fewer days off compared with the week he had taken earlier. The Chief Education Official had granted permission for compassionate leave but Mr Davies returned promptly to resume his duties. This was not because he feared that the Assistants were not up top the task of running the school as he remarked that they had got on well in his absence. His strong sense of duty was probably the motivating factor.[238]

A much happier event was to occur on 1st October, 1907. That was the day his daughter, Lizzie Jane, married Thomas William Lewis, the son of the late William Lewis. The "Merthyr Express" reported a "very pretty wedding" held at Gelligaer Parish Church with the ceremony conducted by Rev Edward J Davies of Vaynor, uncle of the bride. The best man was the curate of St Mary's Church. This union of two families, important in the development of the village, was to arouse considerable interest and not a little excitement. Both Lizzie and Thomas were so well known that practically the whole of Trelewis wanted to be involved to wish them well. This was evidenced by the extensive decorations which marked the event. After the wedding reception, the couple left for their honeymoon in Bournemouth.[239] On their return, they took up residence in Coed Ceirios, one of the larger houses in the village, which was just a stone's throw from Tafelwan where John Davies was to live after his retirement. That retirement was going to be precipitated by a gradual deterioration in his health which is described in the Log.

The first indication of this was in April, 1912, when he writes that he was "somewhat unwell." As a result, the class teachers had to take responsibility for the Terminal Examinations. Mr Davies was quick to add that he would verify the results and supplement what had been done after Easter. Apparently Mr Davies' health must have progressively declined in the months following but it is with some surprise that the entry in the Log for 7th February, 1913, reads: "I regret to report that I have been working for some time in impaired health and I have therefore deemed it my duty to send in my resignation which will expire on 31st March." There had been only the briefest inkling recorded above which had given any indication that all was not well. Everything appeared to be fine in the school. The attendance had peaked with every class having the allotted number on the register, with the Standard 1 classroom being "overcrowded." In the very last statement he was to make in the Log on 31st March, 1913, he states that the school reassembled "in good numbers" after the Easter holiday. This was a real improvement on the old pattern of poor attendance after a holiday break. But very much more had changed as a result of his headship.[240]

Mr Davies' valedictory remarks are brief but heart-felt:

"After 31 years of continuous service as Head-Master, I this day, sever my connection with this school voluntarily, though not without much regret, and bid adieu to the present staff and pupils."

March 31st 1913
John Davies

DAN OSBORNE,
TREHARRIS.

As has been seen, in his very first entry in the Log on 11th April, 1882, he was under no illusion that the school needed to improve under his leadership. No one could deny that during his 31 years of dedicated service that had happened. He was to leave the school in better shape than when he found it and it was with a very real sense of loss that pupils, staff and villagers would feel his departure. This account has demonstrated, beyond all doubt, that the objective which John Davies had set himself all those years before had been secured.[241]

Part Five

SALUTING THE ACHIEVEMENT

Part Five SALUTING THE ACHIEVEMENT (1913 - 1942)

1. OF AN HELPFUL EXEMPLAR

To John Bedford Thomas The TASK-CONTINUING Head
(1st April 1913 - 18th November 1933)

It is not intended to give a comprehensive account of the development of Trelewis School under John Davies' successors. What is being attempted is to show how they followed in his footsteps, encountered some of the same problems but also to note some of their distinctive contributions to the life of the school. John Davies had left them over 30 years of accumulated experience in the entries he made in the Log Book. Included there would be helpful precedents to assist them in dealing with most aspects of school life. His was a useful role model to follow and looking back over his entries in the Log could be of great benefit to them. Judging by the headship of his immediate successor, John Bedford Thomas, that was exactly what he did. Like John Davies, he was determined to raise standards in all

John Bedford Thomas in the back yard of the old school house (Photo Courtesy of Kerry Porter, his great granddaughter)

areas and spared no effort in pursuing this outcome. With justice, he can be described as continuing the task which had been established in the preceding 30 years. He introduces himself in these words on April 1st, 1913: "After completing 10 years service as a Certificated Assistant, I was appointed Head Teacher at the last meeting of the Glamorgan Education Committee and commenced my duties as Head Teacher of this school this morning. J Bedford Thomas." Son of a Miners' Agent in the Rhymney Valley, he had been an Assistant at Pontlottyn school before coming to Trelewis.[242]

Speaking at the presentation evening in May, 1913, to mark John Davies' retirement, in his tribute, he gave an articulate sketch of his future intentions. He commented that the work of the teacher was not only to develop the mental faculties of the child but also to prepare him to be a good citizen by equipping him with the requisite qualities. These he listed as: "courage; truthfulness; cleanliness of body and of mind; a love of fair play; gentleness to the weak; self denial; duty to God and neighbours and regularity and punctuality in all things." All of these, he affirmed, John Davies had tried to inculcate in his pupils and he wished to do the same. Though a newcomer to Trelewis, he had known Mr Davies for a number of years and could testify to "his irreproachable character and sterling qualities." Finally, he expressed the hope that his career would be "as long and successful as Mr Davies' had been." At the commencement of his headship, he had recognized his predecessor's worth and given a brief impression of what the character of his tenure was likely to be. He was intent on following in the well-worn footsteps of John Davies.[243] The chronicle which he was to leave behind covered the next 20 years giving him plenty of time to bestow a worthwhile legacy. His narrative of events was to present a detailed picture of what he wished to achieve. Careful and meticulous by nature, his Log often reveals what he thought and felt about the incidents he was recording.

Before the end of his first month in post, he had prepared a new timetable and scheme of work for the Managers' approval. At the beginning of each day, there was to be a cleanliness inspection. He was starting by showing unmistakably the standards he expected. The staff, too, were made aware of what was required to effect improvement in learning. He stressed the importance of making Arithmetic as realistic as possible; he wished there to be a few moral lessons each week and pointed out the value of doing more outdoor work in Geography and Nature lessons. Within two months, he instructed the staff to have shorter, more memorable recitation pieces learned individually without too much simultaneous repetition. Not content with that directive, he also laid down that there should be more readings of "beautiful passages from good authors." At the beginning of his headship, he revealed himself as someone who knew exactly what he wanted to do and where he wanted to go. Weaknesses, whatever they were, had to be corrected. After the first Terminal examinations in July, 1913, he states that "Arithmetic is weak in Standards 5 and 6 and Welsh needs strengthening." The staff were kept fully in the picture of what was required of them.[244]

Mr Thomas was concerned to remedy any defects in the building he had taken over, without delay. When there was an inadequate water supply due to corroded and inadequate water pipes, discovered in June, 1913, he bothered the Chief Education Official, the County Architect, the Gelligaer Medical Officer of Health and the Water Company until something was done. As parents were keeping their children at home, allegedly because there was no water supply, it was important that the matter was dealt with speedily. New water pipes were eventually installed by 12th September, 1913. His tenacity in getting officials to act was seen again in October, 1913. Together with local inhabitants, he was concerned about the deplorable condition of the road separating the Infants' from the Mixed Department. Eventually their protests caused the road to be resurfaced. He also gained success in: getting the stove replaced in Standard 2 classroom because it was emitting smoke and fumes; replacing dangerous loose coping stones on the wall of the boys' playground and having the school rooms painted and coloured. Most of these improvements came within the first 18 months of his headship and demonstrate his determination to get the best for his pupils.[245]

John Davies would have been delighted with Mr Thomas' desire to improve the teaching and learning of Welsh. Staff were urged to a higher standard of efficiency in Welsh lessons in May, 1914. All but one of the staff could teach the language but their teaching required greater energy and enthusiasm. He was to teach the language to Standard 2 himself as the class teacher could not. Complaints that the staff were still not making the effort they should in teaching Welsh continued in 1915, 1917 and 1919. The Log indicates his feelings about this: "It is a great pity that the parents of Welsh extraction are so indolent and indifferent to the work of their native tongue and neglect to speak it on the hearth." This comment made in 1915, together with his castigation of staff in 1917 for their indolent attitude to Welsh lessons, is indicative of his deep love of the language and of his desire to propagate it.[246]

Mr Thomas' intention to promote Welsh culture and his attention to detail are seen in the programme for St David's Day appearing in the Log for 1916 and 1917. The celebration for 1916 was more varied than usual and included: *Addresses* to scholars on patriotism; *Dramatising* incidents such as Caradoc before the Roman Empire, after the Battle of Crecy, and Welsh heroes like Gruffydd ap Rhys and Owain Glyndwr; *Telling* the children the heroic deeds of our Welsh Regiments in the present Great War; *Singing* of Welsh folk songs; *Welsh recitations*; *Reading* the School Roll of Honour; *Making* of laurel wreaths in memory of fallen heroes and old scholars of the school; *Rendering* of God save the King, God bless the Prince of Wales and Hen Wlad fy Nhadau. That provided a full morning of activity with the customary half-holiday in the afternoon. This detailed description provides a real insight into what schools could do to foster a love and commitment to Wales. The programme for 1917 is equally replete and varied. This time the songs and the recitations are listed. They include: Dafydd y Garreg Wen; Ar Hyd y Nos; Ar Dywysog Gwlad y Bryniau; Nant y Mynydd; Drws y Nefoedd, etc. Tableaux on the dragon, the leek and the harp were presented and for the first time there is mention of an eisteddfod for the two upper classes. Similar programmes were to occur in subsequent years: in 1918 there was an addition to incorporate "the doings of our Welsh lads in the Great War"; in 1923 there is yet another innovation, when parents are reported as being present in good numbers and of their being pleased with the various items. The Head was probably hoping to gain more support for Welsh to be used at home. The tradition of inviting parents to the St David's Day celebrations continued for many years and in 1932 a new feature was incorporated: a fancy needlework exhibition by the Senior girls.[247]

The same problems which John Davies and all Head Teachers had were to beset John Bedford Thomas. The most recalcitrant was that of attendance. In his account, Mr Thomas characteristically gives the fullest possible information because he records practically every monthly and annual attendance return during his headship, stating average number on roll, average attendance and its percentage figure. Close co-operation with the Attendance Officer was established right at the start of his headship. In October, 1913, Mr W Yemm, the Attendance Officer, during his weekly visit to the school, was to issue summonses to the parents of 4 pupils in Standard 6 who kept them at home without reasonable excuse. They had been warned previously by Mr Thomas that this action would be taken if they continued to absent themselves. The roll and the percentage attending improved slowly, the roll reaching a high of 290 by August, 1914. By October, 1914, an average attendance of 94.6% was achieved, entitling the school to an attendance half-holiday. It wasn't until November, 1917, that this percentage was to be exceeded with an average of 95.2% from an average roll of 263. The highest number on roll during his headship was 308 in June, 1926, but the average attendance in any year rarely reached 90%. The last monthly return by Mr Thomas was in October, 1933, which listed 256 on roll and an 88.2% attendance. It was a never-ending struggle to keep the attendance figures up.[248]

The causes for absence remained pretty constant whoever was the Head. Mr Thomas' account closely parallels that of John Davies. His words almost echo those of the latter whenever he comments on the reasons for poor attendance. After a holiday, it took some time for attendance to pick up. There are many instances which could be cited. For example, in September, 1913, on the first day of the Autumn term, only 172 pupils registered in the morning and 136 in the afternoon from a roll of 282. The same thing is reported on the first day of the Autumn Term in September, 1916, when Mr Thomas complained that attendance was poor because many pupils had not returned from North Wales and elsewhere, while others were absent picking blackberries. Friday afternoons were also popular for absentees as was the day before any holiday This was confirmed by Mr Thomas writing: "It is the custom for a large number of scholars to absent themselves from school on the last session before a vacation. This practice is evidently condoned by parents and it should be stopped." For many years, the Whit holiday and the delights of Quaker's Yard fair had increased truancy. The Board of Education, in its wisdom, decreed in 1916, that there should only be one day's holiday on Whit Monday. On Whit Tuesday that year, there were only 207 pupils who arrived in school causing Mr Thomas to declare "The poor attendance will undoubtedly continue this week and the decision to keep the schools open.... is hardly a wise one." John Davies had made a similar statement for the same reason, years earlier.[249]

The frustrations of Mr Thomas concerning absenteeism consistently appear in his entries. Despite regular warnings to parents and pupils he declares: "A large number of parents will persist in keeping their children at home for the most trivial excuses. I am afraid the issuing of a few summonses is the only remedy to bring some people to a proper perspective in this matter." Two years later, he is still complaining of pupils digging potatoes on their parents' allotments during school time. He reported them to the Attendance Officer as "there is abundant time after school to do this work." Holidays were still being given for Band of Hope and Church outings, for teas and celebrations at the Non-Conformist Chapels and St Mary's Church. These provoked a similar reaction to that of John Davies earlier, when Mr Thomas says, with feeling: "These events will have to be held during the summer vacation." His views on these holidays were to continue for some time as he repeated requests for such outings to be held on the same day or outside school time. But continue they did, as previously.[250]

Absence due to sickness is excusable and, there were plenty of cases between 1913 and 1918. The usual array of infectious diseases are recorded: mumps, measles, diphtheria and scarlet fever. (For the first time the Log reports pupils suffering from scarlet fever being removed to the isolation hospital.) Other illnesses also appear including ringworm, St Vitus Dance, rheumatism and scabies. Then in July, 1918, there is an ominous mention of a "new disease, Spanish influenza." This was to decimate attendance of pupils and staff when it reached epidemic proportions. Its effects were to multiply, causing such things as terminal examinations to be cancelled. After some respite, it re-appeared in November, 1918, when over 100 pupils were laid low by it. Even the Attendance Officer succumbed and was off duty for 5 weeks. No wonder the attendance for the academic year ending March 31st, 1919, was the lowest for 5 years. The same repetition of illnesses affecting attendance continued thereafter with other additions such as eczema and croup.[251]

Weather conditions were the other unavoidable feature. Fierce snowstorms, blizzards and torrential rain caused the usual disruption. The school was flooded on 2 occasions in 1914, causing pupils to be dismissed for the day. Snow being driven into classrooms making them very wet; roads being impassable, making it difficult for pupils and staff to attend, caused the inevitable closure for poor attendance in winter months. Despite all these hindrances to good attendance, there were at least 3 times in 1917 when the school gained an attendance holiday because the attendance was over 95%. All credit to Mr Thomas for chipping away at a problem which every other Head had found intractable. He was also concerned when the Registers of the school were not being checked by a School Manager. This happened when Mr Jonah Evans, (previously punctilious in this duty), failed to gain a seat resulting in there being 2 Managers from Bedlinog but not one from Trelewis. Mr Thomas fulminated: "This work is being neglected" as registers were not inspected for some terms. Slowly there was an improvement particularly when Jonah Evans was re-elected and resumed his previous role. Registers, as has been seen, were important for school efficiency, and Mr Thomas wished to achieve a high standard. He made sure too, that Attendance Awards of books and certificates continued to be awarded. Like John Davies before him, parents were warmly encouraged to be present and they came in good numbers. Councillor George Street, who became one of the Managers, regularly monitored Registers and presented the prizes in 1924.[252]

When pupils returned to school after the Summer holiday in 1914, the First World War was nearly a month old. How strange that this major event which was to affect every one in the village for the next few years received so few references in the Log. This contrasts markedly with the Second World War when there are whole swathes of entries connected with the war, mostly listing Air Raid Warnings. The first mention of the war seems to occur in the HMI Report of October, 1914, when Mr W Edwards states that the children "take a keen interest in the progress of the present war." The Log gives very little indication of this as there are such infrequent references. There were items referring to the war included in the St David's Day programmes for 1916 and 1918 such as recounting the heroic deeds of the Welsh Regiments at the front. Education was bound to be impaired by the advent of the war. Teachers and educational administrators were to join in the rush to enlist for their country taking with them their expertise. A male member of staff, Mr J C Williams, is recorded as leaving for war service in December, 1914, after 7 years on the staff. (The school was then short of 2 male Assistants. As there were delays in appointments, there was no teacher to take Standard 4 at the start of 1915). Thankfully, Mr Williams returned fit and well to resume his duties in June, 1919. There is also a brief reference to the war affecting the attendance of pupils in Standard 7 in June, 1918. Those over the age of 13 could claim War Exemption Leaving, which according to Mr Thomas, made them "very indifferent to their attendance." Probably the most gratifying entry for pupils was the granting of a holiday from 13th-18th of November, 1918, to celebrate the Armistice.[253]

There are a number of new features which were introduced into the school during J B Thomas' headship. These include: identifying children who had defective vision, in medical inspections; the beginning of diagnosing what would now be called Special Needs when two names are listed of children "who are mentally defective and incapable of receiving proper benefit from the instruction imparted to the scholars." It needs to be said that identification is one thing; making suitable provision quite another. Socially, school trips

157

now become a more regular part of the summer term programme even to such distant places as Windsor and Clifton Zoo. Over 100 pupils attended an historical pageant at Cardiff Castle just as others had done in John Davies's time. In response to the HMI report for 1914, Mr Thomas started a circulating library for the Upper Standards. Each pupil was to contribute one penny per week until a sum of nine pence or one shilling was raised and a book would be purchased for the Library. When the pupil left, he could retain the book he had purchased or leave it in the Library. This self-help principle was a novel way of producing a library exceeding the attempt which John Davies had made earlier. Sporting success was gained by the School football team which, in October, 1932, won the challenge cup in a tournament sponsored by Trelewis AFC. This was the second trophy to be won by the team that year and speaks well of the skills of the pupils and of the good training they were receiving from staff.[254]

There are very few references to discipline in the Log for these years. One interesting entry is found in 1918. Mr Thomas had reprimanded 3 girls "for twitting another little girl." Next day, they were absent from school and he found out that their father had taken them to Nelson National School, where they had been admitted by the Head, Mr John Jenkins. Immediately, Mr Thomas wrote to Mr Jenkins explaining the circumstances and asking for the pupils to be sent back to Trelewis school. This Mr Jenkins refused to do stating that he had no right to refuse admission to any children whose parents wished them to attend his school, no matter where they lived. J B Thomas could not leave the matter there as he considered that the discipline of the school would be adversely affected if pupils could transfer at will to another school after being reprimanded or punished. So he wrote to the Chief Education Official asking for his observations. As nothing further appears in the school records, one assumes that the girls remained at Nelson National School and Mr Thomas' valid objections were ignored.[255]

Encouragement was given to staff to advance themselves as it was in John Davies' day. There are several reports of staff being short-listed for headships and some gaining promotion. Amongst these were Mr J C Williams who was appointed Head of Bargoed South Boys' School in December, 1922 and Miss Ceridwen Evans, who became Head of Bedlinog Girls' School in 1924. Both had given faithful and valuable service in excess of a dozen years at Trelewis. Pupils, too, are feted in the Log for their successes in the County Scholarship examinations. Early in his headship, there were rarely more than 8 entrants and the numbers passing both Part 1 and Part 2 of the examination were equally small. But as time went on numbers entering and being successful increased. Admission to Hengoed and Pengam County Schools was joined by admission to "Bargoed New Secondary School" in the 1920 account, the first time this school appears in the Log. All the Head Teachers after John Davies were keen on maximising the achievements of their pupils and the Scholarship examination provided a useful benchmark to estimate progress. Mr Thomas was keenly aware of any impediments to pupils' advancement. In March, 1918, he complains vehemently that the year's work had to be done in 9 months as the LEA had decided to end the educational year in March instead of July. John Davies had encountered a similar situation previously and his reaction was identical.[256]

The best, clearest and most objective estimate of J B Thomas' success as a Head and of his contribution to the life of the school is to be found in HMI Reports. Included in the visits of HMI's, and County Inspectors, there are 3 HMI Reports which are written up. The first, made by W Edwards after his visit in October, 1914, gives a full and frank evaluation of what had been accomplished in Mr Thomas's first year. It starts with a most pleasing commendation: "Under the new Master, the year's work has been vigorously started and there is every prospect that a good level of efficiency will be attained." There is praise for: arithmetic being intelligently taught; oral reading being very satisfactory; composition and penmanship efficiently practised; recitations rendered in a pleasing manner; good progress being made in Brushwork Drawing, which had recently been introduced; needlework being on useful lines; raffia work for junior girls and

159

paper modelling for Junior boys; improvements in physical exercises which had been called for by an earlier visit of a Sub-inspector. These far outweigh the aspects which Mr Edwards wished to see improved. He pointed out: the school did not have a library and was scantily supplied with supplementary readers; the requirement of dictionaries for Standard 2 and more poetry books, contour maps and atlases for the senior classes; more attention to spelling in some classes; eradicating the simultaneous answering of questions by pupils; and gaining more general responses to oral questions rather than addressing them to the brighter children. He describes the discipline as being "genial" and praises the general environment for learning in classrooms which had been recently re-decorated. Praise was given to the way that Mr Thomas was trying to improve the knowledge of Welsh. Mr Edwards acknowledged that while the prevailing speech of the school was English, fair progress was being made in Welsh conversational lessons.[257]

This Report, signed by Frank T James, Clerk to the Gelligaer Group Managers, gave rise to much optimism of what could be achieved by a dedicated Head like J B Thomas. Most of the criticisms were directed at the provision of materials which he sought to address immediately. His novel way of trying to provide a school library speedily, has already been noted. But he found officialdom much slower to provide the financial resources required. Ever since he took over the school, he had been pressing for more money to be spent on books and apparatus only to meet with a negative response from the relevant authority. His frustration is revealed in his reaction in October, 1915, when the Clerk told him that his requisition of supplies must be considerably reduced. He says "This is to be deplored!" so eager was he to replenish a good stock of new readers as Mr Edwards had wished. Further delays in requisitions being met were to occur later which displeased John Bedford Thomas. He not only wished to create a pleasant school environment, he wanted the wherewithal to achieve sound teaching and learning.[258]

The next HMI Report, made by HMI Mr H Price, following his inspection on 28th June, 1922, is a most encouraging account of consistent progress. He writes: "There is evidence that the Head Teacher exercises careful supervision and that the teachers discharge their duties in a very conscientious manner. The teaching is calculated to promote accurate thinking and correct expression. The scholars are encouraged to read on their own account and careful record is kept of the books read by the children in the top class. The composition exercises show a wide range of ideas and the efforts of the children are carefully corrected by the teacher." Praise continues for map drawing reading, recitation and arithmetic while brush drawing receives special commendation. Weaknesses of the previous Report appear to have been corrected as the school now has adequate supplies of wall maps and atlases. J B Thomas' pressure had the required effect, or it may be that the ending of warfare had improved supplies. The only negative comment which needed attention was that handwriting could be improved in some classes. The other negatives concerned the building: plugs were needed in girls' lavatories where some outlet pipes were also blocked; two new taps were required to replace broken ones. For anyone who cared to look, Mr Thomas was continuing to assure the school's progress. The Managers would have been delighted.[259]

The final HMI Report on Mr Thomas' headship, recorded in the Log, is for the inspection of Mr Price again, on 5th January, 1926. This confirms his previous findings for there was ample evidence of creditable progress. The English composition of the Upper Standards revealed "careful teaching, judicious supervision and sensible choice of work." Standard 5 was well taught with clear indications of conscientious, systematic teaching, "beneficent control and general sense of orderliness." The school was praised for its tone, sound organisation and intelligent teaching methods and useful, candid reports which were issued every term for each class. Weaknesses were found in Standard 4 "despite the competent and consistent efforts of their teacher." This was put down to the class containing a number of "oldish boys and girls who are not very bright." Matters to be corrected included: improving fluency and expression of boys' reading; training in the use of dictionaries; an immediate order of rulers and set-squares to enable geometrical drawing to be taught. The development of the school under Mr Thomas had won the approbation of HMI and he can be well pleased with what he accomplished.[260]

At the conclusion of this documentation of his headship, it is important to notice the very real stresses and strains which afflicted him during his years of service. This again mirrors what John Davies had also experienced. In April, 1915, he was absent from school for the funeral of his mother, always a debilitating event. Then in April, 1917, he attended the funeral of Lieutenant Hugh Howells, Royal Flying Corps, at Rhymney Bridge. Lieut. Howells had met with a fatal accident while flying in "an eastern County," one of the countless tragedies of the 1914-18 War. Personal affliction escalated for him in the Log of the 1920's, starting with the funeral of his aunt in December, 1922. Next May, he had to take his wife to Cardiff to "see a specialist about her throat." Worse was to follow. Mrs Thomas was taken to Guy's Hospital, London, for "a very severe operation" causing him to be absent from June 25th - July 2nd, 1923. With a serious deterioration in Mrs Thomas' condition, he was again detained in Guy's Hospital during the first fortnight of November. Unusually for him, the entry for November 22nd - November 27th, 1923, is one of the shortest he makes: "Absent from duties - death and burial of Mrs Thomas." John Davies would readily have empathised with the sadness and despair Mr Thomas must have felt on the loss of his wife, for he too had gone through the same process.[261]

The school did not suffer at all as a result of these personal tragedies, as the 1926 HMI report shows. Like John Davies before him, Mr Thomas overcomes his sorrow with his commitment to advance the school. The sound progress which had been seen in the past continues. Inevitably, it was at some cost to himself that this happened. By the 1930's he begins to succumb to illness, albeit unspecified. During a long period of absence from February to June, 1933, Mr Ben Griffiths had to take charge of the school. Mr Griffiths himself was ill for about a month at this time and Mr I T Jones took over. Even when Mr Thomas returned, he was still not fully fit and illness forced him to leave the school again on 1st November, 1933. This time it was really serious and it was with a heavy heart that Mr Griffiths writes on 20th November, 1933: "It is with the deepest regret that I have to record the death of the Head Teacher, Mr John Bedford Thomas on Saturday last, 18th November, 1933." There were to be many who were to share the regret of losing someone, at the comparatively young age of 52, who had done so much for the school and the village. During his residency at Trelewis, he had taken a leading part in the religious and social life of the community. He was a Deacon, Sunday School Superintendent at Trinity Baptist Chapel and one of the pioneers of Trelewis Welfare Association being its first Secretary. Like John Davies before him, he had a strong Christian faith and he expressed it in a life of service.[262]

At J B Thomas's funeral held in Trinity Baptist Chapel on 22nd November, 1933, streets were thronged with people wishing to pay their respect and "every blind in the village was drawn in token of silent sympathy." For the short distance between School House and the Chapel, two long lines of senior schoolboys took up their positions. In the School yard, the remaining pupils and their teachers stood silently. The service at his home and in the Chapel was led by the Pastor of Trinity assisted by local ministers. Eloquent tributes to the many fine qualities in his life were made by the clergy and, appropriately, by John Davies. Then the funeral cortege proceeded to Cefn Hengoed historic Baptist Churchyard, and was led, as far as the Shinrig, by school children. Trelewis Mixed School was honouring one who had served it well. John Bedford Thomas was its first Head to die in service. Hopefully, he would be the last.[263]

To Benjamin M Griffiths   The TWICE ACTING Head
(1st November 1933 - 26th February 1934 and 1st August 1940 - 23rd November 1940)

There were two interregnums when Mr B M Griffiths had to take control of the school as Acting Head while waiting for the substantive Head to arrive. Practically the whole of Mr Griffith's career was spent

163

in Trelewis School. He was admitted as a pupil on 11th April, 1910;[264] in July, 1915, the school was notified of his success in the County School Scholarship; on 6th September, 1920, he joined the staff as a student teacher and left for college on 31st August, 1921, after completing his apprenticeship. As a member of the County Supply Staff, he took up temporary duties at Trelewis on 1st April, 1927, and was appointed to the permanent staff on 1st May in that year.[265] A popular, hardworking member of staff, he gained advancement and recognition without having to go elsewhere. Eventually, it was he who was left in charge of the school during the temporary absences of the Head. This happened during the last illnesses of Mr J B Thomas from February, 1933. However, as indicated above, Mr Griffiths was ill himself for almost a month from March to April and Mr I T Jones took over. It wasn't until June, 1933, that Mr Thomas was to return from his long illness. On 1st November, 1933, he was absent, sick again and, this time, he was not to return. In that month Mr Griffiths then took over as Acting Head until the appointment of Mr D M Davies on 26 February, 1934.[266] Most of the Log for this period is given over to routine matters such as absence of staff, recorded neatly and precisely.

The second occasion when Mr Griffiths took over as Acting Head was after the summer holiday, following the resignation of Mr D M Davies on 31st July, 1940. This was in the early days of the war and the Log, this time, consists of copious entries of air raid warnings. From August to November, 1940, he records no less than 26 warnings when the school had to be dispersed. The longest duration was for over an hour, and the shortest was 15 minutes. The procedure, devised by the school, was for pupils who lived furthest from the school to be paired with those who lived nearest. When the fearsome wailing of the siren sounded, the pair rushed out of school to shelter in the nearby home. The more comforting sound of the all-clear was supposed to signal a prompt return to school. That is not to say that many found excuses to delay their return or just dawdled! Imagine the disruption to education caused by these continuous interruptions. The staff were probably more frustrated by such disturbances than the pupils were. The latter, when they realised that there was no need to be frightened, began to welcome the diversion.[267]

Amongst other references to the war, Mr Griffiths records a member of staff, Mr H S White, leaving for military service in November, 1940 and a visit from Mr D Jenkins, HMI, to gain information about evacuees who were increasingly being housed in the village. What a difference occurred in the Second World War compared with the First. The 1914-18 War gained very few references in the Log Book but the 1939-45 Log is filled with them. Total war was to affect everyone, young and old alike; all were drawn into its orbit. There was no escaping it. Mr Griffiths' other entries were mostly routine including medical inspections, holiday for unveiling of memorial to a local M.P. and staff absences. He kept things decently and in order for the new Head, Mr W Adams Jones. In fact, such was his popularity, that there were many parents disappointed that Mr Griffiths had not been appointed Head permanently.[268]

To D M Davies   The BRIEFLY-WRITING Head
(26th February 1934 - 31st July 1940)

Of all the Head Teachers who contributed to the Log, the one whose entries are the briefest is Mr D M Davies. His very first entry is typical: it simply records him becoming Head on 26th February, 1934, and that is all. There is no introductory statement giving any details of his background or experience, as was usual. Then, in his early entries, he took to leaving a blank line between them which only served to emphasise how brief they were. Because of his brevity, the picture he gives of the school is not as informative as it could be, but it does include some innovative features. For the first time there is mention of: a fire drill in 1936 (with the method of alarm described as unsatisfactory); inspection by the School Dentist in 1937; swimming instruction for the boys at Edwardsville baths in 1939 and for girls in 1940. It also appears that the School Trip had now become a well-established feature of the Summer Term with visits to places like Oxford in 1934; to Cheddar caves in 1936; to Bristol in 1939. More locally, there was a visit to see the SS Doric at Newport in 1935 and visits to School camps at Pembrey, Pendine, Gileston, Rhoose, Ogmore by Sea, (sometimes of a fortnight's duration), began annually in 1935. These latter were to be enjoyed separately by both boys and girls, with some also attending Winter Schools at Rhoose. Residential experiences of this nature, in school time, were to be a highlight for many Glamorgan pupils. Interestingly, the member of staff who accompanied them was replaced with a temporary teacher. As the number of pupils taken away was usually quite small, this meant that those remaining in school did not suffer.[269]

The tradition of celebrating St David's Day was expanded by Mr Davies. For the week following, lessons were to be devoted to "Wales and the Welsh people." This began in 1935, and continued the following year. Royal events gave rise to half holidays, one on 18th November, 1936, because of Edward VIII's visit to the locality, the other on 11th May, 1937, to celebrate the coronation of King George VI and Queen Elizabeth. Pupils were given a tea party and proudly took home with them coronation mugs and other mementoes which were kept for many years to come. (The Log does not mention this - but those that received them remember!) School concerts were given over two nights in January and December, 1937. An end of term Christmas Party is recorded annually even in December, 1939, after the war had started. There is also mention of an Armistice service being held on 11th November in 1937 and 1938, but not in 1939. Perhaps war with Germany made it inappropriate.[270]

The Second World War was to have a much greater impact on pupils and far more prominence in the Log than the 1914-18 War. On 4th September, 1939, at the end of the Summer holiday, Mr Davies writes: "Owing to outbreak of war between GB and Germany, the school which should have re-opened today remains closed for an indefinite period." A week later it did open. Within days, the first Dispersal Drill was held which was to become standard practice during air raid warnings, as described previously. Drill practice was repeated three times in May, 1940 and the very first real Air Raid Warning requiring dispersal occurred on 15th July, 1940. In all, there were 5 such dispersals before the end of July but fortunately three of them happened towards the end of afternoon school so there was no significant interruption to lessons. There were to be more incidents which brought home the reality of war to the school. An ARP Depot and First Aid Post had to be set up in the Standard 7 classroom, but because of pressure on space it was soon transferred to the Infants' Department. In November, 1939, afternoon school was to begin at 1.00 p.m. instead of 1.30 p.m. with closure at 3.30 p.m. This enabled pupils to go home in daylight and also saved on electricity and fuel. The emergency situation caused by the war was to require even more savings to be made. Pupils would not have been pleased in May, 1940, when their Whit holiday was cancelled "because of the German invasion of the Low Countries" according to the Log. Some marked their displeasure by absenting themselves, only158 turning up out of 189.

The School roll was to increase significantly by the addition of evacuees seeking shelter in the seemingly less threatened village of Trelewis. In the first month of the war, the school had received instructions for the incorporation of evacuated children in school registers. Just over 8 months later, on 3rd June, 1940, the first evacuees arrived, 45 boys from Broadway Junior School, Sheerness, Kent, with two members of staff. 5 more pupils joined them before the end of the month. Already the official circular which said that no more than 40 evacuees were to be admitted had been exceeded and the number was destined to grow further. The coming of evacuees was to create additional problems for the school. They had to be integrated harmoniously with the existing pupils, not an easy matter when there were so many differences between them in things like background, accent and experience. Assimilating them into a completely new environment as well as providing efficient continuity for their education was to present quite a challenge. Practical matters such as finding neighbouring houses where the evacuees could shelter during air raids added to the problem. Mr Davies, however, only had to contend with this situation for one month, before he left the school at the end of July.[271]

Prior to his account of the outbreak of war and its impact, Mr Davies provides details of his concern for the building. Soon after his appointment as Head, he got the County Architect to visit the school to see the poor state of the Yard and the walls, together with the defective weather board on the girls' lavatories. When Mr Jenkins, HMI, called in March, 1935, he too was made aware of structural defects, (windows in Standard 5 room and ceiling in Standard 3 room). Mr Davies wished to have the building properly maintained and was prepared to keep up pressure for this to happen.[272] In his first monthly return on attendance in April, 1934, he records a school roll of 235 with a 92.8% average attendance. This had increased to 94% within a month, the best recorded during his Headship. By the annual return for 1939, the average number on roll had fallen to 171.4, with an average attendance of 90.9%. Illness and weather were indicated as being the main causes for poor attendance. The illnesses recorded were influenza, tonsillitis, measles, scarlet fever and diphtheria. He also states that poor attendance towards the end of term in December, 1939, was due to "shopping expeditions." Winter weather in January/February, 1940, caused attendance to fall to 78.8%, with lavatories frozen. Water was only able to be restored for hand washing. Things did not change very much for attendance no matter who was Head![273]

Because of the absence of detail in his Log, it is difficult to gain a composite picture of the quality of education which was provided. There is very little reference to curricular matters or to the pupils' progress. On one occasion, in 1936, he comments on the weakness of arithmetic in the lower Standards, but very little else. He records pupils' successes in the County Scholarship examination with his customary brevity. Six pupils gained places at Pengam and Hengoed in 1936 and two for the Bargoed Technical Institute. In 1937, eleven out of 24 were successful while in 1938 and also in 1939 there were 15 out of 22 who gained places. These were commendable results and Mr Davies' comments could have been more extravagant.[274] For the most reliable appraisal of his headship, the HMI Report for 1939 provides valid evidence. Although there were a number of visits of HMI's,

County Inspectors and Organisers during his tenure, this is the only formal Report to be found in the Log. Most of the other visits appear as statements with little other information.

On 7th March, 1939, Mr A G Prys Jones, HMI, made a two day inspection. He corroborated Mr Davies' finding that Arithmetic was the chief weakness with many pupils failing to work out simple problems. On the other hand, he noted that there had been a good start to simple Algebra in the top class. He also asked for there to be more variety in the subjects for English composition. There was a good report on: the correlation of Geography and History in the Upper Standards; fluent and clear reading (except in a few cases of "retarded children"); and the introduction of Bookbinding to Handwork lessons. He commented on the variation in the "calibre of children" from class to class but praised the "unusually large number of pupils" who gained admission to secondary schools the previous year. Describing the premises, he notes that there were 6 classrooms but no Hall, with accommodation for 258. While the structure was in good repair, there had been no re-decoration for some years and ventilation was poor, requiring new windows to be installed. His visit resulted in windows being replaced in September, 1939 and anthracite stoves being installed in 4 classrooms, replacing 1 coke-burning stove and 3 open fires. HMI Reports still had the power to effect improvements.[275]

Mr Prys Jones makes a telling remark about the School roll, pointing out that there had been a decline of about 100 in the past decade as the 1939 enrolment was only 171. The years of depression and industrial conflict had very obviously taken their toll on the population of the village. Many must have left for pastures new to have caused such a decline in the numbers attending Trelewis School. Turning to the quality of the education they were receiving, Mr Jones describes it as "commendably good." The Head and the 6 Assistant Teachers, (4 of them certificated), "all work harmoniously together." Schemes of work have been thoughtfully drawn up and the Head Teacher's reports on the progress made in all subjects are "thorough and helpful." So, while his Log might keep us in the dark because of its paucity of information, Mr Davies more than makes up for the deficiency in his written reports to others. He was to receive the following accolades from HMI: "Appointed 5 years ago, he carries out duties zealously and efficiently; he has done much to infuse fresh vigour into the life of the school." That is a praiseworthy description of a Head Teacher's role. Mr Davies had not only continued the tradition which John Davies had established but enhanced it.[276]

Frank T James, Clerk to the Gelligaer School Managers, was to sign this copy of the HMI Report in the Log on 3rd May, 1939. Whether its complimentary nature was to encourage Mr Davies to seek further advance in Headship is not clear. The fact is that, within two months, he had applied for and gained a Headship elsewhere, possibly of a larger school. It was on 31st July, 1939, that he made his final entry in the Log: "Having been transferred to Hendre Junior Mixed School, Caerphilly, I cease active duties in this school today, the last school day of the term. My transfer takes place as from August 19th next." He ends with this brief, valedictory statement confirming the title which was bestowed on him at the start of this account.[277] Before he left, the School gave presents to Mr Davies showing its appreciation for what he had done. Mr Ivor Davies, on behalf of the staff, presented him with a volume of Rupert Brookes' poems. The Senior Girl added to his reading material by presenting him with books by G K Chesterton and Thomas Hardy. The Sheerness Teaching Staff gave him a Writing Case. The Head of the Sheerness School then thanked Mr Davies, warmly, for his kindness to the evacuees and wished him every success in his new sphere. With these expressions of thanks and gratitude, D M Davies was to leave Trelewis and Mr B M Griffiths, for the second time, became Acting Head at the start of the Autumn Term.[278]

To W Adams Jones   The LOG-CONCLUDING Head
(25th November 1940 - 19??[279])

The school had to wait until 25th November, 1940, for a new Head to succeed Mr D M Davies. His first entry is even briefer than that of his predecessor: "I commenced duties as Head Teacher today. W Adams

Jones." It was he who was to record in the Log the death of John Davies in 1942. He also concluded the second Log Book of the school in 1947, the last of Trelewis School Log Books to be deposited in Glamorgan Archives. It is this feature of his Headship which has led to the above appellation. The other unique aspect of his entries in the Log is his tiny handwriting, certainly the smallest of all the Head Teachers. Neatly and precisely, he continues to chronicle the early war years and the increasing ramifications on the school. There were two air raid warnings on the very first day of his headship and they continued apace. Five occurred in December, 1940, one of them at 12.05 p.m. causing him to detain all those children who had their lunch at school. In 1941, there was one dispersal needed in January (on a very snowy day), one in February, three in March, and then a gap until three warnings in July. The war disrupted education and children were constantly reminded of it. Evacuees continued to arrive in Trelewis from Birmingham and from Cardiff. On 20th February, 1941, 20 girls from Tinkers' Green School, Birmingham, (2 Infants, 4 Juniors and 14 Seniors), were admitted and took over the Standard 7 classroom. How young some of these evacuees were to be leaving parents and home for a completely new life amongst strangers. In June, 1941, 27 evacuees from Cardiff (15 boys, 10 girls and 2 Infants) were admitted. These were absorbed into classes according to age. With the threat of bombing on Cardiff, there was the promise of safety not too far away, further up the valley.[280]

The school had to make the necessary provision for their education. On 27th February, 1941, Mr A Jenkins, HMI, came to discuss the consequences of the school receiving evacuees. This was followed, pretty promptly, by a visit from the Director of Education himself, (the first time that title has appeared in the Log), to look at the accommodation. He was to give instructions for Standard 2 to use the First Aid post classroom in the Infants' Department after adjustments had been made to the room. By the 24th March, 1941, the transfer had been made. Other aspects which affected evacuees were: the immunisation of those from Sheerness in December, 1940, and January, 1941; arrangements for the playground and the school to be left open for the use of evacuees in the Easter, Whitsun, and Summer holidays, 1941. The new experiences which befell them were not always propitious. In March, 1941, one of the Kent evacuees, while playing after school, fell into the water in the nearby quarry. He was rescued by some men working in the local allotment, given artificial respiration and rushed to Merthyr General Hospital in a critical condition where his condition improved. That quarry had claimed the lives of other youngsters previously and was to do so again. In July of the same year, another of the Sheerness pupils broke his leg while playing after school and was taken to Merthyr Hospital. Trelewis might escape the bombing but there were other dangers for the unwary.[281]

The attendance figures for evacuees were to be better than those of the indigenous pupils. In the first annual return which Mr Adams Jones submitted in April, 1941, evacuees were shown as having a 92% attendance while Glamorgan pupils had 88.9%. The average number on roll was 191 for Glamorgan pupils and 51 for evacuees. Whether that trend was to continue is not discernible. Weather conditions still adversely affected attendance. Heavy snowfall during January, 1941, took its toll. The bus service was suspended and trains were delayed causing 2 staff to be late in arriving. No milk was delivered because of the conditions. In October, 1941, 4 out of the 6 classrooms were flooded because of an unusually violent thunderstorm and the school had to be closed for the day. Heavy rain and thunder and lightning in November, 1941, meant that electric light had to be used for morning sessions for a week. The heavy rain caused pupils to stay in school at lunch time and the staff organised impromptu singing. Such extra-curricular activity had not been recorded previously. Snow and ice in January and February, 1942, made the playground dangerous for some days. Pupils were always ready to test their prowess at sliding as far as they could and as fast as they could over the ice. Lavatory tanks also froze over and pupils were warned not to use them - except in dire emergency![282]

Sickness was the other inhibitor of attendance: epidemics of influenza which also affected staff, diphtheria and chicken pox, are all recorded. Nurse Evans continued to inspect the children at regular intervals and she found cases of scabies and impetigo. Pupils still discovered their own reasons for non or late attendance as was seen in May, 1941, when there were a large number of morning absences following the change to Summer time. Normal routine was continued as far as possible, though as has been shown, the war led to plenty of diversions. Pupils were encouraged to participate in National Savings for the war effort. The sum of £75.1.7½ was raised for the Gelligaer Area War Weapons week in April, 1941. The savings habit grew in the school and, almost a year later, in February, 1942, the magnificent sum of £450 was collected for the Gelligaer Area Warship week. This far exceeded the target figure the school had set. The war intruded in other ways on the life of the school. Netting was placed over the school windows in May, 1941, to protect against splintering glass; the ARP room was supplied with a stirrup pump, storm lantern, 2 two tier bunks, 4 mattresses, 24 blankets, 3 torches, 3 spare batteries and 5 steel helmets. Seeing all this largesse bemused pupils if they ever went to the ARP room and confirmed that the tentacles of war could reach even this small village.[283]

The St David's Day celebration was held in the Church Hall in 1941, possibly a new venue. The programme consisted of: plays by the senior classes; choral singing and individual competitions adjudicated by the staff. Competing before one's peers from the stage of the village hall was to be a different and exciting, though nerve-racking experience for those who participated. It would be interesting to know what the evacuees made of this demonstration of national identity. They, together with the whole school, listened to Mr Griffiths delivering an address on St David and the Log states that "the celebration proved edifying and entertaining." All would have enjoyed the traditional half-holiday which followed. Having joined in their first recognition of a patron saint, the evacuees might have wished there had been more acknowledgement of St George in their schools back in England. There were other interruptions to the usual lessons. Prior to the Easter holiday, in April, 1941, the pupils received, as a treat, a Film Exhibition on the growth of the cocoa bean in West Africa. How many of them considered it a pleasure remains questionable. More to their liking would have been the resumption of swimming instruction for senior girls and boys in the Summer Term.[284]

The war did not interrupt the celebration of Christmas in 1940. The end of term Christmas party was held in the Church Hall. It is interesting to find the school utilising the Church Hall increasingly for its activities. The lack of a school hall was compensated for by this local provision. John Davies, whose efforts had led to the erection of the Church Hall, would have been delighted to see it being used for the benefit of pupils at Trelewis School. The Log does not mention a Christmas party in December, 1941. Instead it describes a carol concert being held with individual items being given by pupils and staff. At its conclusion, every child was presented with two new three-penny pieces, one from Mr Joshua Harries, the local grocer, and one from the staff.[285]

Mr Joshua Harries was an increasingly important figure in the village. Owner of the Gwalia Stores Grocers, children were amazed when they visited it to see its then, ultra-modern system of conveying cash for purchases to a central cash desk. They gazed, in wonder, as small receptacles containing their money were dispatched effortlessly on overhead wires with any change being returned in similar fashion. If Mr Harries could afford such an expensive contraption for his store, he could certainly afford the three-penny pieces they received from him. This was not the only time that children received presents from the school at Christmas time, although it is the only one recorded in the Log. Maggie Pryce Jones, a former pupil, mentions at least two previous occasions when this happened. The first was during the hardship of the inter-union strife of the 1930's when Mr Griffiths, seeing the lack of money for Christmas, asked if the children would like to make calendars as presents. The children were delighted that they had a gift to offer their parents in such straitened times. Some years later, Maggie describes how her brother Davy and pupils at the school received gifts at Christmas of balloons, balls, pencil sets and a little brooch. It was that brooch which she gratefully received from him as her present. These may have been small gestures by the school but they were of enormous worth to the pupils who received them.[286]

In the period up to the death of John Davies, there is not much recorded by Mr Adams Jones of curricular developments at the school. Though there were again visits by HMI and County Inspectors, there is no HMI Report on the school at this time. He does record the success of 6 boys gaining places in the 1941 scholarship examination for Pengam, 4 girls for Hengoed, 1 boy and 2 girls for Bargoed and 2 boys for the Junior Technical School, out of the 18 pupils who sat. The sound traditions established by John Davies, J B Thomas and D M Davies were being continued despite the vicissitudes of war. On 26th February, 1942, W Adams Jones writes: "Mr John Davies, a former Headmaster of the school, passed away yesterday at the age of 91. A letter of sympathy is being addressed to relatives." This almost concludes the survey of the work done by his successors at Trelewis school although Mr Adams Jones was to continue as Head for over a decade longer. All of them had a worthy exemplar to follow and none of them would have disappointed John Davies. One can think of the great pleasure John Davies revealed when recounting the successes and achievements of his daughter, Lizzie Jane, in the Log. The same pride can be seen in the Log for 7th June, 1943, in the results of the County Entrance examination: "Of the 17 entrants, 16, (9 girls and 7 boys) have secured places in the secondary schools. The school for the first time, secured top place in the Gelligaer Area. This honour was secured by 10 year old David Adams Jones, who obtained 284 marks out of a possible 300. The 4th, 10th and 13th places were also filled by the school." This was a vintage year and heading the list was David Adams Jones, the Head's son, who went on to a distinguished career in the Welsh Office. Others of those pupils were to gain notable success, one receiving a knighthood for his scientific research. From that village school, the potential for advancement was sky-high and all because of the dedicated, consistent hard work of Head Teachers and staff like John Davies and his successors.[287]

There are more references to the war in the Log. The final Air Raid Warning would appear to be on 15th July, 1941, lasting from 3.05 to 3.40 p.m. Fire watching began on the School premises, in the Standard 7 classroom, on March, 24th, 1942. Three men were to be on duty each night from 8.00 p.m. This continued until November, 1943. In June, 1942, all pupils were issued with gas masks and instructed in donning and removing them. These new items of equipment were to cause much amusement especially when pupils conversed when wearing them. Parents were often cajoled to make bags with straps to carry the gas mask box, resulting in unhealthy competition to see whose was the most fashionable. You felt inferior if you merely had the standard cardboard box container with its flimsy string! The jubilation of the village when victory in Europe was declared is reported in the Log. The school was closed on May 9th, 1945, for the VE Day celebrations. But on May 10th, when the school reopened, the attendance was only 60% "due to the fact that parents and children of the village were on the streets singing and dancing until the early hours of the morning." Bonfires, street parties and other festivities made this joyful occasion unforgettable.[288]

It was on January 31st, 1947, that W Adams Jones completed the second Log Book of Trelewis Mixed School. He reported that the weather was bitterly cold with the water system frozen and temperature in the classrooms at 9.00 a.m. not above 38°. Heavy snow was to continue and the attendance for the week was 58.7%. The legendary winter of 1947 was taking hold. The Log might conclude with this cold, frosty scene but a warm glow replaces it when one reflects on what had been achieved by the school and its pupils in the war-torn years which would now continue with the resumption of peace.[289]

2. OF AN ESTEEMED RESIDENT

Living Through Change

In the 29 years of his retirement, John Davies was to live through a period of momentous change. Historians, often reticent in using hyperbole, have seen fit to make use of the adjective "great" on a number of occasions for pivotal happenings in these decades. Starting with "The Great War 1914-1918", which had such great loss of life, to "The Great Depression 1929-1934", which caused such great misery, the adjective is more than merited. There was great change occurring on a national scale in Wales throughout this period between the wars. The impact of the 1926 General Strike was particularly felt in mining communities like Trelewis. It was the miners, threatened with a cut in wages, who began the nation-wide strike between 4th and 12th May, 1926. But it was to be of no avail. While their supporters soon returned to work, the miners were left to fight on alone until December, 1926, when they were forced to give in, drifting back to work, with wages still reduced and hours increased. There is at least one reference to the strike in the School Log for May 21st, 1926, which states that owing to the strike and the necessity to feed school children, only one day's holiday would be taken at Whitsun.[290] The soaring of unemployment in the 1930's as a result of the great depression also left its mark on the Welsh valleys. By August, 1932, over a quarter of a million people were unemployed in Wales out of a population of two and a half million. This was to lead to a massive exodus from Wales to find employment elsewhere in the developing light industries. Birmingham, Dagenham, Slough, etc., were just a few of the places where Welsh accents were to increase. It is estimated that nearly half a million people were to leave by 1939.[291] The accession of Edward VIII in 1936, had given a small ray of hope, when, seeing the effect of the recession in South Wales on his visit there, he declared that "something must be done." His abdication in less than a year, without decisive action being taken to fulfil his promise, was a real disappointment. Some slight relief was given by the government declaring part of the South Wales coalfield a "special area" with the objective of introducing a greater variety of industries. But it took until 1938 for real progress to be made when the first government-assisted trading estate opened at Treforest. This relieved some of the prevailing unemployment for 2,500 employees found work in the 60-70 firms sited on that estate.[292]

Between the two world wars, historians have chronicled many significant events. There were international upheavals, like the Spanish Civil War 1936-9, when 174 Welshmen, mostly miners,

Tawelfan, at the top of Trelewis, where John Davies lived in retirement. As Headmaster he lived in the accomodation beside the school.

joined the International Brigade to fight fascism. There were national advances like the granting of women's suffrage in 1918 when the Representation of the People Act gave the vote to women over the age of 30 as a belated concession for the part women had played in the war and for the abandonment of their militant suffragette tactics. Women's suffrage was extended, in 1928, to all over the age of 21. At long last, they gained the right to vote on the same terms as men. As has already been shown, amongst all the recorded milestones, there were to be some with a particular Celtic importance. Included in these was the struggle for Irish independence. In 1922, the Irish Free State had come into being and this probably gave impetus to the demand for Welsh autonomy. Shortly afterwards, in 1925, an independent nationalist party for Wales, (Plaid Genedlaethol Cymru), was founded and the coming of depression was to strengthen its numbers. Unlike the Irish nationalists, those in Wales eschewed the use of force to gain their ends preferring persuasion as their weapon.[293]

John Davies was to witness the failure of the League of Nations to prevent wars and secure the peaceful resolution of international disputes. The rise of Hitler and the consequent onset of war in 1939 was to take him back to the situation he had encountered a year after his retirement: the return of a world at war, for the second time in his lifetime. The fond hope of 1918, that there had been a war to end all wars, was not to be realised. Towards the end of his life, there was much discouragement from such things as the disaster of Dunkirk. Then there was to follow the heroism of the Battle of Britain and, before he died, he was to see the beginning of the turn of the tide. The USA entered the war in 1941, after Pearl Harbour; success was starting in North Africa, but ultimate victory was still some way off. There was to be much blood, sweat and tears shed before Trelewis was to host joyous celebrations on VE Day and VJ Day in 1945.

Witnessing New Developments

Taff Merthyr Colliery

Some of the most notable of all the momentous happenings in John Davies' retirement years were to occur in Trelewis itself. Amongst these, the opening of Taff Merthyr Colliery in 1926, was to have substantial consequences for the village. It grew in size as a result of the influx of workers for the second pit in the neighbourhood. More importantly, it was to have its social cohesion and strong community spirit shattered by the industrial conflict which was to centre on Taff Merthyr. The pit was sunk between 1922 and 1924 in the valley bottom, on a site midway between Trelewis and Bedlinog, by the Taff Merthyr Steam Coal Company, a joint enterprise of the Ocean Coal Company and the Powell Duffryn Group. It was to be one of the last deep mines opened in South Wales under private ownership and also one of the most modern. From its inception it utilised electricity, new machinery and methods. In 1934, it opened a splendid pithead baths, equal if not superior to those opened at Deep Navigation Colliery, Treharris, in 1932 (which were a replacement for those erected there

179

Courtesy Alan George

in 1916.) The conditions and facilities on offer were attractive to miners in the locality and further afield. Many from Bedlinog were keen to find employment at Taff Merthyr because the mines in their village were closing. Others from Treharris and Nelson similarly sought work there. The opening of a colliery halt in September 1927[294] and a growth in bus transport ensured that miners from a wider area could be employed. By 1936, there were 1,380 underground workers and 195 on the surface at the colliery which, by then, was producing 600,000 tons of steam coal annually.[295]

To house at least some of its workers, the Taff Merthyr Steam Coal Company built a housing estate on the side of the mountain above Trelewis, under a mile away from the colliery. The Company gave this the impressive name "Taff Merthyr Garden Village" as it followed the principles of the Garden Village movement which had already established dwellings in Wales, notably in Rhiwbina (Cardiff) and Barry. The houses in Garden Villages varied in appearance some being semi-detached, others built in clusters of 3 or 4. All had gardens front and rear and were equipped with modern conveniences: indoor

Taff Merthyr Garden Village (aka Stormtown) just above the village of Trelewis

toilet; hot and cold running water; electric light; bathroom etc.[296] They were far more substantial and comfortable than the traditional residences for South Wales miners. The ever-practical tin bath for use in front of the fire was no longer required in the Garden Village! Housewives lovingly and laboriously polished the wood block parquet-floors which to them was evidence of real luxury. For all who lived in one of these Company houses it was a dream come true. For the Company, it was to give an almost inextricable hold over its workers, (even more so than the 19th Century Company Shop), because losing employment at the colliery would also mean forfeiture of tenancy of the Company house.

Possibly to prevent the new residents of Taff Merthyr Garden Village getting ideas above their station, the older inhabitants of Trelewis soon began to call the development "Stormtown," a name which the newcomers were to find most appropriate. The houses they lived in were readily exposed to the elements, catching the full force of wind and rain in their hillside position. Mr J B Thomas in the Log of Trelewis School records that 12 new scholars were admitted from the new houses on 29th August, 1927. A year later he comments on very

181

poor attendance due to rough weather and adds "the worst attenders are the new element from the Taff Merthyr New Houses. Very little excuse is needed, however, from these scholars to absent themselves from school." His attitude to these new arrivals was probably typical of most of the original inhabitants.[297] Before the new houses were built, there were just two or three habitations on the mountain-side: Gilfach Maen farm at the very top and two small cottages sited below. The naming of the streets in the Garden Village also differed from those erected on Bontnewydd land. Instead of prosaic English names like Field Street and Railway Terrace, each row of the Garden Village was given a Welsh name. The two lower streets of semi-detached houses were called "Heol Isaf" (Lowest Street) and "Ael y bryn" (Brow of the Hill). Being more spacious than those built towards the top of the mountain, they were intended mainly for colliery officials. (The Sergeant of Police for the colliery lived there!). Sandwiched between was "Brondeg" (Fairbreast) which only contained two detached houses, the biggest dwellings in the estate. It was here the Under-Manager had his residence. "Maen Ganol" (Middle Stone) with "Maen Gilfach" (Gilfach Stone), the summit of the estate, were the streets which completed the rest of the development.

Children growing up in the Garden Village had a ready-made, natural playground for their enjoyment. The grassy slopes which surrounded them were ideal for slides on makeshift pieces of cardboard in summer. In winter, more elaborate, homemade sledges gave endless hours of fun in the abundant snow. Between their houses and the colliery were plentiful supplies of ferns which could become spears, bows and arrows, guns, roofing for the dens they constructed; in fact, they could be anything which their fertile imaginations decided. Right next to their houses were two large quarries with two very deep ponds which over the years became adventurous but dangerous sites for their play. There were young lives lost there skating on the ice in winter or swimming in the cold water in summer. The Trelewis Welfare grounds were to provide a much safer environment and the slide, swings and roundabouts were much enjoyed. The sloping football pitch which was provided was to give an unfair advantage to the home side who knew how to utilise it against their opponents.

In 1936, the Aberdare Circuit of the Methodist Church constructed a chapel in Brondeg. This was the Taff Merthyr Garden Village Methodist Church. Spiritual as well as material provision was being made for the inhabitants. It rapidly gained a strong congregation and a thriving Sunday School (especially before the Whitsun Treat and the Annual Outing to Barry Island.) Whitsun was an especially memorable time. The Sunday School Anniversary was always held on Whit-Sunday. Parents would ensure that their offspring had new clothes (mainly bought from Treharris Co-op or Bargoed Emporium) because the children were on open display in chapel on the specially elevated stage, for three services. From there, they nervously said their recitations and sang their solos to an appreciative, proud congregation. On Whit Monday there was the impressive March of Witness around each of the streets of the Garden Village. No band and no musicians accompanied the procession but the singing of the hymns was not affected in any way. Loudly and melodiously, the voices of young and old filled the air. After the march, it was back to the chapel for the Whit Tea. The array of coloured cottons which adorned cutlery and cup handles provided a dazzling but useful spectacle. (They ensured that the owners would be re-united with their property.) The day finally ended with the Whit Sports, on the field at the end of the chapel road with monetary rewards for the exuberant winners of the three-legged, egg and spoon races and other non-Olympic events. More fun was to come because the Whit holiday was not over without a visit to Quaker's Yard Fair, the acme of enjoyment for generations of Trelewis children. The delights of the dodgems, the raciness of the rides, the surprises of the side-shows, the tastes of toffee apples and candy floss were indulged in until every penny was emptied from their pockets. Then the long walk, up the Mill Road, back to the village, the annual trek home for a satisfied group of youngsters whose normal routine would resume on the morrow.

8379   GENERAL VIEW, TRELEWIS.   ERNEST T. BUSH

The other special occasion, eagerly awaited each year, was the Sunday School outing to Barry Island. Trelewis Platform would be crowded with chattering, excited children and their parents waiting the arrival of the special excursion train. Each compartment of the non-corridor, non-toilet train, was rapidly filled amid arguments as to who was to sit next to the windows. The journey was a delight in itself because it was travel into the unknown. The route followed was not the usual one taken by passenger trains as it used the track which the Barry Railway had constructed principally to transport coal to the docks. The high spot, literally, was the crossing of the Walnut Tree Viaduct at Taff's Well, one of the outstanding engineering achievements in South Wales. As the train slowly passed over its 7 lattice girder spans for 1,548 feet, everyone rushed to the windows to catch a glimpse of the fairy-tale Castell Coch, or the valley road, 120 feet below, with what appeared to be toy vehicles on it.[298] Then it was on to remote, less-frequented stations like Wenvoe before, at long last, the train chugged its way to the Promised Land - Barry Island.

It always seemed as if every other Sunday School in South Wales had chosen the same day for their visit, such were the crowds. The rush to

184

claim sufficient square metres of sand on the beach was a joy to behold. Provided the tide allowed it, Trelewis folk usually managed to commandeer their share for varied activities. Paddling; swimming with untutored doggy-paddle; building sand castles; burying the unsuspecting up to their necks; playing cricket, rounders, football in teams; riding recalcitrant donkeys and much more, were to see the hours fly past. The sights of chapel worthies with knotted handkerchiefs over their heads and ladies of an uncertain age getting their feet wet while holding their dresses aloft, gave additional amusement. Before leaving for home, the coins, which had been painstakingly saved in the weeks before, rapidly disappeared. The money-relieving slot machines proved too great a temptation: the flicking of ball-bearings; the manoeuvring of the crane which hovered over enticing rewards; the laughing policeman ; the drunken sailor and other attractions all claimed their victims. Promising so much, those contraptions delivered so little. Any remaining money was soon dispatched on the Barry Island Shows, more sophisticated but more expensive than those at Quaker's Yard Fair. The day, invariably sunny, had once again lived up to all expectations. Still excited, still noisy, but very satisfied, all made their way back to the station hoping to find the correct train back to Trelewis. The annual and, for most, the only trip to the seaside had come to an end.

The Garden Village Methodist Church was to give the children of the locality a further cause for pleasure. When weddings were held there, (and there were a number in the course of the year), crowds of children would turn up in Brondeg with other well-wishers. Their motive in being there was rather more mercenary than to give their greetings to the bride and groom. A tradition grew for the children of Stormtown called the "scram-bull" in their vernacular. When the bridal car drew up to transport the happy couple from the chapel, a strong rope was held across the road in front of the car to prevent its leaving. The custom was that it was not removed until the best man drew from his pocket a load of coins which were thrown to the waiting, eager children. They would then scramble to retrieve as many pennies and halfpennies as they could. It was this scramble which gave the name to the profitable pastime. Even before the bridal car moved off, another tradition was to tie tin cans and other clattering articles to the bumper so that the departure was accompanied by a barrage of noise, as well as cheers and waves. At this time, there were not many cars to be seen in Garden Village. True, there was a handful of corrugated garages constructed on the land at the end of Brondeg, next to the chapel. Whenever cars were parked outside them, by their supposedly wealthy owners, they would attract numbers of inquisitive and appreciative children to look on with envy.

Such were the joys and pleasures of growing up in the houses of the Taff Merthyr Steam Coal Company, which were just up the road from Tawelfan where John Davies lived in his retirement. But he was to witness, regrettably, bitterness, stress and hardship throughout the village springing directly from Taff Merthyr Colliery which was at the heart of industrial disputes in the 1920's and 30's.

Strife between Unions.

As early as November, 1926, as miners began to drift back to work following the 7 month long strike, there were 500 men working at Taff Merthyr. At a meeting held at the Bontnewydd Hotel, they agreed to form a Works Committee which, together with management, was to provide sick and funeral benefits, legal aid and was to refer any disputes to arbitration. In addition, it was agreed that the committee would be non-political. The coal owners warmly welcomed this development. Within a week, the Taff Merthyr Works Committee was to inaugurate the South Wales Miners' Industrial Union (SWMIU). This Union was soon labelled the Company or Scab Union and was to come into severe conflict with the South Wales Miners' Federation, (SWMF or the Fed), the self-proclaimed champion of miners' rights. The SWMIU, with the encouragement of the mine owners, gained support in other valleys and, by 1927, it claimed it had 21 branches and 30,000 members. Bitter rivalry between the Unions was to continue into the 1930's with Taff Merthyr being right at its centre. The Fed embarked on a campaign to get Taff Merthyr miners to join it instead of the SWMIU. While there were numbers who wished to do this, the Fed complained vehemently that they were prevented from doing so because management forced them to join SWMIU or lose their jobs. The loss of their job would also result in the loss of their home if they lived in the Garden Village! Troubles were bound to result from the conflict of interest. The other local colliery, Deep Navigation, where the SWMF was dominant, was inevitably drawn into the struggles between the rival Unions. A strike there by the Fed in 1931, resulted in no production. To the chagrin of the Fed men and the delight of the coal owners, at the very same time Taff Merthyr raised 2,000 tons a day with 1,600 miners working.[299]

Recriminations and worse were to follow as the situation deteriorated in subsequent years when the SWMF determined to weaken and, if possible, end the supremacy of the SWMIU at Taff Merthyr. In October, 1934, when the Fed was holding meetings outside the pit, at the start of shifts, to persuade miners to transfer to them, 12 miners, who wished to do so, were dismissed by the Taff Merthyr Steam Coal Company. With increasingly likely rumours spreading that at least 250 more were to be sacked, a tense and difficult period began. First, the night shift went on strike, then the day shift, leaving only 200 men working within a short time. The whole episode was to provoke violent clashes between the strikers and those who continued to work. Hundreds of police were drafted in to the area during this time, some from Swansea, some from as far away as Liverpool and Birmingham. Their task was to maintain order and to accompany working miners to the pit. Such was the seriousness of the matter that even the Chief Constable of Glamorgan, Captain Lionel Lindsey, was in attendance. His tactics, which included baton-charging, were to produce in the mining community a growing disrespect for the police. The "Western Mail" recorded that "after almost every strike, there were complaints about the over-vigorous action of the police."[300]

When there were still 600 men on strike, after some six weeks of angry, brutal confrontation, the Company reluctantly agreed with the SWMF to hold a ballot. But the caveat the Company made was that only those who were still working could vote, not those on strike. The

SWMIU forestalled their rivals by holding their own ballot first, when 542 men out of the 654 at work voted in favour of remaining with the SWMIU. Uneasy tension was to continue and it wasn't until October, 1935, that those who had opted to join the Fed were re-employed. Thereafter, the Company, with much hesitancy and disinclination, finally conceded that their workers would be allowed to join whichever Union they wished. But the fear that Taff Merthyr miners had of displeasing the management took longer to disappear. When another ballot was held at the pit in 1937, there were still 453 who voted in favour of the SWMIU with 448 voting against. It wasn't until 1939 that disputes between the two Unions were ended when the SWMIU merged with the SWMF. That did not mean that the animosity and bad feeling between fellow miners arising from the preceding years were to dissipate. The effects and the scars took much longer to heal, if they ever did.[301]

The small, neighbouring village of Bedlinog was to gain some notoriety as a result of its part in the disputes between the two Unions. The leading light there, in support of the Fed miners, was the local ironmonger, Edgar Evans. Born in 1900, he became a member of the Communist party as a young man. From 1926-1943 he was Branch Secretary of the Communist Party in Bedlinog and in 1934 was elected as a Councillor on Gelligaer Urban District Council.[302] He led a core of activists, holding meetings in a hut on Bedlinog Square which was called "The Kremlin" by locals. In October, 1935, serious disturbances and riots broke out in the village with clashes between the SWMF and SWMIU. The police arrested Edgar Evans together with numbers of his supporters. This resulted in the largest mass trial ever being held at Cardiff. At the trial, the police alleged that it was Evans who was responsible for the majority of the upheavals caused by the Taff Merthyr dispute. These statements were made: "He takes an active part in all industrial trouble .... He has spread pernicious views and caused trouble for 8 Years .... The police look upon him as a menace to the youth of Bedlinog." On the charge of incitement to riot, he was sentenced to 9 months imprisonment. At the trial, 53 men and 3 women were found guilty on March 25th, 1936, with most of the men receiving hard labour and imprisonment, some for up to 15 months. Others were bound over to keep the peace. The remarks of the Judge provoked great resentment in the valley community when he vilified the characters of some of the accused. Margaret Jenkins was called "that wild woman." Sentencing her he said: "You were the person who committed the first act of violence by pulling a man off his bicycle. Because you are the mother of 7 children and have a respectable husband, you will be bound over. I am going to keep this matter hanging over your head for three years."[303]

The supporters of the Fed were incensed at the punishments which were handed out to those who, they felt, were merely defending the rights of miners against the Company bosses. Evidence of the strength of that support was seen when some 10,000 people turned up at a mass meeting which was addressed by S O Davies, M.P. At the meeting, the trial was described as a deliberate effort "to encourage police brutality against the workers." This particular incident deepened the resentment which already existed between the two Unions. When, eventually, the prisoners were released there was great rejoicing in the streets. A heroes' welcome awaited them. Large banners, hung between the terraced houses, proclaimed: "You have suffered for a principle. We are proud of you." Crowds of people gave their heroes a rapturous welcome home. Not so the authorities. Edgar Evans was deprived of his civil liberties for 10 years. It was not until 1947 that he regained his seat on Gelligaer Council.

The disturbances caused by these years of conflict between striking miners and those who continued to work was to have an effect on life in Trelewis that was little short of calamitous. Social, religious and everyday life were to be radically affected. The windows of houses belonging to "scabs", as they were called, were broken, doors tarred, and their livestock let loose on the mountain. Wives of striking miners left wreaths outside the homes of those still working, an ominous, cruel warning of repercussions. The "Merthyr Express" could report that "the strike at the Taff Merthyr colliery arising out of the conflict between the South Wales Miners' Federation and the Miners'

189

Industrial Union….is causing the greatest anxiety in the district." It also told of the chairman of the Taff Merthyr Branch of the SWMIU being "violently assaulted by a hostile crowd in High Street, Trelewis, as he was proceeding home."[304]

Anyone who appeared to support members of the SWMIU was victimised and, if shopkeepers or others did so, their businesses were boycotted, This happened to the Landlord of the Ffald-gaiach Inn for serving a non-striking miner. When a bus driver for the Gelligaer Urban District Council received threats of retaliation for transporting workers to Taff Merthyr, his fellow drivers refused subsequently, to transport SWMIU members. The social cohesion and strong sense of collective identity, typical of a mining village, was being ruptured. Societies and clubs, which had harmoniously contained both SWMF and SWMIU members previously, were split and forced to cease their activities. This happened to the Trelewis & District Male Voice Party, the Trelewis Bowling Club and the Taff Merthyr Workmen's Silver Band. Football teams expelled those who had not supported the strike. In view of all this deep-seated conflict, no wonder the "Western Mail" reported: "It is something that is making the valley a place of fear and terror." [305] Even chapels, in which people had sung hymns, worshipped and prayed together, succumbed to the prevalent mood of ill-will. In some, whenever families of SWMIU rose to sing the hymn that had been announced, the supporters of the SWMF sat down. In others, when services were attended by members of the SWMIU, their opponents stayed away.[306]

Parents refused to send their children to classes where teachers would not show displeasure to pupils from SWMIU homes. The impact of these unusual and unpleasant circumstances is brought out in the fascinating account given by Maggie Pryce Jones of her growing up in Trelewis during these troublesome times. She lived in Pen-y-groes-heol, just down the hill from John Davies' home. Her father was employed at the colliery and was a member of the Fed. Early on, she learned, the hard way, that "our village was in bondage to the colliery owners for whom most of the men worked." With her friend Megan, she heard for the very first time the words "strikes", "scabs" and "blacklegs", words which were soon to resonate with grim reality for her. When they knew their meaning, Megan's reaction was: "I wouldn't want to be one of those people in a village as small as ours." Maggie went on to describe incidents which occurred in the troubles: boulders being rolled down the mountain on to the railway line to prevent coal leaving the colliery; young men being arrested and sent to Swansea prison; the very real suffering of children whose fathers would not strike. Maggie's teacher, Mr Griffiths, asked her to find out when her friends, Mary Winters and brother Huw, would be returning to school after being absent for a week. She called at their house which had tar splattered on it and broken windows. A distraught Mrs Winters told her that the children were much too scared to return to school because of people shouting "scab" through the letter box and hurling things at the house. In sad tones she said: "People who have sat by us in chapel for years have turned their backs on us." The children did, however, agree to go back to school when Maggie promised to take them. She also suggested that they ask Mr Griffiths to dismiss them before the rest of the class so that they could leave school before their peers.[307]

The picture she paints captures the pain, the suffering and the fear which came to dominate everyday life in the village. One young mother, living in Maen Gilfach, corroborates this. Whenever she went shopping in the village in these years, she would always take her baby daughter with her, wrapped in a shawl, Welsh fashion. She surmised that no one would be so cruel as to attack a nursing mother. Some of her neighbours thought the same and insisted on accompanying her to assure their own safety.[308] But the children from the homes of striking miners did not escape their share of the misery either. Food shortages, caused by lack of wages, led to hungry children becoming under-nourished. The school, with help from the parish, tried to combat this by giving them, each day, a table-spoon of malt extract from the enormous jar provided for that purpose. Money was so tight that footwear and clothes could not be replaced. Again the school was able to identify those who needed boots and, with aid from the parish, it provided them. Even when the strikes were over and the imprisoned miners released, any feelings of victory were pretty hollow. The cost which had to be paid was too high: the hardship and distress caused to so many individuals, young and old; houses stripped of furniture to pay the bills; the continuing way in which activists were still penalised (e.g. by never being offered overtime); the aftermath of suspicion and recrimination. Taff Merthyr colliery may have brought modernity and even some prosperity to the locality but it had also contributed much loss and suffering.[309] One is left wondering what John Davies' reaction, in his declining years, would have been to these sad events in a village where he had spent so many happy times.

Continuing To Serve

In his early years in the village, John Davies had involved himself with the work of local building societies as housing needs developed. His determination to be of service to the wider community can be traced, not only during his years as Head, but in his retirement as well:

in St Mary's Church

His Christian convictions and Anglican background were to find plenty of opportunities to express themselves. He was one of the founding members of St Mary's Church which he continued to serve throughout his life. Regularly his voice could be heard reading the lesson there. His wisdom and expertise were also to be deployed to good effect as Churchwarden and Church Secretary. The wider denomination of the Church in Wales benefited, too, from his serving as representative in Church Congress meetings. It was for leaving his mark on much of the religious and social life of the village that John Davies will be remembered. He was the main instigator of the campaign to erect a Church Hall which came to play an ever-increasing role in the community. In the Fourth Schedule of leases for Bontnewydd estate, 608 square yards of Bontnewydd farm land were conveyed to the Vicar and Churchwardens for the building of a Church Hall. At its opening, in November, 1932, the timing of sessions at Trelewis School was altered to enable pupils to attend.[310] The "Merthyr Express" described this event as "a red letter day in the

history of Trelewis." A large attendance came to the opening
ceremony, presided over by the Vicar of Bedlinog, with the Lord
Bishop of Llandaff, the Right Rev Dr Timothy Rees, on his first visit
to Trelewis, performing the dedication. Most of the local dignitaries
were present including David Hughes, M.E., Manager of Taff Merthyr
Colliery, John Davies, J Bedford Thomas, T W Lewis, Josiah Harries,
and Jonah Evans. In his speech, John Davies, Secretary at St Mary's
gave a resume of the background to the project. Plans for a Church
Hall had first been prepared before the Great War but nothing came
from that until, a few months earlier, the Vicar revived the scheme.
Now, thanks to the Curate and Church members, the sum of £1,000
had been raised to build the Hall. Concluding his speech, Mr Davies
hoped that the young people would not regard the Hall as a substitute
for Church but as something supplementary. His only regret was that
he wasn't younger so that he could enjoy the benefits of the Hall in the
same manner as the youth of the village. For him, this event was "one
of the proudest moments of his life." With that, he sat down to great
applause. T W Lewis, (William Lewis' son and John Davies'
son-in-law), Vicar's Warden, continued the speeches in which he
described his hopes for the Hall. It was to be a place designed to "oil
the wheel of life and help the members to understand each other
better." Youngsters would gain healthy recreational opportunities,
come into closer contact with clergy and with adults who could teach
them something. The future of the Hall would be promising and bright
if these hopes were realised.[311]

These two speeches have been quoted in some detail because of the
Bishop of Llandaff's response. He said how delighted he was to visit
Trelewis and congratulated the members on the fine achievement of
building such a magnificent Hall. Then he spoke of the "splendid
laymen" of the parish, referring to John Davies and T W Lewis. He
had listened that afternoon to "men of the right type, men of truly
amazing gifts who spoke choice and elegant English." It had been a
genuine pleasure to listen to them. His remarks were interrupted by
applause at this point. The villagers were only too well aware of the
calibre of the two men, but it was satisfying to have this confirmed by

John Davies, with paper in hand, at turning of the first sod for the building of the Church Hall at Trelewis.

the bishop. "With such men," he said, "St. Mary's could look forward to greater achievements in the future." In conclusion, he thanked the vicar, curate and members for writing "a new chapter in the history of the parish." The Church Hall was to be of enormous benefit to the religious and social life of the village and John Davies more than deserved the plaudits which he received.[312]

The "handsome, new Hall" seating over 500, with a large stage, "suitable for cantatas", had two dressing rooms either side, a kitchen and the usual offices. It was erected by a local builder, Sam Williams, Glynbargoed House, whose little daughter presented Rev J F W Leigh (eldest son of the late Dr W W Leigh, JP), with an inscribed gold key to open the building formally. The Hall was located about 100 yards further along the High Street from St Mary's. Its main access was up a steep flight of steps which were to prove a problem for the disabled and elderly. As it was the only building in Trelewis with a stage, it soon became the main venue for concerts and dramatic productions of all descriptions. Many a happy hour was spent there by the villagers particularly when dances were added to its activities. In fact, there were to be a number of romances begun with an encounter on that dance floor!

Maggie Pryce Jones again provides her insight into the value of the Church Hall which John Davies had so encouraged. She was much indebted to the curate, Rhys Emmanuel and his German wife Helga, who went out of their way to support and help her. Their kindness was a source of inspiration and provision in the difficult days when young Maggie was left with the responsibility of bringing up the family following the death of her mother at the young age of 39. She records that the Emmanuels had brought with them a new spirit to the village which was to be in evidence during the upheaval caused by the strikes. When money was in short supply in many village households, they organised a Christmas party in the Church Hall to which Church and Chapel children were all invited. The children participated in a Nativity play before enjoying a meal far better (and larger), than many had seen for some weeks. Afterwards they sang carols as their parents joined them. The Church Hall, then and later, lightened what were dark days for children. The Emmanuels also established a children's club in the Church Hall, on Tuesday evenings, which became very popular. The vision and faithfulness of John Davies and others in establishing a Church Hall was to be rewarded a hundred-fold.[313]

as Guardian of the Poor

To his Church activities and concern for the local community, John Davies was to add service as a Poor Law Guardian. Since the Poor Law Amendment Act of 1834, Unions of parishes had established a Board of Guardians to relieve the distress of the poor who were unable to care for themselves. Gelligaer Parish was part of the Merthyr Tydfil Union. John Davies was to follow in the footsteps of William Lewis who had also served as a Guardian during his lifetime. It was not a sinecure to hold such a position. Meetings were held fortnightly and the business and activities of the Board of Guardians multiplied over the years. Responsibilities ranged from oversight of the Union Workhouse, Infirmary and Cottage Homes, to outdoor relief, care of the elderly, the infirm and children. There was always much business

Nelson Council School (Now called Llancaeach Junior School)

to transact and the results of the Guardians' deliberations were to be felt throughout the parishes of the Union. The Guardians were elected for a three year term and, in some parishes, these elections were fiercely contested. John Davies was to represent the Bedlinog/Trelewis Ward for 12 years which shows the confidence the community had in his ability and in his commitment to serve it well. The comment of the "Merthyr Express" was that "he did a great deal of social work in the Ward." This assessment of him was attested by Dr W W Leigh, J.P., who, at John Davies' retirement presentation, stated that the poor "would always find in him a true friend during his tenure of office" for he had always looked after the interests of the Ward in a careful manner. (In 1929, the Local Government Act abolished Boards of Guardians and their powers passed to the Public Assistance Committees of County and County Borough Councils.)[314]

as Head of Nelson Council School

With all of these multifarious activities, one would have thought that retirement from Trelewis School for John Davies was a welcome relief especially as he had not been in good health. But, in just over a year and a half, he was back in harness again, this time as Head of Nelson Council School. Once more, his public spirit and willingness to serve prompted him to respond to the shortage of male teachers occasioned by the outbreak of the Great War. There had been a quick and numerous reaction to the recruiting campaigns which had followed the outbreak of war on 4th August, 1914. The "Merthyr Express" reported in October, 1914, that there had been a "remarkable response" to Kitchener's appeal for men. Over 70 men from Trelewis had joined up since the war started and their names had been prominently displayed on the door of St Mary's Church by the curate, Rev W J Williams. The same thing was happening in Nelson. The campaigns and the advertisements in the "Merthyr Express" in these early days of the war were having a real impact. Every psychological pressure was applied for men to enlist. Here are some of the "Merthyr Express" adverts:

"A SOLDIER OF THE KING

After the war, every man who has served will command
his country's gratitude. He will be looked up to and respected
because he answered his country's call.

The regiments at the front are covering themselves with glory…
There is rapid promotion for intelligence and zeal. Hundreds who
enlisted as private soldiers have already become officers because
of merits and courage and thousands have reached
non-commissioned rank…..

ENLIST TODAY

GOD SAVE THE KING"

A week or so later a different form of pressure was applied:

"IS YOUR NAME ON A ROLL OF HONOUR?

There is room for YOUR name on your firm's roll of honour…
Ask your employer to keep your position open to you….
Tell him now…..
Your King and Country want YOU…
TODAY"[315]

197

Whether it was the result of these campaigns or not, E T Owen, the Headmaster of Nelson Council School, joined the St. John Unit of the Welsh Field Ambulance (RAMC) in December, 1914, leaving the school at short notice. He had been Head there since November 16th, 1908, and was well-respected and regarded by parents and pupils alike. John Davies was to abandon the ease of retirement to fill the vacancy until 1919. After much searching, the Log Book of Nelson New Council School Mixed Department was eventually found in Llancaeach Junior School. This now provides a rich source of evidence for John Davies' contribution to the life and work of that school.[316]

The Nelson New Council School Mixed Department had opened on 28th September, 1908, in temporary premises and, surprisingly, with a temporary Head Teacher, Mr D J Jenkins (on Supply). Standards 1, 2 and 3 were accommodated in Calfaria Chapel and Standards 4, 5, 6 and 7 in Penuel Chapel. There was nothing new about schools starting their existence in chapel premises. Examples have already been seen in Trelewis and Treharris. But it seemed strange to open a new Council School initially without a permanently-appointed Head Teacher. This anomaly was corrected in just over a month when E T Owen took over as Head. The use of temporary premises, however, was to continue for some time. On 22nd March, 1909, the Infants Department opened with Class 1 based in Salem Chapel and Class 2 in Ebenezer Chapel. Supervision of staff and pupils in such scattered buildings presented the Head with additional problems to which were added deficiencies in chapels' sanitary arrangements, ventilation, etc. Some relief came on 23rd December, 1909, when new school premises were officially opened. The new school had: 3 rooms to accommodate 50 children each; 2 rooms for 40 and 1 room for 32. In total, 262 pupils could be fitted into the building which also had a central hall. In May, 1911, the number on roll had reached 332 and chapel premises were still being used. There is also reference to the Head having to take Standard 7 to temporary premises in February, 1912. Penuel ceased to be used by Standards 4 and 5 on March 13th, 1913, when the Infants'

Department was accommodated in a new building on the school site.[317]

The first pupils of the school were initially drawn from Llanfabon National (Nelson Non-Provided) School, with both names appearing in the Admission Register. By April, 1909, the average number on roll was said to be 260 and this had increased to 343 by May, 1913. A year later, the roll had declined to 261 but this was probably due to the opening of the Infants' school in its own building from April, 1913.[318] The Admission Register indicates much coming and going of pupils between Nelson Council School and the Llanfabon School. This transfer of pupils suggests a growing rivalry between the two. It seems that parents would move their children from one school to the other only to move them back again, presumably when their hopes of an enhanced experience had not been realised. The Admission Register also shows a continuing influx of people into the locality, although on a much reduced scale from that of the late 19th Century. The column indicating "School last attended" for the years 1908-1914 records pupils arriving from Hereford, Southampton, Hebden Bridge Yorkshire, Chester, Cambridge, Staffordshire, Bristol, Reading, Gloucester, Stroud, Devonport, Woodford Green, Crosby, etc. Most of the admissions, however, were from the school's own Infants' Department, Llanfabon and the Welsh Valleys.[319]

The HMI Reports on the school during these formative years were encouraging. The first of them, by Gomer Jones, HM Sub-Inspector, in May, 1911, stated that the "general condition is very promising both in instruction and discipline." He commented on the 2 classes having to occupy temporary premises a short distance away. But apart from asking for improvements: in penmanship; in more ordered response from some classes; in using mental calculations better related to everyday life, his report is complimentary especially for the Infants' Department. The Infants were: intelligently directed; bright and happy; being taught on modern lines and were progressing satisfactorily. Mr Jones approved of the fact that children under 5 were being "excluded wisely at the present," possibly not to add pressure on the accommodation. Further visits by Gomer Jones were made in June and July, 1913. On this occasion, he asked for: regular inspection by the Head Teacher; sundry improvements in Standards 2, 3 and 4 and more time to be given to practical mensuration. John Evans, also an HM Sub-Inspector, visited in April, 1912, and wished to see better maintenance of the Admission and other Registers. In addition, he inquired about the School Garden as Gardening had been approved as a School subject by the Board of Education in December, 1911. Because of site problems, the course did not commence until November, 1912 and, in further visits, Mr Evans checked on its progress. Each time he made practical suggestions for the layout and educative use of the garden. In September, 1914, he made several other observations including: the importance of seasonal lessons in nature study and the introduction of a scheme of work to teach Welsh and English History contemporaneously up to the present. Surprisingly, there was no comment on the outbreak of the 1914 War![320]

The last Report on the School before Evan T Owen left for War Service was made by W Edwards, HMI, on November 5th, 1913. His main comment centred on the need for the Head to supervise the School regularly. Staff absence through prolonged illness and the failure to replace staff quickly when they left had put additional pressures on him. Mr Edwards instructed that the staff "should be strengthened immediately for the Head to do his work of supervision." This was so much needed for two reasons: "the children of this growing district are often very backward when they are admitted" and "the inexperience of many teachers." Mr Edwards concluded that the tone and discipline of the School "seem exceedingly good" with Mr Owen seeking to rectify such deficiencies as existed. Given more time, Mr Owen would be able to visit classes more frequently and advise the staff appropriately. The accommodation provided for the Mixed Department (6 classrooms plus the Hall), following the Infants having their own premises, now appeared to be adequate.[321]

All of these reports reflect credit on Mr Evan T Owen. He had got the School off to a good start in far from ideal circumstances. It seemed such a pity that just as the staffing had been strengthened with more Certificated Teachers, (including 2 graduates), and the Head had been freed from taking a class, the 1914-18 War broke out. Within 4 months, the Chief Education Official had formally acknowledged Mr Owen's enlistment into the Armed Services and stated that "John Davies, Trelewis, has been appointed Certificated Assistant at this School" to take up duties on December 1st, 1914, at a salary of £135 p.a. In little over a week, Mr Owen had left the School making his last entry in the Log on December 11th, 1914: "The Head Teacher leaves this evening to take up duties with the RAMC of the Welsh Army Corps. Mr John Davies, Certificated Teacher, will take charge of the School." A rather brief farewell, with no mention whatever of John Davies' long professional experience as a Head. It was now up to John Davies to lead Nelson Council School during wartime conditions and to find out whether his skills, after retirement, were still up to the task.[322]

Seeing again the firm, clear handwriting of John Davies, writing for the first time in the School Log on December 14th, 1914 was a pleasure. Characteristically, he starts by putting his arrival into context: "Mr Evan T Owen left on Friday last, the 11th inst., for military service with the RAMC and, by this morning's post, I received notification from the Chief Education Official of my appointment as temporary Head Teacher. My presence in the school during the last fortnight, taking part in terminal examinations, has enabled me to get an insight into the state of work and the methods adopted in the several classes. An effort shall be made to carry on everything as heretofore with the least possible change or friction." He obviously set himself a more limited objective for his headship at Nelson than that which had guided him previously. Showing real sensitivity as to how his coming might be viewed by the existing staff (and Mr Owen), he affirms that he wants to consolidate what had been achieved rather than to adopt a more radical approach. His intention was that his role was to be a caretaker Head. He was not going to use his abundant knowledge and wisdom to make far-reaching changes.[323]

The Log confirms that his intention was realised as the usual pattern of activities in the School continued as before. There were, inevitably, differences in the way that Mr Owen and Mr Davies recorded them. For instance, Mr Owen was punctilious in listing the attendance figures for each year ending on May 31st. Mr Davies, however, merely noted that monthly returns of attendance had been sent to the Clerk of the Group, except that in June, 1917 and June, 1918, he did record the attendance figures for Year ending, May 31st. These proved to be very similar. For 1917: Average No. on Registers - 246; Average Attendance - 210 = 85%. For 1918: Average No. on Registers - 255; Average Attendance - 220 = 86%. Also, whereas Mr Owen had recorded the weekly readings of gas and water consumption, Mr Davies did not. The amount of detail given about other routine aspects of school life also varied between them e.g. John Davies gave more information about the celebration of St. David's Day: "Special programme for St. David's Day consisting of short addresses, patriotic songs and playlets." This had always been a prominent feature of his headship which he wished to continue at Nelson.[324]

There were only two discernible innovations that can be seen in the account which John Davies has left. One was an addition to the school curriculum. In December, 1918, a course in Manual Training and Cookery for the Upper Standards was introduced. This was probably on the initiative of HMI and the County Organiser for Manual Instruction. A room was prepared for the purpose in the Infants' Department and, by 1919, pupils were also attending for instruction from Llanfabon National and Trelewis Mixed School. (John Davies was not averse to sharing facilities to enrich educational experience.) [325] The other was an addition to the school's extra-curricular activities. In March, 1915, a concert was held in which the children performed the operetta "Birth of the Union Flag." This was to raise money to purchase pianos for the School. (John Davies was always ready to improve amenities for pupils and ever eager to develop their creative talents.) All agreed that the concert was "a decided success." There was added pleasure on the following evening, when the concert was repeated, to have Evan T Owen presiding as he was home on leave. The person responsible for the performance was Mr J Rhys Williams, B.A., who had practised the songs and drills in Music and PE lessons in the preceding two weeks. It could well be that this was the only concert given in these years as no other entertainments are recorded in the Log during Mr Owen's or Mr Davies' headships. Within a year, Mr Williams, the Class Teacher for Standard 6, had left for War service. His departure left a staff comprised of females, apart from Mr Davies.[326]

It seems surprising that the War figures only very spasmodically and incidentally in the Log. In our media dominated age, when world events are known as they unfold, the impact of war on a school would be more fully reported. But apart from recording the departure of Mr Evan T Owen, the next mention comes in February, 1916, when J R Williams enlisted. The two of them made welcome visits to the School during their service: Mr Owen, in May, 1917, returning from the BEF in France for an afternoon visit, gaining "a hearty reception from teachers and pupils"; Mr Williams, also serving in France, made his visit in October, 1917. There is a brief mention too of some of the unfortunate consequences of war. In April, 1917, Mr Davies was granted leave of absence to attend the funeral in Llangeitho of his nephew, Captain Rev. T G Jones, C.F., who had died at a London hospital of wounds received in France. There is no mention of other fatalities amongst parents or of former pupils despite the appalling loss of life which occurred. More mundane consequences are mentioned. Because of the war there had been difficulties in procuring registers, so in June, 1917, the staff had to use spaces in old registers until new registers were received. A truncated terminal examination had to be held in March, 1918, because of deficiencies in "exam books and other materials." Only tests in essentials could be held. In December, 1918, again, just oral examinations could take place because of shortage of materials. The war had ended on the eleventh hour of the eleventh day of the eleventh month and was reported with

203

joy in the Log for November 11th, 1918: "The glad news of the signing of the Armistice with Germany reached the village this morning and naturally caused considerable excitement and rejoicing. No orders were received to close the school but very few children attended in the afternoon." The next day, instructions were received to close the school for the rest of the week.[327] Peace had come and John Davies could look forward, ere long, to resuming tranquil or, in his case, hectic retirement. But in all of his time at Nelson there was no respite from routine matters which had dogged his footsteps throughout all of his professional career.

The constants of attendance, holidays, weather, illness and staffing are prominent features. There is no mention of an attendance holiday being secured between 1914 and 1919 as the highest percentage attendance seen in the Log was 86% and there are plenty of comments that the attendance was unsatisfactory. When, in 1916, the Chief Education Official stated that only Whit Monday (not Tuesday), was to be observed as a holiday, the inevitable consequence was, as John Davies' experience could have foretold, a depleted attendance for the rest of the week. He would have been pleased, though, that there were not so many interruptions for occasional holidays as he had witnessed at Trelewis. Polling Days, Nelson Fair day, Church occasions, funerals still required the closure of the school but these seemed more controlled. Weather in the Valleys often affected attendance, as has been seen. Blizzards, rain and the cold kept pupils away. Illness too made its impact. Measles and influenza were noted as they reached epidemic proportions. Throughout 1915 to 1919, each year, there were at least 3 visits from the School Nurse, who also visited parents as required. There were 2 medical examinations by Doctors as well. Very few, if any, visits had been recorded before so it was of real benefit to see regular medical inspection occurring. There were pupils who were excluded on orders of the Nurse. With the recurring phrase that all the children present were "under observation by the nurse" one wonders, for what? Could this have been a polite way of describing the activity of the "nit Nurse?" In December, 1918, the Nurse was able to report on the favourable general physical condition of the pupils. Staff sickness was a continuing feature and further problems became apparent when staff were absent. In 1916, there were two teachers away and Mr Davies says how difficult it was to carry on in such circumstances. Even when there was a full complement, he observed: "it is still impossible to carry out in detail the prescribed syllabus in all subjects." He had plenty of experience to draw upon in dealing with all of these well known problems which he had encountered on many occasions.[328]

There are other fascinating observations to be seen during John Davies' time at Nelson. The practice of serving as Uncertificated Teachers began to decline as more of them were leaving for training. The Log tells us of staff going: to Barry Training College and University College, Reading, in 1915; to Bangor Normal College, in 1917. (Earlier, others had left for Portsmouth Training College in 1910 and Dudley Training College in 1913.) Staff were realising the personal advantage of being fully professionally qualified. [329] Information is also provided about the social background from which Nelson pupils came. This is derived from the Admission Register of Llanfabon National School which records the Occupation of Parent. (The Admission Register for Nelson Council School did not have a column for this.) Looking at the entries for 1914 - 1919, over 70% of fathers are listed as Miners. The only other occupations listed which exceed a single figure are: Farmer 6; Quarryman 5; Haulier 4; Soldier 3; Tipper 3; Fireman 3; Electrician 2; Gardener 2; Clerk 2; Policeman 2; Repairer 2. The remainder were: Licensed Victualer; Auctioneer; Publican; Shoemaker; Painter; Contractor; Baker; Butcher; Grocer; Ganger; Bootman; Carpenter; Fitter; Clerk in Holy Orders; Printer; Fisherman; Mines' Examiner; Railway Packer; Colliery Overman and a Horse Slaughterer. This gives a realistic commentary on the home backgrounds of Nelson pupils. Many of those listed had moved to Nelson to work in the mines, some from considerable distances. On finding that things were not necessarily better, some families returned from whence they came, in less than a year, as did one family from Fulham. The Admission Register also records pupils leaving to go abroad to Australia and Canada. It lists 2 pupils without father or mother and 6 pupils who were fatherless.[330] The information from Nelson Council School's Admission Register throws light upon the extent of transfer between the Nelson Schools, which was mentioned earlier. During John Davies' Headship, there were at least 18 pupils who left for Llanfabon National (Non-provided) School. During the same period there were at least 27 pupils admitted from Llanfabon. This rivalry possibly continued until they were amalgamated in 1960.[331]

There was some consternation in the school on February 19th, 1917. Mr Davies speaks of "a disorganised morning" when the class teachers' bunches of keys went missing. But with the help of the Sergeant of Police, it was discovered that a working collier lad had stolen them and gained access to the premises. The miscreant was summoned to appear at Bargoed Magistrates' Court on February 24th, 1917, when Mr Davies was called as witness for the prosecution. He was to remember his Headship at Nelson for being the only time recorded, during his career, which required him to appear in court. Presumably he had been involved previously in the legal process, e.g. providing details for persistent truants to be dealt with but there had been no mention of his having to witness in court.[332] Headship can impose diverse stresses and strains on the individual and a strong, resilient constitution is very necessary. Fortunately for John Davies, he had all that was needed for the task. There is no record of his being absent through illness at Nelson except for a fortnight in February, 1919, towards the end of his time there. This was a boon considering that it had been illness which had resulted in his retirement at Trelewis. Earlier, in January, 1919, he had been given leave of absence to attend the funeral of his housekeeper (Mrs Jane Treasure).[333]

It is difficult to evaluate the contribution which John Davies made to Nelson Council school in the time he spent there. There is no HMI Report written up in the Log to give an objective assessment. Whether this was due to the exigencies of war and a recognition that so many experienced staff were away on active service is not known. It could be that HMI Reports were recorded elsewhere. There was no shortage of visits to the school by Inspectors. John Evans, HM Sub-Inspector, visited 3 times in 1915, twice in 1917 and twice in 1918 apart from other visits, each year, to conduct the Labour examination. But there are few details of what his purpose was or of his conclusions, other than he inspected registers and work in the School garden. In September, 1916, there was a short visit from Mr L J Roberts, HMI, (the first time his name appears) and he saw some of the classes working. W Bryn Davies, the County Primary Inspector, made two visits each year in 1915, 1916, 1918, and 3 visits in 1917 again with little detail given other than inspection of registers, approving arrangement of classes and seeing classes at work. In October, 1916, Miss Stevens, the County Organiser for Domestic Subjects, saw several classes doing needlework. J H Mathias, Manager, made regular visits each year to inspect registers. Apart from logging these visits, there is no comment on the quality of the education which the pupils were receiving.[334]

Trying to make a judgement based on the success which pupils gained is also difficult. In July, 1916, 5 of the 7 pupils who sat, passed the entrance examination for the Higher Elementary School at Caerphilly. These would appear to be the first successes for secondary education recorded in the Log since one boy passed for Pontypridd County School in Evan T Owen's first year of Headship. In June, 1917, 2 of the 3 candidates who sat the scholarship examination for Pontypridd County School, passed Part 1. In that year there were 11 candidates sitting for entrance to Caerphilly Higher Elementary School. The Log is very non-committal about what the eventual success was only stating that "very satisfactory results were secured."[335] So without recognised benchmarks to adjudge his performance, all that remains is John Davies' own concluding statement which sums up his time at Nelson.

The School had re-assembled after the Easter holiday on April 28th, 1919, with a full staff and a "very fair attendance." On April 30th, 1919, John Davies makes his final entry in the Log: "I, this day, relinquish my position as Head Teacher in this school and, in doing so, I feel it my duty to acknowledge the valuable assistance I have received from the Staff, some of whom have been here during the whole period, and others during the greater part thereof, in the discharge of my duties. The most cordial of good understandings and co-operation have prevailed throughout. I wish Mr E T Owen who resumes work tomorrow (May 1st), after an absence of 4 years and five months, every possible success." [336] John Davies had served the school well showing his characteristic efficiency, goodwill and determination to succeed. From the start, he had recognised that his was to be a holding operation until Mr Owen returned, not to seek kudos for himself. In this he had succeeded admirably, leaving the School with the benefit of his accumulated experience.

The "Merthyr Express" welcomed the safe return of E T Owen and provided some details of his war service. After enlistment in the RAMC, he was speedily promoted to Sergeant. Later, he was commissioned in the Lincoln Regiment and was severely wounded serving in France. It also reported the welcome received by ET Owen and J R Williams when they returned to Nelson School. John Davies heartily congratulated them on their meritorious service and returning unharmed to resume duties at the school. He also paid high tribute to the ladies of the staff for their "faithful service and loyalty to him." In reply, Mr Owen said he was touched by the warmth and sincerity of his welcome home. Finally he acknowledged his indebtedness to Mr Davies "for the conscientious work he had done."[337] This recognition is important because, in the Log, one might have expected Mr Owen to be more fulsome in appreciation and gratitude to John Davies. But his first entry, on May 1st, 1919, merely stated: "Mr Evan T Owen resumed duties as Head Teacher after being demobilised from the army." The next day, he wrote: "Mr John Davies this day terminates his service at this school." No mention of how fortunate the School had been to have such an experienced Head Teacher in his absence or even thanks that John Davies had voluntarily come out of retirement to serve. In all his references to Mr Davies, he called him a Supply Teacher. On May 13th, 1919, his last comment was that the Chief

Education Official had notified the school that John Davies was to be paid at "the maximum rate for Supply Teachers viz £280." That was the same rate as Mr Owen himself was to be paid from April 1st! [338] Whatever lay behind Mr Owen's references, nothing can detract from what John Davies had done and the personal sacrifice he had made during the war years. His health had not been good; he had looked forward to a relaxing and well deserved retirement. Yet the call to be of service in his neighbourhood could not be denied. All credit to him for being public-spirited enough to forego his own well-being for the benefit of the community. When he left Nelson Council School, he had completed 50 years as a Teacher, 46 of them as a Headmaster. Very few could equal such a lifetime of service.

3. OF AN INSPIRATIONAL CAREER

Receiving Grateful Thanks

At Trelewis, there was an outpouring of appreciation, felicitation and recognition which greeted John Davies when he resigned as Head in 1913. There was nothing muted or half-hearted about it. Admittedly, this was after 31 years of loyal service there, but no one could be left in any doubt of the great esteem in which he was held for what had been accomplished under his Headship. The tiny village of Trelewis was often marginalised by the "Merthyr Express" at this time and reports of some of the things happening there often appeared under news for NELSON. Not so on John Davies' retirement. A full column was devoted to it under the headlines: **Presentation at Trelewis - Schoolmaster's Retirement - Long and Faithful Service Appreciated.** There followed a very detailed account of the pleasant presentation evening spent at the school on May 29th, 1913, when the inhabitants turned out "in strong numbers to do honour to their old friend, Mr John Davies, who had just retired from the headmastership of the schools after holding this position for upwards of 31 years." The Reporter commented on the huge respect he had won from all with whom he came in contact witnessed by what local people had done when they knew he was retiring through ill-health. Immediately they felt that "his faithful devotion to duty should be recognised in a tangible manner" and raised a substantial amount of money to present him with a testimonial.

What a gathering there was of appreciative villagers and hundreds of school children "who were delighted to see their popular master" receive his presentations. Befitting the occasion, there was an impressive programme of solos, duets, recitations and even an overture which all enjoyed. The meeting was presided over by Dr W W Leigh, J.P., Glynbargoed, who was joined by other important members of the community including T W Lewis (Mr Davies' son-in-law), Councillor Jonah Evans, the curate of St Mary's and the minister of Ebenezer Chapel. Dr Leigh started the tributes to his "old friend" who was regarded by the village as being part and parcel of the school. J C Williams, Assistant at the School, then presented Mr Davies with a gold chain on behalf of the teaching staff. He said how much Mr Davies' work and leadership had been appreciated by them and how they all "keenly regretted his retirement." Mr David Davies, Cashier of Ocean Colliery, Treharris, had been chosen to make the presentation of a handsome gold watch as he was the oldest pupil of Mr Davies still living in Trelewis. The inscription on the watch read: "Presented to Mr John Davies on his resigning the headmastership of Trelewis Council School after 31 years faithful service by old pupils and friends as a token of appreciative esteem. May 29th, 1913." When making this presentation, David Davies testified to the value of the tuition he had received as could "many former pupils now holding important positions throughout the country." Wishing John Davies a well-earned rest, he asked him to accept the gift "as a small token of the respect and esteem in which he is held by his old scholars and friends." The repetition of the word "friend" so many times during the evening speaks volumes about the affection felt for John Davies.

As one might expect, John Davies was quite overwhelmed by all that was said that evening. Now that his health was failing and not being "so young as he used to be", the time had come to leave. He reflected fondly on the past: his appointment to Bontnewydd School; his service under the Gelligaer School Board and subsequently. (His comments on past pupils will appear below.) What pleased him was that he had got on well with officials and that the school "had always gained a good report." He earnestly hoped that the new Head would receive the same whole-hearted support as he had done. While his own future was still a mystery, he was "old enough and wise enough to know that happiness is not gained by indolence." His intention was that "he would still be of service to the inhabitants in many ways." As has been shown, he more than fulfilled that wish. Concluding with thanks to all for the kindnesses received, typically, his final words are: "I can only say that amidst my many faults and failures, I have always tried to do my duty." The Reporter added in brackets (Loud Applause.)[339]

The "Merthyr Express" report on John Davies's death also mentions an additional gift on his retirement, which emphasised the affection and praise which he had engendered. An illuminated address was bestowed upon him. In the late 19th and early 20th Centuries, such addresses were given to mark special occasions or outstanding performance. Persons of prominence or importance would be presented with an illuminated address as a mark of respect and gratitude for what they had accomplished. They were beautifully written and decorated by hand, hence the description "illuminated", because the use of gold, silver and bright, lavish colours lit up the document, in the tradition of a medieval manuscript. The text would appear in formal style with an abundance of fulsome praise. Those awarded such an expression of approbation would ensure that it was displayed conspicuously. [340] Nowadays, in our less formal age, illuminated addresses have fallen out of fashion, but not completely. To celebrate the Diamond Jubilee of Her Majesty, Queen Elizabeth II, in 2012, the Parliament of the Isle of Man, (the Tynwald), commissioned an illuminated address to convey their loyal greetings and congratulations. As a method of communicating real appreciation and tremendous regard, it seems it is still of value. John Davies would have been thrilled to receive such recognition which he would keep as a permanent reminder of how highly he was thought of in the village where he had spent most of his life.

Unveiling Trelewis War Memorial (John Davies is seen on platform at right)

Perhaps the outstanding tribute to him was seen on Sunday, May 31st, 1925. On that day, the Trelewis War Memorial to the 45 young men who had sacrificed their lives in the Great War was to be unveiled. This notable event was to command a whole page of the "Merthyr Express" with two photographs and some almost poetic reporting. The headlines this time were: **TRELEWIS WAR MEMORIAL - IMPRESSIVE SCENES AT UNVEILING CEREMONY - A worthy tribute to fallen heroes.** The Report started: "Sunday last will long live as a day of sacred and proud memories in the minds of the residents of Trelewis and it will be spoken of as such in the story handed down to the generations yet unborn. Fully 3,000 people stood in silent

Trelewis War Memorial
To the men who died in the Great War

1914 ✝ 1918.

The Memorial will be unveiled by

Mr. JOHN DAVIES,
Late Schoolmaster, Trelewis.

On WHIT-SUNDAY, MAY 31st, 1925,
At 3.30 p.m.

:: PROCESSION ::
Headed by The
Treharris & District Workmens' Silver Band.
Ex-Servicemen.
Police.
Members of Memorial Committee.
Members of U.D.C.
Ambulance Brigades.
Fire Brigades.
R.A.O.B.
Friendly Societies.

W. R. Davies, Treharris Printing Works.

Courtesy Merthyr Library

admiration as the Union Jack which had veiled a majestic and beautiful monument was unfurled, revealing the little mining town's tribute and memorial to the 45 gallant men of Trelewis who laid down their lives in the great war." A stormy night and a rainy morning had preceded the ceremony but then the weather turned out gloriously fine. "The Great War, like unto the storm, was a thing of the past and a great peace had taken its place."

The War memorial was an imposing structure. A life-size figure of a mourning soldier, made of Sicilian white marble, with head reverently bowed and hands resting on an upturned rifle, had been erected in a peaceful location adjacent to Captain's Hill. The site had been presented by Mr Daniel Lewis of Bontnewydd Farm, keeping up his father's beneficence. It was a beautiful, even awe-inspiring recognition, by this tiny community, of the debt it owed these gallant men. But who was to have the honour of unveiling it? Some thought a local worthy such as Captain Lewis of Brynffynon would be chosen. Others considered that it would be better to have someone who was more closely associated with the men who were being commemorated. The obvious choice, therefore, was to be John Davies who knew practically all of those named on the memorial and had been their Headmaster.

The respect and regard of the whole village for him could not have been more marked when he unfurled the Union Flag covering the memorial before the crowded audience. All the inhabitants had turned out for this moving and historic ceremony taking place almost in the shadow of the winding gear of Deep Navigation Colliery.[341] Earlier there had been a large procession through the village led by the Treharris Workmen's Silver Band. A dense crowd of spectators had lined the road leading to the memorial controlled by a large body of police under the command of Superintendent Goronwy Griffiths, Treharris. The dignified Memorial Service was led by the three local ministers and then John Davies rose for his important task. Of the 45 names on the pedestal, two of the youngest were aged only 19, most were in their twenties and the oldest was aged 46. John Davies had seen most of them in their formative years with their lives stretching out before them. Now, he had the sad duty of commemorating their untimely demise in this act of remembrance. He was honoured but also moved by the task he had been assigned. Remarking on the unveiling, he said: "We have today performed an honourable but sad and solemn ceremony……. All suffered in the Great War, but nothing compared to these who gave their all." His thoughts that day were of those he had known as pupils at the school who had concentrated on "the acquisition of learning, preparatory to the battle of ordinary life." Now the remains of some were interred in foreign soil, some unknown were laid "Ei enw dyna'i gyd" - ("His name and nothing more.") He congratulated the ex-servicemen present on their safe return (some with medals, some with scars and disfigurements) and wished them well for the future. Finally he made an eloquent appeal for all to maintain the monument "worthy of their fallen heroes" and to seek an end to war by supporting the work of the League of Nations and the propagation of the Gospel. Then would come true the words of the Psalmist: "He maketh wars to cease to the end of the earth", which he also quoted in Welsh.[342]

The Memorial was then dedicated followed by the Last Post and floral tributes were placed at its base by relatives of the fallen and various societies. The Reveille, singing of "Guide me O Thou Great Jehovah", "God Save the King" and the Benediction marked the conclusion. Everyone who was there could not fail to be affected by the solemnity and significance of what they had witnessed. The village had wanted to give a worthy accolade to those who had given so much. The beautifully impressive memorial did just that in its simple but nonetheless eloquent inscription on the grey granite pillar:

Erected by the inhabitants of Trelewis
To the Glory of God and the Immortal Memory of
The men of this village who died for their country
In the Great War 1914-1918
They died that we might live
Gwell Angau Na Chwilydd

That Welsh phrase, ("Death rather than Dishonour"), was to be the most common inscription used on Great War Memorials.[343]

It was the Caiach Lodge of the RAOB which had first started the movement for a memorial. But when villagers learned that the memorial was only intended for members of the Lodge they wanted something for the whole village. So in September, 1919, a meeting was held in the vestry of Ebenezer Chapel to discuss how to proceed. A committee was formed chaired by T W Lewis and including John Davies amongst its members to raise money for a War Memorial. Various fund-raising activities were begun. Trelewis School participated on 2 occasions in 1919 when the School was closed for a carnival and sports to be held. When the original fund-raising committee stalled with the fund reaching £161.15.9, a fresh committee led by Mr Ivor Lewis (but still including John Davies), made the final push to raise the £250 required. Of all the interested parties, at the forefront of raising money for the impressive war memorial, was the Trelewis Ex-Servicemen's Club which became part of the British Legion after it was founded in 1921. Previously, it had also been active in supporting the families of those killed in the war. For many years it was to be a focal point in the life of the village, using as its base one of the original huts left by those who had sunk Taff Merthyr Colliery. In all, it took over six and a half years and the overcoming of many difficulties before the objective was accomplished with an estimable memorial constructed by Messrs David Williams and Sons of Abercynon.[344]

Towards the end of the twentieth century, the War Memorial had become neglected and even subject to vandalism. Did anyone remember what John Davies had said at the unveiling? He had expressed the hope that the memorial would be well-preserved and be worthy of pilgrimage. The British Legion, inspired by its women members, wished to rectify a deplorable situation. It was decided to raise funds to move the memorial to a more prominent and safer spot, opposite the main road, near the Ffald bridge. On June 23rd, 2002, about 500 people took part in the re-dedication of the War Memorial. There were 300, mostly ex-servicemen, who marched from the Millennium

Park through the village to the new site, led by the Salvation Army band. Local clergy officiated at the service of hymns and prayers. The Mayor was also in attendance and the Chairman of the Trelewis Cenotaph Project, Shirley Bufton, presented him with the symbolic deeds of dedication. The laying of wreaths and poppy crosses was followed by the Act of Remembrance. At the close, light refreshments were served at the Bontnewydd Hotel and in Trinity Church Hall. The report in the "Merthyr Express" was much briefer and less lyrical than that of the 1925 ceremony but it had a much larger, coloured photograph than on the former occasion. John Davies would most certainly have approved that the names of those inscribed on the memorial were not going to be forgotten, despite the passage of 77 years. Age was not going to weary them: they were still to be remembered. In his speech in 1925 he had said: "What comfort and consolation have we to offer if the names of the brave boys reared, nourished and loyal to the village and country are not transmitted down to posterity."[345]

Giving Motivating Hope

All of the accolades bestowed upon John Davies by the village, sprang from a potent mixture of respect and gratitude, which was well-deserved. His long, dedicated career as Head and his concern and support for the well-being of the community influenced countless numbers of people: pupils, teachers, parents and villagers all benefited from his presence. For Trelewis Mixed School, he helped create a tradition where none had existed before. Persistently and steadily, he dedicated his time and energy to improving the school and establishing solid foundations. His determination and resilience ensured that he left the school vastly better than when he found it. Staff, be they Pupil, Uncertificated or Assistant Teachers, were encouraged in their professional development. There were those who went on to highly-successful careers, having learned from the example they had seen in John Davies. Generations of pupils had their lives improved because of the education they had received under his influence. Villagers had observed his integrity, moral uprightness, devotion,

Trelewis War Memorial, now standing near to where Trelewis Halt once stood

realism, perseverance in adverse circumstances and his strong sense of purpose. He was, in every way, a pillar of the community. Rev D Ffrydwen Lewis, Minister of Ebenezer, speaking at his retirement, had said that holding a very important position for such a long period of time and in such a praiseworthy manner meant that: "His influence is impossible to measure." How wonderful that his pupils had been taught by a man of high moral character. He had not only trained and taught but created a desire for knowledge which was of greater value than the teaching itself. His conclusion was that John Davies' influence "would run like a river from generation to generation."[346]

So it was to prove. The reason for the impression John Davies made on so many arose from his view of teaching. For him, his whole life was dominated and inspired by the conviction that teaching was not a profession but a vocation - a calling. He saw the power that education had to shape the characters and the futures of his pupils. His aim was to motivate them to achieve their best despite their background or situation. For this, they needed hope which always brings with it the possibility of improvement. While Alexander Pope might say "Hope springs eternal in the human breast", for many, the spring becomes weakened through the harsh realities of life. That was undoubtedly true for numbers of those living in Trelewis at the same time as John Davies. His belief in hope as an anchor, a stimulus and an incentive, might be difficult to achieve but it was still his objective. That was the culture which he had tried to create in the school. His pupils were central to his thinking. Speaking at his retirement, he wondered where the thousands of pupils who had passed through the school were now. Many were in Trelewis or the neighbourhood but some were scattered all over the world. He could not find words in the English language that were adequate so he used the words of the Welsh bard, Evan Evans (Ieuan Glan Geirionydd, 1785-1855) in his poem "Ysgoldy Rhad Llanwrst":

Pa le, pa fodd, mae heddiw	Where are they, how are they today
Y lliaws yma fu	That once thronged here
'N cydchwarae a chyd-ddysgu,	Playing together, learning together,
A chydymgomio'n gu?	Fondly conversing together?
Mae rhai mewn bedd yn huno	Some are sleeping in a grave,
A'r lleill ar led y byd:	Others are scattered across the world;
Nad oes yn gloch a ddichon	There is no bell that is able
Eu galw heddiw 'nghyd.	To call them together today.[347]

He hoped that those now "on the prairies of America, on the veldt of South Africa and the bush of Australia" would look back with pleasure on the time that they had spent at Trelewis School, remembering what they had learned there.[348] He trusted that the school had made a significant contribution to their lives. From what has been described already, his successors had the same sentiment and continued his work. So even in his retirement there were pupils of Trelewis School who were to be motivated by hope.

A good example is Maggie Pryce Jones whose book "Kingfisher of Hope", (which has already provided insights into the life of a school child in the inter-war years), exemplifies what John Davies had been seeking for his pupils. It was hope which sustained her even when problems and difficulties surrounded her. Encouragement from Mr Griffiths at Trelewis School had been as oxygen to her hope. The talisman of her vivid anticipation was the appearance of the kingfisher at seminal times in her life. On the night before she sat the Scholarship examination she saw it, albeit fleetingly. Her spirits were raised, providing her with renewed confidence that she would be successful, which indeed she was. She proceeded to Hengoed for a grammar school education which she revelled in. Gaining her School Certificate, a brighter future seemed about to open up only to be dashed by the untimely death of her mother. Forced to leave school to spend her time and talents caring for her father and raising the young family, appeared to put paid to her cherished hopes of being transported out of her valley on the wings of education. But there was still a resilience which, in her more mature years, after resolutely serving her family's needs, enabled her to fulfil at least some of her dreams. She carved out a new career in local politics, studied at Merthyr Technical College, entered the Civil Service and developed her creative writing skills. Hope had not deserted her and was to lead her to a fuller, richer life. At the very end of her book, when she comments on the changes occasioned by the closure of the local collieries, she concludes with a statement which characterises her unbridled optimism: "Will our rivers, one day, run clear again and my kingfisher return to fish then?"[349]

Entering Final Rest

After a lifetime of service to his community, John Davies was to die on February 25th, 1942, at the age of 90. He had been in failing health for several months and passed away peacefully, in his sleep. It is difficult to express adequately his all-round contribution to Trelewis over so many years as there are so many facets to it: educational, religious, social and personal. The comment of the "Merthyr Express" was: "His passing removes one who had played a great part in the religious and educational life of the District." John Davies was to scorn delights and live laborious days in his fixed intention to serve the locality to the best of his ability. He was a generous supporter of all religious and charitable organisations. Typical of this was his presidency of the Trelewis Auxiliary of the British and Foreign Bible Society. Nothing was too much trouble for him. He was to leave a worthy memorial in the school he steered in its formative years; his beloved Church was a beacon light in the neighbourhood; his good and sound work on behalf of the community provided its own testimonial. The end and the reward of toil should be rest but John Davies remained active in the 22 years after his second retirement. Even some 6 months before his death he was still reading the lesson at St Mary's! He loved to keep on keeping on until, finally, illness took its toll, slowed him down and stopped his activity.[350]

On Saturday, February 28th, 1942, St Mary 's Church was packed for his funeral service. Past and present members of Trelewis School joined scores of villagers, in grief and sorrow for someone who had affected the lives of so many of them. There were no fewer than 10 clergy present at the service and 4 Head Teachers including W Adams Jones and D M Davies. At the private burial at Gelligaer Churchyard were his daughter and son-in-law, 4 grandchildren and his brother, Canon E Jenkin Davies. The interment at St Catwg's was further recognition of the esteem in which he was held. William Lewis, the founder of Trelewis, had been honoured there some 38 years previously at his death. It was fitting that the longest serving village Headmaster of Trelewis Mixed School should be laid to rest with similar commendation and gratitude.

EPILOGUE: A PERSONAL TRIBUTE

As I come to the end of this survey of the life and work of John Davies, I feel it necessary to add my own panegyric. The solid foundations which he had laid for Trelewis School were to benefit me when I became a pupil there in 1936. My father worked in Taff Merthyr Colliery and we lived in the Garden Village. He was determined that I would not have to work underground, as he had done, and I was always encouraged to work hard at school. In 1943, I was one of the vintage successes in the Scholarship examination and my horizons were expanded as I entered Lewis' School, Pengam. The first member of my family to go to University, I became a Teacher. Proceeding upwards through the profession, I eventually finished my career as Headmaster of an 11-18 Comprehensive School which could trace its foundations back to the reign of Elizabeth 1. My thanks are, therefore, due in a large measure to the early training I received in our village school at which my progress began.

As I have read and researched over the past few years, my admiration for John Davies, has grown more and more. Of course, he was not perfect: no Head Teacher is if you consult their staff! But from all the evidence I have gathered, the positives far outweigh the negatives. Reading his words in the Log Book, I have almost felt as if I have heard his intonation in some of his comments. I can empathise with the trials and tribulations of his headship; I can rejoice in his successes and triumphs. Above all, I can identify with his thrill of being the channel through which a pupil gains knowledge, understanding and hope. Aristotle wisely commented that: "Education is the best provision for old age." It shapes and moulds us and has a life-long influence. John Davies knew the truth of that and realised that it is not so much what is poured into the pupils but what is planted which really counts. His objective was to train his charges to think clearly and to act rightly. In so doing, he can be proud of his life-long work. They say a successful teacher can affect eternity: he can never tell where his influence will reach. Although John Davies never knew it, I am so glad that his legacy reached right down to me as a result of the ideals and culture which he established in Trelewis School. He had contributed to the rise of meritocracy in the twentieth century, when advancement came to depend not on who you were or who you knew but on what you were and what you knew. That enabled many youngsters from ordinary homes, like me, to enrich their lives with fulfilment, success and happiness. So, it is fitting to express heartfelt gratitude and appreciation to John Davies, on behalf of all of those who benefited from his influence on an insignificant and tiny valleys' school. Instead of being chained to the local environment, we were set free by education, many to join the vast army of teachers and preachers who became Wales' greatest export in the modern era. We will all be forever indebted to the work of John Davies and his successors for giving us a better future.

Concluding my tribute, I recall, with pleasure, that made by Oliver Goldsmith to the village schoolmaster in "The Deserted Village", his epic on Irish rural life in the eighteenth century (learned by me for School Certificate!) Briefer, more balanced and far more eloquent than mine, Goldsmith depicts a teacher, modestly doing a good job in a simple place, spreading numeracy and literacy amongst his pupils. His word-picture describes the man, his moods and his impact on the village. He neither idealises nor trivialises his schoolmaster but realistically shows him at the centre of his community gaining its affection and esteem. Giving a humorous account of the teacher's character, the poem never loses sympathy for him. Rather it recognises that he is the source of knowledge and the communicator of cultural heritage to succeeding generations. Simple words and melodious phrase blend perfectly together to provide a masterpiece that is worth remembering. While I could never attain to that standard in my study, I still feel a similar amalgam of respect and admiration which characterises Goldsmith's description. I trust that, despite my deficiencies, I have faithfully presented a fully-orbed portrait of John Davies and his impressive contribution to the development of Trelewis. For me, he will always be the quintessential Village Headmaster.

REFERENCES

Part One   SETTING THE SCENE (1851 - 1882)

1 Glamorgan Archives, *Trelewis Mixed School Log Book 1878 -1914* E/CG 41/2 - referred to below as TML (1).
2 Information kindly supplied by Lucy Smith, Archive Volunteer at Ceredigion Archives and Greg Buick, whose great grandfather was John Davies.
3 Gwent Record Office, *Llanover Parochial School Log Book   1872- 1891* CE.A.93.1
4 Gwent Record Office, *Plan of Llanover Parochial School 1872* D1210.768
5 Gwent Record Office, *Wage Book for 1872* D1210.731 and *Wage Book for 1875-6* D1210.732
6 Ceredigion Archives, *Ciliau Aeron Board School Log Book*
7 George Borrow, *Wild Wales* John Murray 1862 (Latest edition - Wrexham 2009) pp. 465, 466
8 Hywel Wyn Owen & Richard Morgan, *Dictionary of the place names of Wales* (Gomer, Llandysul, 2007) plus information from Greg Buick's researches into the 1601 mortgage for Bontnewydd
9 Glamorgan Archives, *1875 Ordnance Survey Map Gelligaer and Llanfabon Parishes* Glamorganshire Sheets   XIX.12; *1879 Ordnance Survey Map Merthyr Tydfil, Llanfabon and Gelligaer Parishes* Glamorganshire Sheets XIX.11
10 John Hutton, *The Rhymney Railway Volume 1* (Silver Link Publishing 2004) p.9
11 *Merthyr Express,* March 8th 1879
12 Greg Buick the grandson of Thomas William Lewis kindly provided a trunk full of documents all relating to the Bontnewydd Estate of William Lewis and Daniel Lewis. The information on Leases is derived from An Assent dated 27th October 1947. (The documents are referred to below as: Docs: TWL)
13 www.genuki.org.uk, *Chapels' Data base*
14 TML (1) p.23
15 ibid pp. 53,54,70, 83, 84, 87, 105
16 ibid pp. 70, 117
17 ibid pp. 6, 13, 23, 50
18 ibid pp. 79, 88, 90, 92, 96
19 *Merthyr Express,* January 11th 1879
20 ibid February 8th 1879
21 TML (1) pp.124, 126
22 Glamorgan Archives, *Treharris School Log Book 1881-1893,*   EMT 22/2
23 TML (1) p.35
24 *"The Aelwyd Modulator"* The Gwyn Publishing Company, Llangollen, (GPC 0901) - Copy (and relevant information) kindly supplied by my friend Ralph Davies who was taught Tonic Sol-fa notation and who still uses it!
25 TML (1) pp. 54, 57, 60, 61, 62, 64, 65, 67, 68, 84, 91, 93, 97, 116, 124,
26 Gwent Record Office, *Llanover Parochial School Log Book* CE.A.93.1 p.28
27 TML (1) pp. 10, 33, 71, 73, 76, 79, 86, 89, 100, 113, 115, 128
28 ibid pp. 3, 12, 14, 32, 72
29 ibid pp. 26, 27, 32, 34
30 ibid pp. 6, 12, 17, 25, 26, 28, 32, 33, 35, 41, 42, 47, 49, 51
31 ibid p. 43
32 Michael Eyers, *"The Masters of the Coalfield"* (Pontypool 1992) pp. 105-107
33 TML (1) pp. 10 14
34 ibid pp.28, 31
35 ibid pp. 44, 48, 50
36 ibid pp. 45, 47
37 ibid pp. 46, 51, 52
38 Glamorgan Archives, *Penybank Mixed and Infants' School Log Book 1879-1898,* E/CG 10/1 pp. 1, 39
39 *Merthyr Express,* January 11th 1879, February 1st 1879
40 TML (1) pp. 57, 72
41 ibid pp. 53,54, 55, 56, 60
42 ibid pp. 60, 78, 87, 90, 92
43 ibid p.54

44 ibid pp. 54, 56, 61, 64, 66, 68, 70, 78, 89,
45 ibid pp.58, 62, 63
46 ibid pp. 54, 57, 60, 61, 64, 65, 67, 68, 70, 71, 76, 78
47 ibid p. 72
48 ibid pp. 69, 70, 71, 73, 74, 76, 77,
49 ibid pp. 86, 87, 88, 89, 91
50 ibid p. 102
51 ibid pp. 107, 112, 113
52 ibid pp. 93,100
53 ibid pp. 114, 115
54 ibid pp. 115, 116, 117
55 ibid p. 118
56 ibid pp. 120, 125, 126, 127
57 ibid pp. 117, 120, 121, 122
58 ibid pp. 115, 117, 119, 120,
59 ibid pp. 119, 121, 122, 123, 124
60 ibid pp. 124, 125, 126
61 ibid p. 124
62 ibid p. 121
63 Docs: TWL: Second Schedule No. 6 dated 1.5.76 for Capel Ebenezer, the lessees being Davies and Kinsey - a lease for 99 years at a rent of £2.7.9
64 TML (1) p. 126
65 ibid pp. 115, 121, 127,128, 129, 130
66 ibid pp.118, 128, 129, 137
67 Glamorgan Archives, *Treharris School Log Book 1881 -1893* E/MT 22/2 - (referred to below as THSL.) p. 10
68 TML (1) p. 131
69 ibid p. 134
70 THSL p. 28
71 TML (1) p. 132

Part Two   STARTING THE WORK (1882 - 1892)

72 TML (1) p. 133
73 ibid p. 138
74 ibid pp. 151, 210
75 ibid pp. 164, 198, 202, 222
76 ibid pp. 150, 154, 156,
77 ibid p. 158
78 ibid p. 164
79 ibid pp. 190, 201, 212, 213, 226, 227, 228, 237, 251, 252
80 ibid pp. 147, 163, 180, 182, 185, 188, 189, 191, 196, 199, 221, 234, 242, 246, 249, 255
81 ibid pp. 180, 224, 225, 226, 230, 231, 235, 237
82 ibid pp. 152, 167,
83 ibid pp. 153, 157
84 ibid pp. 141, 146, 161, 172, 183, 193, 205, 217, 232, 244, 257
85 ibid pp. 141, 150, 153
86 ibid pp. 158, 159, 170, 191, 201, 214
87 ibid pp. 185, 189, 203, 204
88 ibid pp. 222, 228, 248
89 ibid p. 227
90 ibid p. 238
91 ibid p. 239
92 ibid p. 172
93 ibid pp. 180, 181, 183
94 ibid pp. 146, 161, 172, 183, 193, 205, 217, 232,
95 ibid pp. 238, 239, 244
96 ibid pp. 134, 135, 145, 148, 160, 163

97 Arthur Wright, *The History of Lewis' School Pengam* (Newtown,1929) pp. 179, 180
98 TML (1) pp. 149, 172, 217, 225
99 ibid pp. 170, 177, 190, 200, 204, 214, 216, 251, 252, 257
100 ibid pp. 186, 187, 193, 205, 227
101 ibid pp. 230, 231, 236, 242
102 ibid pp. 246, 250, 251, 255
103 ibid pp. 152, 161, 165, 169, 177, 198, 213, 217, 227, 232, 239, 241, 244, 257
104 ibid pp. 148, 163, 215, 219, 241, 253
105 ibid pp. 142, 170, 188
106 ibid pp. 147, 175, 181, 192, 221
107 ibid pp. 163, 196
108 ibid pp. 170, 175, 188, 192, 250
109 ibid pp. 146, 161, 172, 173, 193, 205, 217, 235, 239, 246, 247, 250, 252
110 ibid pp. 138, 163, 174, 176, 200, 209, 211, 212, 223, 234, 235,
111 ibid pp. 139, 141, 146, 154, 156, 168, 170, 195
112 S J Cutis, *History of Education in Great Britain* (London, 1953) p. 283
113 TML (1) pp. 236, 249, 250
114 ibid pp. 134, 135, 149, 156, 157, 168, 170, 174, 176, 180, 182, 186, 187, 189, 191, 196, 201, 208,
    214, 222, 227, 226, 234, 250, 251
115 *Merthyr Express,* November 19th 1932
116 *Kelly's Directory of Monmouthshire and South Wales* (London 1884) pp. 330-334: (London 1891)
    pp.237 -240.
117 TML (1) p. 117
118 Glamorgan Archives, 1900 Ordnance Survey Maps (Surveyed 1873, Revised 1898) Glamorgan
    Sheets XIX 11 and 12
119 Docs: TWL - *Assent (27 October 1947)* Second Schedule Nos. 1-35
120 ibid - Assent Second Schedule Nos. 26, 55, 78
121 ibid - Agreement 2nd November 1885 between William Lewis and Ffald-Gaiach Building Society
122 ibid - Agreement 20th May 1886 between William Lewis and John Lewis together with Bill for the
    Contract.
123 Glamorgan Archives, 1900 Ordnance Survey Maps (Surveyed 1873, Revised 1898) Glamorgan
    Sheets XIX 11 and 12
124 *Kelly's Directory of Monmouthshire and South Wales* (London 1891) pp. 237-240
125 TML (1) p. 174
126 ibid pp. 186, 215, 223, 232, 238
127 ibid pp. 174, 205
128 The Honourable Society of Cymmrodorion, *"The Dictionary of Welsh Biography Down to 1940"*
    (London 1959) p. 200

Part Three   SUSTAINING THE EFFORT (1892 - 1902)

129 S J Curtis.& M E A Boultwood, *Introductory History of English Education since 1800* (London,
    University Tutorial Press, 1966) p. 73
130 TML (1) pp. 256, 265 279, 340,
131 ibid pp. 259, 260, 261, 262, 267, 368, 370
132 ibid pp. 271, 272, 328, 329, 330, 331, 360, 366, 367
133 ibid pp. 300, 304, 309, 341
134 ibid p. 343
135 Iona & Peter Opie, *The Lore and Language of Schoolchildren* (New York, NYRB, 2001) p.211
136 TML (1) pp. 259, 271, 281, 282, 291, 296, 297, 301, 322, 337, 342, 352, 353, 356, 375,
137 ibid pp. 260, 261, 262, 264, 265, 270, 272, 276, 277, 278, 281, 285, 286, 287, 288, 289, 290, 291,
    294, 295, 296, 297, 300, 302, 303, 304, 305, 307, 308, 309, 312, 313, 314, 315, 325, 327, 333, 335,
    336, 337, 340, 345, 346, 347, 348, 350, 351, 352, 357, 358, 359, 360, 362, 363, 366, 367, 368, 369
    370. The sheer number of entries about occasional holidays and the fact that they occur often on
    consecutive pages underline the impact they would have had on the school.
138 ibid pp. 260, 261, 262, 264, 265, 266, 267, 270
139 ibid pp. 273, 275, 276
140 ibid pp. 271, 276, 279, 280, 281,

141 ibid pp. 282, 285, 286, 290, 291, 292, 293, 294
142 ibid pp. 276, 278, 287, 289, 290
143 ibid pp. 295, 296, 297, 300, 302, 303, 304, 306
144 ibid pp. 283, 298, 310, 323, 334, 343, 354, 365, 376, 398
145 ibid pp. 263, 266, 269, 287, 288, 291, 300, 302, 305, 314, 317, 330, 325, 338, 340, 346, 350, 373
146 ibid pp. 295, 297, 308, 362
147 ibid pp. 310, 323, 334, 354, 365, 376, 317
148 J B Thomas, *"The Origins of Teacher Training at University College Cardiff"* Journal of Educational Administration and History, Volume 16, Issue 1, January 1984 pp.10-16
149 Glamorgan Archives, *"Log book of Merthyr Vale Mixed School 1897-1953,"* EMT 13/3 p.50
150 ibid pp. 53, 54, 55, 56, 76, 85, 91, 93, 100, 109, 111, 119, 143, 145, 146
151 S J Curtis & M E A Boultwood, *Introductory History of English Education since 1800* (London 1966) pp.369-371
152 TML (1) pp. 263, 265, 267, 279, 283, 294, 305, 308, 310, 312, 318, 329, 376
153 ibid pp. 279, 326, 331, 339, 340, 352, 356, 364, 374,
154 Annual Reports of Committee of Council on Education 1894-95 p. xi, (London, Her Majesty's Stationery Office)
155 TML (1) pp. 308, 309, 312, 316, 317, 321, 329, 332, 344, 347, 361, 364
156 ibid pp. 325, 336, 342, 344, 349, 350, 370, 372
157 ibid pp. 318, 339, 340, 341
158 ibid pp. 313, 318, 321, 335, 345, 374
159 ibid pp. 289, 325, 326, 333, 339, 342, 364, 373, 374
160 ibid pp. 282, 295, 351, 358, 359, 368, 370, 373
161 Glamorgan Archives, *"Rules for Management of South Wales & Monmouthshire Certified Truant and Industrial School"*
162 www.Tredegar.co.uk/forum/topic.asp?TOPIC_ID=2255
163 TML (1) pp. 357, 361
164 ibid pp. 172, 173, 193, 232, 239, 247, 250, 252, 257, 275, 276
165 ibid pp. 271, 283, 286, 291, 298, 301, 310, 325, 328, 340
166 Docs: TWL *"Agreement between William Lewis and Gelligaer School Board",* 17th April 1900
167 TML (1) pp. 363, 369, 371, 373, 374, 375
168 Docs: TWL *"Second Schedule of Assent"* 27th October 1947 (Thomas William Lewis and his sister, Mary Edwards had become trustees and Administrators of the Bontnewydd estate following the death intestate of their elder brother Daniel in 1927.)
169 Docs: TWL *"Draft Documents for Lease of Bontnewydd Hotel",* 1899/1900; *"Draft assignment between Margaret Roberts & Others with Watkin Lewis."* 1902.
170 Kelly's Directory of Monmouthshire and South Wales 1901
171 TML (1) pp. 303, 326, 327, 359, 366
172 ibid pp. 337, 339

Part Four   SECURING THE OBJECTIVE (1902 - 1913)

173 S J Curtis & M E A Boultwood, *"An Introductory History of English Education since 1800"* (University Tutorial Press London 1966) p. 168
174 F Smith, *"A History of English Elementary Education"* (University of London Press 1931) p.347
175 TML (1) pp. 402, 406, 407, 408, 415, 416, 418, 425, 426, 442
176 ibid pp. 411, 414, 423, 427, 429, 432, 439, 440, 444, 445, 455, 463
177 S J Curtis, *"History of Education in Great Britain"* (University Tutorial Press London 1953) p.327
178 TML (1) pp. 414, 416, 442
179 ibid pp. 380, 388, 392,
180 ibid pp. 400, 436, 439
181 ibid pp. 447, 452, 460, 466
182 ibid pp. 379, 457, 460,
183 S J Curtis & M E A Boultwood, *"An Introductory History of English Education since 1800"* (University Tutorial Press London 1966) p.174
184 S J Curtis, *"History of Education in Great Britain"* (University Tutorial Press London 1953) pp. 325-6
185 TML(1) pp. 436, 443, 446, 447, 456, 460

186 ibid pp. 440, 448, 453, 456
187 ibid p. 443 Also information from *"Western Mail"* 27th July 1909; *"National Pageant of Wales - Railway arrangements"* (GWR 1909); *"National Pageant of Wales 1909 - Order of Proceedings"* (E. Rees, Cardiff 1909); and Hywel Teifi Edwards, *"The National Pageant of Wales"* (Gomer Press 2009.)
188 ibid pp. 450, 454, 456
189 ibid pp. 375, 377, 384
190 ibid pp. 429, 430, 438, 439, 440, 445
191 ibid pp. 385, 386, 387
192 ibid pp. 413, 418, 425, 426, 432, 439
193 ibid pp. 386, 406, 413, 418, 421, 439, 445,
194 ibid pp. 380, 407, 408, 421, 426, 431,
195 ibid pp. 378, 390, 428, 429, 441, 444, 452, 445
196 ibid pp. 389, 390, 447
197 ibid pp. 392, 407, 411, 448
198 ibid pp. 377, 379, 384, 386, 387, 390, 395, 397, 399, 409, 410, 427, 430, 438, 441, 445, 465
199 ibid pp. 379, 382, 385, 387, 391, 393, 394, 400, 402, 414, 415, 418, 422, 424, 428, 429, 430, 437, 438, 441, 446, 447, 451, 452, 453, 454, 455, 460, 461, 462, 464, 466
200 ibid pp. 403, 408, 411, 416, 420, 433, 446
201 ibid pp. 380, 387, 392, 398, 402
202 ibid pp. 396, 405, 428, 436, 446, 447, 449, 450, 452, 454, 455, 460, 462, 464, 465
203 ibid pp. 378, 390, 391, 399, 400, 402, 410
204 ibid pp. 396, 397, 398, 400
205 ibid pp. 403, 404, 405, 406, 411
206 ibid pp. 414, 415, 416, 417, 418
207 ibid pp. 420, 423, 424, 425, 427, 428, 431, 432
208 ibid pp. 433, 434, 438, 444, 449, 456, 463, 465
209 ibid pp. 378, 391, 394, 397, 404, 413, 422, 430, 433, 440, 443, 446, 451, 453, 459, 461,465
210 ibid pp. 382, 383, 395
211 ibid pp. 381, 384, 389, 393, 400, 426, 430, 436, 437, 439, 443, 449, 462
212 ibid pp. 391, 393, 396, 397, 400, 402, 409, 419, 421, 423, 427, 430, 443,
213 ibid pp. 383, 398
214 ibid pp. 425, 434, 438, 448, 453
215 ibid pp. 407, 417, 437, 464
216 ibid pp. 388, 401, 412, 419, 435
217 ibid pp. 377, 381, 390, 395, 396, 403, 409, 417, 420, 428, 434, 442, 447, 452, 456, 462, 466
218 ibid pp. 419, 457
219 ibid pp. 384, 393, 394, 436, 442, 449, 450, 454, 455, 462
220 S J Curtis & M E A Boultwood, *"An Introductory History of English Education since 1800"* (University Tutorial Press London 1966) pp. 62, 78, 374, 375
221 TML (1) pp. 382, 416, 423, 463
222 ibid pp. 386, 391, 397, 401, 402, 404, 409, 419, 421, 422, 423, 424, 426, 427, 429, 430, 432, 434, 443, 444, 463,
223 ibid pp. 398, 420, 428, 433, 400
224 Docs TWL
225 Glamorgan Archives, *Glamorgan Sheet XIX:12* Ordnance Survey 1920 (Surveyed 1873, Revised 1915)
226 TML (1) pp. 457, 459
227 ibid pp. 379, 421,423
228 Docs: TWL, also Kelly directory 1910
229 Docs: TWL (Lease No76 dated 1 May1906)
230 Kelly's Directories 1906, 1910, 1914
231 TML (1) pp. 401, 443
232 Gwyn Briwnant Jones and Denis Dunstone, *"The Vale of Neath Line"* (Gomer 1999) p.134; V Mitchell & K Smith, *"Welsh Valleys - Cardiff to Dowlais"* (Middleton Press 2009) p.102; V Mitchell & K Smith, *"Welsh Valleys - Pontypool to Mountain Ash"* (Middleton Press 2005) pp. 87, 88, 89;

John Hutton, *"The Rhymney Railway Vol. 2"* (Silver Link Publishing 2004) p.49

233 City of Cardiff Central Library Capital Collection, *"Souvenir Programme of Royal Visit"* (S Glossop 1912); John Hutton, "The Rhymney *Railway* Vol. 2" (Silver Link Publishing 2004) p.65

234 TML (1) p. 462

235 ibid pp 381, 454

236 ibid p. 391

237 ibid pp. 444;453

238 ibid pp. 406, 407

239 *Merthyr Express,* 5th October 1907

240 TML(1) pp. 461, 464, 465

241 ibid pp. 133, 46

Part Five SALUTING THE ACHIEVEMENT (1913 - 1942)

242 TML(1) p. 467 and *Merthyr Express*

243 *Merthyr Express*, 7th June 1913

244 TML(1) pp. 468, 469, 470, 472

245 TML(1) pp. 470, 473, 477, 478, 489, 497

246 ibid p.488 then continued in Glamorgan Archives, *Trelewis Mixed Log Book 1914- 47* listed below as TML(2) pp.26, 56, 80

247 TML(2) pp. 10, 32, 49, 62, 74, 81, 94, 100, 104, 137

248 TML(1) pp. 476, 490, 496, 499; then TML(2) pp.9-13, 15, 18, 22, 25, 27-32, 36-40, 43, 45-49, 51-62, 64-71, 76-96, 99-108 (The attendance returns almost occur on consecutive pages!)

249 TML(1) p. 491, TML(2) pp. 7, 29, 31, 38, 41, 69, 73, 78, 79, 92

250 TML(1) p. 493, TML(2) pp. 77, 83, 84, 96, 102, 106

251 TML(1) pp. 482, 483, 485, 486, TML(2) pp. 30, 53, 55, 61, 64, 65, 67, 68, 74, 79, 80, 83, 93

252 TML(1) pp. 485, 490, TML(2) pp. 7, 21, 25, 33, 34, 40, 43, 48, 50, 56, 58, 60, 61, 66, 73, 76, 80, 82, 85, 86, 89, 93, 94, 96, 98, 100, 102, 104, 105, 107, 108

253 TML(1) p. 500, TML(2) pp. 10, 32, 62, 66, 71, 76

254 TML(1) p. 482, TML(2) pp. 6, 7, 16, 76, 133, 139, 141, 147

255 TML(2) p. 43

256 TML(1) p. 494, TML(2) pp. 19, 41, 54, 63, 67, 76, 77, 80, 81, 82, 84, 90, 92, 95, 96, 99, 102, 103, 104

257 TML(1) p. 487, TML(2) p. 500

258 TML(2) pp. 13, 16, 23

259 ibid p. 97

260 ibid p. 112

261 ibid pp. 11, 52, 99, 101, 102, 103,

262 ibid pp. 143, 145, 146, 147, 150 and *Merthyr Express* 1933

263 *Merthyr Express,*- as 21 & TML(2) p. 150

264 Glamorgan Archives, *Trelewis Admission Register* ECG41/4

265 TML(2) pp. 19, 85, 91, 118

266 ibid pp. 143, 145, 146, 147, 150, 152

267 ibid pp. 232, 233, 234, 235, 236

268 ibid pp. 234, 236,

269 ibid pp. 156, 167, 170, 172, 174, 180, 182, 183, 184, 186, 189, 198, 205, 215, 216, 228

270 ibid pp. 162, 181, 183, 187, 193, 194, 204, 205, 222

271 ibid pp. 217, 218, 219, 220, 227, 228, 230, 231

272 ibid pp. 154, 163

273 ibid pp. 154, 155, 163, 180, 182, 194, 196, 200, 206, 209, 217, 222, 223, 224

274 ibid pp. 177, 178, 202

275 ibid p. 218

276 ibid p. 210

277 ibid pp. 230, 231

278 *Merthyr Express,* 31st August, 1940

279 The date is probably between 1955 and 1961. I have not been able to discover the exact date. The current Head Teacher of Trelewis Junior School and her immediate predecessor, have not provided any information for this study despite several requests.

280 TML(2) pp. 236, 237, 238, 239, 241, 242, 243, 244, 245, 250, 251
281 ibid pp. 242, 243, 244, 245, 248, 250, 251,
282 ibid pp. 239, 240, 244, 252, 253, 254, 256, 258
283 ibid pp. 237, 240, 241, 245, 246, 247, 250, 254, 255, 257
284 ibid pp. 242, 245,
285 ibid pp. 238, 255
286 Maggie Pryce Jones, *"Kingfisher of Hope"* (Llandysul 1993) pp.36, 52
287 TML(2) pp. 249, 272,
288 ibid pp. 251, 259, 261, 275, 289
289 ibid p. 299
290 Kenneth Morgan ,*"Wales 1880-1980"* (OUP Oxford 1982) p.285 and TML(2) p.115
291 ibid p.231 Also David Williams, *"A short history of Modern Wales"* (John Murray London 1961) p. 124
292 Kenneth Morgan, *"Wales 1880-1980"* (OUP Oxford 1982) p.226
293 ibid pp. 206, 209, 290, 291
294 Edward A Evans, *"South Wales Valleys"* (Easingwold 2005) p. 45
295 Ray Lawrence, *"The South Wales Coalfield Directory"* Vol. 2 p. 464 (Typescript Copy in Cardiff Central Library.)
296 Dennis Morgan, *"The Illustrated History of Cardiff's suburbs"* (Derby 2003) pp.143-147
297 TML(2) pp. 119 124
298 James Page, *"Rails in the Valleys"* (Newton Abbot 1989) pp. 14, 75, 76
299 Hywel Francis and Dai Smith, *"The Fed"* (Cardiff 1998) pp.91-97, 203, 215
300 D. Smith, *"The Struggle against Company Unionism in the South Wales Coalfield 1926-1939"*, Welsh History Review, vol. 6 No 3 (June 1973) p. 354ff.
301 Ray Lawrence, *"The South Wales Coalfield Directory"* Vol.1 pp.216-218 (Typescript Copy in Cardiff Central Library.
302 Biographical Note from Archives Wales on Edgar Evans (Bedlinog) relating to documents held at Swansea University Ref. Nos. GB0217 SWCC; MNA/PP/24
303 D. Smith, *"The Struggle against Company Unionism in the South Wales Coalfield 1926-1939"* Welsh History Review, vol. 6 No 3 (June 1973)
304 *Merthyr Express,* November 3rd 1934
305 Hywel Francis and Dai Smith, *"The Fed"* (Cardiff 1998) pp. 222-223
306 W H Davies *"The right place, the right time"* (Swansea 1973) p. 72
307 Maggie Pryce Jones *"Kingfisher of Hope"* (Llandysul 1993) pp. 2, 26, 29, 31,
308 Information supplied by Mrs A Dunning, Maen Gilfach, Trelewis, when interviewed just after her 100th birthday in 2012!
309 Maggie Pryce Jones, *"Kingfisher of Hope"* (Llandysul 1993) pp. 35, 47, 48
310 Docs: TWL Also TML(2) p.142
311 *Merthyr Express,* 19th November 1932.
312 ibid
313 Maggie Pryce Jones, *"Kingfisher of Hope"* (Llandysul 1993) pp, 52, 64, 65
314 Glamorgan Archives, - Catalogue note Ref: UM/1-2, Merthyr Tydfil Poor Law Union. Also *Merthyr Express*, 7th June 1913 and February 28th 1942
315 *Merthyr Express,* August 8th 1914; October 17th 1914; December 5th 1914; December 19th 1914
316 Most grateful thanks are due to Mrs A Birkenshaw, Secretary, and Mr R James, Caretaker of Llancaeach Junior School who searched assiduously until they found the School Log Book and Admission Register. Even the key to unlock the Log Book was found! Thanks too to the Head Teacher, Mrs L Greenhaigh for allowing me to consult the Log and Registers. (The Nelson Council School Mixed Department Log Book will be referred to below as: NCSL.)
317 NCSL pp. 1, 4, 7, 17, 27, 29, 37, 38, 45
318 ibid pp. 2, 8, 10, 29, 47,
319 Nelson Council School "AL" Admission Register commenced on September 28th 1908
320 NCSL pp. 31, 32, 37 38, 39, 43, 46, 47, 48, 51, 54
321 ibid pp. 49-51
322 ibid p. 55
323 ibid p. 56

324 ibid pp. 40, 41, 42, 43, 44, 47, 57, 58, 63, 75, 81
325 ibid pp. 78, 81, 85, 86, 87
326 ibid pp. 59, 66
327 ibid pp. 66, 74, 78, 80, 81, 84, 87
328 ibid pp. 59, 60, 61, 62, 63, 66, 67, 68, 69, 70, 71, 72, 73, 74, 75, 76, 77, 78, 79, 80, 82, 83, 85, 86, 87
329 ibid pp. 23, 49, 62, 63, 77
330 The Glamorgan Admission Register, which provides these details for Llanfabon National School, starting with Admission No. 1 in September 1914, was found in Llancaeach Junior School. The two Junior Schools amalgamated in September 1960 and that is probably when this Admission Register was transferred to Llancaeach.
331 The "AL" Admission Register was supplied to Nelson Council School Mixed Department on September 28th 1908 and starts with Admission No.1 on that date and ends with Admission No.2035 on June 11th 1934. The subsequent Admission Register has not been found in the School. (The school was notified in June 1953 that henceforward it was to be known as Llancaeach Mixed Primary School. Despite the Head writing that the usual spelling of the name was "Llancaiach" the designated name has continued to this day.)
332 NCSL pp. 72, 73
333 ibid pp. 85, 86
334 ibid. pp. 57, 58, 60, 61, 62, 65, 67, 68, 69, 70, 71, 72, 73, 75, 76, 78, 79, 81, 83, 84, 87,
335 ibid. pp. 22, 69, 75, 76
336 ibid. p.88
337 *Merthyr Express*, 10th May 1919 and 17th May 1919
338 NCSL p. 89
339 *Merthyr Express,* 7th June 1913
340 ibid Feb. 28 1942,
341 *Cardiff Times and South Wales Weekly News,* June 6 1925
342 *Merthyr Express,* June 6th 1925
343 Angela Gaffney, *"Aftermath. Remembering the Great War in Wales"* (Cardiff 1998) pp. 71, 125, 149
344 ibid and *Merthyr Express* 6th June 1925, and TML(2) pp. 75, 78
345 *Merthyr Express,* 6th June 1925 and 12th July 2002
346 ibid 7th June 1913
347 The translations from the Welsh throughout are kindly supplied by my friend Nerys Davies
348 *Merthyr Express,* 7th   June 1913
349 Maggie Pryce Jones, *"Kingfisher of Hope"* (Llandysul 1993) pp.27, 40, 68, 123
350 *Merthyr Express,* Feb 28th 1942 and 24th February 1934